D1490342

ACROSS THE PERILOUS SEA

Across the Perilous Sea

Japanese Trade with China and Korea from the Seventh to the Sixteenth Centuries

Charlotte von Verschuer

translated by
Kristen Lee Hunter

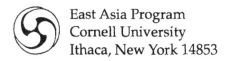

East Asia Program
Cornell University
Ithaca, New York 14853

The Cornell East Asia Series is published by the Cornell University East Asia Program (distinct from Cornell University Press). We publish affordably priced books on a variety of scholarly topics relating to East Asia as a service to the academic community and the general public. Standing orders, which provide for automatic notification and invoicing of each title in the series upon publication, are accepted.

If after review by internal and external readers a manuscript is accepted for publication, it is published on the basis of camera-ready copy provided by the volume author. Each author is thus responsible for any necessary copyediting and for manuscript formatting. Address submission inquiries to CEAS Editorial Board, East Asia Program, Cornell University, Ithaca, New York 14853-7601.

Number 133 in the Cornell East Asia Series
Copyright © 2006 by Kristen Lee Hunter. All rights reserved
ISSN 1050-2955
ISBN-13: 978-1-933947-03-7 hc / ISBN-10: 1-933947-03-9 hc
ISBN-13: 978-1-933947-33-4 pb / ISBN-10: 1-933947-33-0 pb
Library of Congress Control Number: 2006933388

24 23 22 21 20 19 18 17 16 15 14 13 12 11 10 09 06   9 8 7 6 5 4 3 2 1

Original French edition published in 1988 by Institut des Hautes Études Japonaises du Collège de France, Paris, as Le Commerce extérieur du Japon des origines au XVIe siècle.

Cover illustration from the illustrated scroll entitled Kōbō Daishi gyōjō'e ("Illustrated Biography of Great Master Kōbō"), artist unknown, 14th century. Important Cultural Property, owned by the monastery-temple Tōji in Kyōto.

This scene, from the third of twelve scrolls, shows one of the ships that carried the Japanese embassy including the monk Kūkai (Kōbō Daishi) to Tang China in 804. Courtesy of Tōji.

CAUTION: Except for brief quotations in a review, no part of this book may be reproduced or utilized in any form without permission in writing from the author. Please address inquiries to Kristen Lee Hunter in care of the East Asia Program, Cornell University, 140 Uris Hall, Ithaca, NY 14853-7601.

Contents

PREFACE

It seems timely to reedit the present history of Japanese foreign relations and focus on an understanding for cohesion in the community of East Asian relations in light of the fact that the Japanese authorities have recently been intensifying relations with their Asian neighbors. In Japanese studies, as in all other disciplines, research fosters progress; I should, therefore, explain why this book, first published in 1988 as *Le commerce extérieur du Japon des origines au XVIe siècle*, remains a reference. This present English edition has been methodically revised, taking into account recent scholarship and the more accurate data on ancient measures now available. The selective bibliography of the original monograph has been expanded to reflect the full array of sources upon which the study was based, with the aim of improving its utility to academics and nonspecialists alike. Most of the secondary literature referenced emanates from the long-standing tradition of Japanese historiography, whereas Western-language inquiry into premodern Japanese foreign relations was then, and still is, in its infancy. Those seeking an in-depth discussion of the state of the field may wish to consult an article I published in the Winter 2000 issue of *Monumenta Nipponica* titled "Looking from Within and Without: Ancient and Medieval External Relations." Here, however, my intent simply is to place this book within the context of contemporary scholarly trends.

Since World War II, historical studies of Japanese foreign relations in premodern times have focused principally on institutional and diplomatic aspects. The exchange of official embassies between Japan and its continental neighbors has drawn greater attention than private trade between the archipelago and China and Korea. Within the domain of interstate diplomacy, historical revisionism sometimes has colored the interpretation of past events. Pre- and postwar Japanese historians, for example, regarded the ancient Korean kingdoms as Japanese tributaries and considered Japan's diplomatic position in premodern East Asia equal to that of China. It was also thought that Heian Japan eschewed Sinification in an effort to promote a distinct Yamato culture. Furthermore, the once-avid Japanese interest in the Parhae kingdom (Japanese,

Bokkai; Chinese, *Bohai*), which straddled what is now North Korea and northeastern China (formerly Manchuria), declined greatly in the postwar era.

A new generation of scholars emerged in the 1970s and 1980s, and with them many of these approaches were entirely revamped, resulting in many innovative interpretations. Nevertheless, the fundamental research of their predecessors, who scrutinized the primary sources and compiled them for publication, continue to be esteemed. Materials on early Japanese foreign relations are scattered throughout archives in Japan and elsewhere in East Asia. In the current age of unprecedented worldwide access to electronic and printed information, it is all too easy to forget that Japanese scholars in the mid-twentieth century had no recourse to photocopying: they were obliged to visit libraries, archives, and temples to examine documents and manually transcribe excerpts for their treatises.

I was the beneficiary of these predecessors' fundamental work when I conducted doctoral dissertation research in Japan prior to 1983. Having been influenced by the Japanese academic milieu, I concentrated on diplomatic relations in the eighth and ninth centuries. With my thesis completed, I chose to extend the chronological parameters of my work to encompass the entire premodern period. I soon found that patterns in foreign relations before the sixteenth century were very complex, and my research eventually led to *Le commerce extérieur du Japon des origines au XVIe siècle*. The book's primary objective was to outline the characteristics of Japanese relations with China and Korea up to the sixteenth century, and to survey the main primary sources which (I have to admit) gives the book a somewhat lexicographical character. The main focus clearly was to assess interstate commerce, trade commodities, and the balance of foreign trade. French historians had put aside narrative history for the study of material culture and, influenced by that trend, I became more intrigued by the economic, rather than diplomatic facets of Japanese foreign relations. This change in emphasis has paralleled Japanese historians' burgeoning interest in anthropological perspectives.

In the 1980s Japanese scholars, theretofore preoccupied with institutional and diplomatic history, showed greater interest in the agents of foreign relations—namely, monks, diplomats, and merchants. There was also a growing awareness that intergovernmental dealings were but one aspect of Japan's relations with the continent and that private trade and diplomatic exchanges were conducted at the same time. Historians were also mindful of the ambiguities inherent in the conventional native-foreign dichotomy that predominated in analyses of external relations. Upon closer inspection, it was evident that within Japan's territorial confines and along its periphery were a multiplicity of social groups with varying degrees of allegiance to Japanese central authority. Murai Shōsuke, in particular, has styled as "marginal men" those islanders who engaged in extralegal commerce in the fourteenth to sixteenth centuries. In addition, interest in the experiences of sojourners as depicted in travel diaries, foreign trade goods, and the significance of specialty items in East Asian societies flourished. These factors resulted in a more multidimensional understanding of international relations.

This volume addresses many of these themes and provides a comprehensive inventory of the variety of merchandise traded in each period. It is further enriched by material culled from the diaries of monks, diplomats, and merchants. While many such diaries have been consulted, still others await examination. The piracy and illicit activities of inhabitants of islands in the East China Sea, especially from the thirteenth century onward, are outlined, but both issues warrant further investigation. The same holds true for interactions with northeast Asia and the islands south of Kyūshū before the fourteenth century, study of which began in earnest only within the last decade. I hope that this publication will highlight areas for future research. Toward that end, the bibliography has been supplemented with an addendum of both classic and recent publications that deal with these topics.

Within a chronological framework, this book traces Japan's transformation over nearly a millennium from an importer of continental luxury items, raw materials, and techniques to an exporter of high-quality handicrafts. Chapter 1 explores Japanese diplomatic relations with China, the kingdom of Parhae, and the kingdoms of the Korean peninsula from the seventh to the ninth centuries. During this period exotic goods acquired through interstate exchange were available exclusively to elite courtiers, and imported handicrafts also served as models for domestic manufacture in workshops affiliated with the court and select high-ranking aristocrats. Japan was able to procure such valuable products in exchange for relatively modest outlays of plain woven silk and sometimes gold, pearls, or agates. Consequently, the court pursued official exchanges with the continent until the early ninth century, when it ceased to dispatch embassies abroad.

Thereafter, as revealed in Chapter 2, products continued to circulate between the Japanese archipelago and mainland Asia primarily via Chinese merchants. The Heian court administered commercial trade through the agencies and procedures originally developed to govern diplomatic relations. With an ever-growing demand for foreign goods by estates and court nobles, the court's efforts to monopolize imported merchandise and control foreign trade ultimately failed as its administrative power waned.

In the Nara and Heian periods, perfumes, medicines, fine silk fabric, ceramics, and Chinese books were among the most desirable imported articles. Their significance in Japanese aristocratic circles is detailed in Chapter 3, which also describes Japanese exports—gold dust, mercury, sulfur, and art crafts such as paper, swords, folding fans, and artifacts adorned with mother-of-pearl inlay or gold-lacquer ornamentation—that were admired on the continent.

Chapter 4 documents the process by which Japanese agents supplanted Chinese merchants in the transaction of international commerce beginning in the thirteenth century. Because of the gap between the jurisdictions of the Kamakura Bakufu and the court, local leaders in Kyūshū achieved a measure of independence in conducting foreign trade and capitalized upon it to send frequent missions to China. The Bakufu and Buddhist temples too sponsored overseas missions. Trade with Korea in this era was eclipsed by exchanges with China, which supplied a most-coveted import: currency.

From the fifteenth century onward, Chapter 5 asserts, international trade became a more commercial source of revenue for Japanese local leaders and government entities. Imported items that had formerly often served for luxury uses now were commercialized on the domestic market in a higher proportion than in preceding periods. Japan succeeded in exporting greater quantities of its manufactures to China and Korea than those countries demanded, not withstanding the limitation to the number of trade delegations imposed by both China and Korea. It is indeed ironic that Japan, which had never articulated an explicit trade policy of its own, availed itself of Chinese and Korean state-controlled trade practices to further its own commercial objectives.

An undertaking of this scope could not have been realized without the magnanimity of many colleagues. *Le commerce extérieur* *du Japon des origines au XVIe siècle* benefited greatly from the invaluable advice and suggestions for improvement offered by Francine Hérail and encouragement by Bernard Frank for its publication. Father Grootaers's expertise with Chinese texts was of considerable assistance, while Ishii Masatoshi was a font of knowledge and made available his personal file on trade in the Heian Period. Their collective efforts continue to be sincerely appreciated.

Joan R. Piggott's vision that *Le commerce extérieur du Japon des origines au XVIe siècle* might one day be more readily accessible to a broader audience through an English edition brought about the collaboration between author and translator. Throughout, she has steadfastly championed this volume's publication and has been instrumental in all aspects of the manuscript's development. Cornell University's East Asia Program generously funded the project through the award of the Robert J. Smith fellowship in Japanese studies to translator Kristen Hunter, whose expertise in the field of East Asian foreign relations, bibliographic research, and constructive suggestions have enriched the English edition. *Across the Perilous Sea* owes much to the counsel of Charles A. Peterson, who meticulously studied an early draft, Cornell East Asia Series managing editor Karen K. Smith for coordinating preparations for publication, and Arnie Olds for assuming the onerous task of designing the book. Their contributions are deserving of special recognition and heartfelt thanks.

CHARLOTTE VON VERSCHUER
Paris, June 2005

CHAPTER 1

TRIBUTARY EXCHANGES
From the Seventh to the Ninth Centuries

"China is an extraordinary country, endowed with a well-organized legal system; we ought to make regular visits there," declared the Japanese scholar and medical expert E'nichi in 623 C.E. upon returning from his stay in China.[1] The history of Japan's foreign relations proves that this remark was not the opinion of merely one man. Was not this same principle embraced by Japan in the Meiji era (1868–1912) in its relations with Western countries? E'nichi returned from China in 608 with an official Japanese delegation—one of six embassies sent to China during the seventh century by the Yamato court to deliver tribute consisting of native products.

International relations in this period were conducted within the framework of the Sinocentric tributary system, a system founded upon a non-egalitarian ideology that was blatantly hierarchical. Akin to the imperialism of other oriental and occidental civilizations, this doctrine was predicated upon Confucian thought, which conceived of a social order between superiors and inferiors regulated by benevolence on the one hand, obedience on the other. At the apex of this system was the Chinese emperor, called the Son of Heaven, who by dint of his righteousness was superior to all men. Through his virtuous conduct, manifested in rites, he maintained order and governed "all under Heaven," that is, China proper and beyond. Under this authority an aristocracy of princes and high dignitaries endowed with titles and powers was created; they were dubbed vassals and presented tribute to the sovereign as a token of their obedience. Beyond China's frontiers, the leaders of other countries also were encouraged to bring tribute and acknowledge their allegiance. In accordance with Chinese terminology they "were subject to the beneficent influence of the Son of Heaven." The sovereigns of these countries then had titles bestowed upon them by the Chinese court and were considered "exterior vassals." But this tributary system did not give the emperor administrative control over non-Chinese territories, unless they were occupied by military forces. Rather, it was based on what we might call cultural imperialism.

From the seventh to the ninth centuries, roughly seventy countries, tribes, and city-states regularly sent local products as tribute to the Chinese court. Embassies from a good number of these came each year. China at that time was the most developed country in the Asian world and, in some cases, tributaries depended on it for subsistence. China, in principle, was the arbiter of peace in the region. Its tributary system officially survived for more than two millennia, until the end of the last dynasty—the Qing—in 1911.

Japan was among these seventy countries of the tributary network. According to the Chinese annals, a native group from the Japanese archipelago sent its first delegation to China in the first century C.E.[2] Japan, which did not yet have a state structure, needed to establish relations not only to obtain China's military support but also to import its artisanal techniques, writing system, administrative organization, and systems of thought (divination, Confucianism, and Buddhism). The Japanese local sovereigns apparently seized upon tributary exchanges to acquire knowledge. Indeed, nearly all of the embassies sent to China were accompanied, at least from the seventh century onward, by numerous students and monks responsible for studying various aspects of Chinese civilization and bringing back handicrafts and scientific books.

Tributary embassies were not always the sole link to the continent. In the fourth and fifth centuries, numerous emigrants from the Korean peninsula, fleeing from troubles that plagued their countries, sought refuge in Japan. Japanese authorities welcomed these immigrants with open arms, according to the *Nihon shoki*, the official history compiled in 720, and settled them near the seat of government, sure of the benefits that would be gained from them. These Koreans were in fact scribes, ceramists, sericulturists, weavers, saddlers, stock breeders, ironsmiths, and smelters, and they assumed an important role in the transmission of artisanal techniques to Japan. Thus, thanks essentially to several waves of immigration from the Korean peninsula and the dispatch of official delegations to China, Japan was able to absorb the civilization of the region's most advanced country. It did so with such zeal that not only writing and technology, but also Chinese principles of government and the concept of social hierarchy soon were considered Japanese assets.

Let us remember, here, that there was no "Japan" in the sense of a centralized country. The Yamato rulers adopted the name "Japan" (Nihon) at the end of the seventh century, and even after that, they did not rule over the entire Japanese archipelago, but controlled more or less thoroughly sixty-eight provinces which were located between the south of Kyūshū and the Tōhoku region. This rule became even looser from the eleventh and twelfth centuries onward, and a political regionalism continued to exist until the Tokugawa period (1603–1868). However, in this book we will use the terms "Japan" and "Japanese" for convenience, meaning no political entity but things and people geographically located in the Japanese archipelago, regardless of any links with the administrative centers. The same is true for our meaning of Korea and China.

The Japanese monarchs developed imperialist ambitions similar to those of the Chinese: from about the seventh century on, the Yamato sovereign considered himself a supreme monarch who "ruled over all under Heaven" and received tribute from foreign vassals. This role was reinforced by Shintō tradition, according to which the *tennō* was a descendant of the sun goddess Amaterasu. Japan found its vassals on the Korean peninsula, then occupied by the three kingdoms of Silla, Paekche, and Koguryô, and on the southern islands of Tanegashima and Yakushima. The Japanese annals (*rikkokushi*) note—reality or fiction?—tribute-bearing missions from these countries to the Yamato court from the sixth century onward. The Japanese monarch thus imagined he ruled the "universe" and claimed a position equal to that of the emperor of China. "Empress" Suiko (r. 592–628) expressed her idea in two letters addressed to the Chinese court in 607 and 608: "The Son of Heaven (*tenshi*) in the land of the rising sun sends this letter to the Son of Heaven in the land where the sun sets" and "the Emperor (*tennō*) of the East greets the Emperor (*kōtei*) of the West."[3]

Nevertheless, the fact that this same Japanese "emperor" sent tribute to the Chinese court cannot be denied. The paradox of being at the same time sovereign and vassal must have posed a moral dilemma for Japanese rulers for many centuries. Their attitude was supercilious in certain periods, submissive in others. One might speculate that material gains were an essential consideration. Indeed, at times, Japan's diplomatic position changed according to the state of the commercial trade.

What was the reality in the seventh century? Japan sent ten missions to China, where the Tang Dynasty had succeeded the Sui in 618. The Japanese court complied with certain rules of tributary etiquette but refused to follow others. It presented its native products as tribute and in exchange accepted gifts from the Chinese court. During audiences before the Son of Heaven, Japanese delegates took their places among the representatives of other tributary countries, but Japanese monarchs no longer were invested with titles by the Chinese court (they had been given them until the late fifth century) and their missions most likely were no longer supplied with tallies, which normally were obligatory. In their letters accompanying tribute shipments, Japanese sovereigns, at least Suiko, omitted any statement of allegiance to the Chinese Son of Heaven.

But Japan was not the only country that failed to obey. Other countries clashed with Chinese cultural imperialism in every era. In the second and first centuries B.C.E., the Wusun kingdom, an exterior Chinese vassal, concurrently received tribute from other countries. The Xiongnu, a nomadic people who reached their greatest strength in the first century C.E., proved a formidable adversary, capable of extracting gifts of appeasement from China. Nanzhao, situated in modern Yunnan, in the eighth and ninth centuries sent tribute sometimes to China, sometimes to Tibet, and finally proclaimed their monarch "emperor" to demonstrate their autonomy. In the eighth century, the Khitans, China's northern neighbors, refused vassalage and later enthroned their own emperor. Finally, in the fourteenth and fifteenth centuries, the Mongol empire of Samarkand hardly considered itself a Chinese vassal at all and in turn received tribute from several kingdoms. Therefore one might imagine Japan's position among the resistant vassals. Until the sixteenth century, however, Japan's foreign diplomatic and economic relations were nevertheless consistent with the tributary framework, whether it be a period when they refused or agreed to submit tribute.

Tribute in the Seventh Century

Of what did tribute, the material expression of diplomatic relations, consist? All official delegations took numerous products from their own countries as presents for the foreign monarch, usually China's, and in exchange received for their governments goods that could be quite valuable. The volume of trade therefore was proportional to the number of embassies. In the seventh century, arrivals and departures seem to have been plentiful: the *Nihon shoki* records about thirty Japanese missions sent to China and approximately one hundred delegations, principally Korean, that came to visit the Japanese court. The Japanese annals depict the Korean delegations as tribute-bearing embassies. It is difficult to verify their status and number because they are hardly mentioned in the official Korean histories, which, nevertheless, frequently mention the submission of tribute to China. In turn, the sovereign country also sent representatives supplied with gifts for their foreign vassals. In this way, for example, some Chinese ambassadors accompanied Japanese envoys on their return to Japan.

On the subject of the content of tribute and presents, the annals provide only fragmentary information. In 599 Suiko Tennō's court hosted an envoy from the kingdom of Paekche who presented a camel, a donkey, two goats, and a white pheasant to the throne.[4] Three years later another Paekche delegation came to Japan, led by the monk Kwallûk, laden with books about the calendar, astronomy, and exorcism techniques. Kwallûk stayed in Japan and three men were named to be his disciples and study science.[5] In 605 the empress commissioned two images of the Buddha, one in bronze standing 4.8 meters tall, the other in embroidery. When the Koguryô king heard the news, he sent a contribution of three hundred ounces of gold.[6]

In 607 ambassador Ono no Imoko departed for China and returned the following year in the company of a Chinese envoy. On that occasion the court erected a new guest house in Naniwa, in the vicinity of modern Osaka. The Chinese ambassador then received an audience at the Yamato court and the presents, according to the Japanese account, were displayed in the central court of the palace. Their content, however, was not mentioned. The Chinese guest then returned to his country accompanied by a new Japanese embassy. A few years later two scholars, Korean monks from Koguryô, arrived in Japan. One of them was educated in the Chinese classics, and also had mastered the techniques of making pigment as well as ink and paper; moreover, he taught the Japanese how to construct a water mill (the primary source of mechanical energy known to ancient civilizations).[7] This mill, however, did not become widespread in Japan until several centuries later.

The following account dates from the year 618. A mission from Koguryô came to report an invasion—though already repelled—of Chinese forces into their territory, and they offered as tribute two Chinese prisoners of war, tambourines, flutes, bows, crossbows, and a camel. Five years later, an embassy from Silla presented to the

Yamato court a carved image of the Buddha, gilt steles, relics, a large banner and twelve small ones. These objects were placed in Japanese temples right away.[8] In 625 a monk delegated by the king of Koguryô came to Japan and immediately was raised to the rank of abbot.[9] Some years later, in 642, tribute from Koguryô consisted of gold and silver.[10] A 647 mission from Silla then brought a peacock and a parrot as "special presents."[11]

In 653 Kôtoku Tennô (r. 645–654) dispatched an embassy to China bearing tribute that, according to Chinese sources, consisted of, among other things, amber and agate. Upon their return the ambassadors were rewarded with promotion to an exceptional rank for having received an audience with the Son of Heaven and for having obtained numerous books and invaluable products in China.[12] Three years later, another Japanese delegation brought back from Paekche a parrot and other objects, and the delegation of the following year received a camel and two mules from Paekche.[13]

An amusing episode was reported for the year 659. A Koguryô envoy went to market carrying a bear fur, which he offered for sale for sixty pounds of silk floss. When the market official heard this, he began to laugh and left. Can we deduce from this tale that foreign envoys also brought items to sell? This is the only such written evidence from the seventh century. The account further notes that a Koguryô painter residing in Japan rented seventy bear furs that he used as cushions to greet his compatriots who had come on a mission. The guests were surprised and embarrassed, however, and left his residence.[14]

The ensuing years were marked by significant upheavals on the Korean peninsula. In 660 Japanese troops were sent to assist the kingdom of Paekche, which had sustained an invasion of Chinese and Silla troops. Japan and its ally were vanquished, and Paekche was occupied by its enemies. In 668 Silla invaded Koguryô and soon became the sole ruler of the peninsula. After these wars Japan experienced a new wave of immigration. Four hundred Paekche refugees were authorized to settle in Ômi Province (modern Shiga Prefecture) in 665, and the following year 2000 more immigrants from Paekche were settled in a northern region.[15] Japan had also welcomed other foreigners in previous years. In 660 roughly 100 Chinese prisoners were sent from Paekche and later domiciled in Mino Province (Gifu Prefecture).[16]

Other smaller groups came at other times. Some groups, composed of artisans and technicians, were sent by the Korean kingdoms, but others came on their own initiative. They apparently benefited from the right to reside in Japan. Nevertheless, toward the end of the century, they could no longer reside in the provinces situated near the government center, but only in the northern regions of the country, where they were awarded allotments of land and stipends. They thus cleared uncultivated lands and increased the population of individuals subject to taxation. Among the immigrants, those who were considered nobles, scholars, or scientific specialists were even granted official rank—notably in 671 and 686—and entered the service of the court.[17] The proportion of immigrants among the families attached to the Japanese court can be seen in an official register from the year 815. Recorded therein were the names of 1,182 families living in the capital or in the five adjacent provinces, of whom 324 were considered to be of Korean or Chinese descent.[18] Thus, the circles of the lesser Japanese nobility encountered a relatively sizable foreign presence during these periods of immigration prior to the eighth century.

Let us return to the information pertaining to tribute. In 667 a Tanra delegation arrived in Japan. The Tanra, a tribe that occupied Cheju-do, an island situated south of Korea, had opened relations with Japan in 661. The annals note the presents given to the envoys in exchange for tribute: 14 bolts of brocade (*nishiki*; 1 bolt, *hiki*, measured 12 meters), 19 bolts of tie-dyed silk (1 bolt, *tan*, measured 12 meters), 24 bolts of red silk, 24 bolts of dark blue hemp (*nuno*), 58 bolts of mauve hemp cloth (*nuno*), 26 axes, 64 billhooks, and 61 knives.[19] The following year, gifts consisting of 50 bolts of silk taffeta (*kinu*), 500 pounds of silk floss (*wata*; 1 pound, *ton*, corresponds to about 168 grams), and 100 animal furs intended for the Silla king were bestowed on the ambassadors from Silla.[20] In 671 one of many missions from Silla came to present tribute, accompanied by a buffalo and a pheasant as "special gifts."[21] Another embassy received as gifts for of the Silla king 50 bolts of silk taffeta, 50 bolts of plain-woven raw silk (*ashiginu*), 1,000 pounds of silk floss, and 100 furs.[22]

A Chinese mission that came to Japan in 673 received as presents armor, bows, arrows and, in addition, 1,673 bolts of plain-woven raw silk, 2,852 bolts of hemp cloth, and 666 pounds of silk floss. These gifts perhaps included rewards for this very large delegation of six hundred.[23]

The *Nihon shoki* contains six reports concerning tribute brought by Silla embassies between 680 and 690. Tribute generally consisted of gold, silver, sometimes copper and iron, as well as brocade, silk taffeta, hemp cloth, animal furs, animals (horses, mules, dogs) and, in one case, exotic birds, medicines, and metal dishes. Aside from the regular tribute offering, the Koreans also presented to the court a "special tribute" consisting of supplementary gifts comprising gold, silver and, in some cases, embroidered banners, mauve-tinted brocades, or bronze Buddhist images.[24]

We thus are informed about the products that circulated between the continent and Japan in the seventh century. Nevertheless, the *Nihon shoki*, which is practically the only source of information on the period, scarcely mentions the volume of trade. Indeed, products are cited only in regard to some twenty Japanese and foreign embassies, even though the same source attests to more than a hundred arrivals and some twenty departures. The volume of trade thus seems more considerable than the annals would suggest. Furthermore, these accounts mention only trade conducted under official auspices, that is, tribute and presents, but one can assume that the immigrants themselves did not come empty-handed. Did they conduct their own exchanges, like the Korean envoy who attempted to sell a fur in the market? On this subject the sources remain silent, but archaeological excavations of fifth-century burial mounds in Japan have unearthed iron ingots identical to those of the Korean kingdom of Silla. These ingots could have served as a means of payment. The Chinese chronicles of the Wei Dynasty (fifth–sixth centuries) assert that the Koreans and the Japanese used Chinese pieces of iron to trade, in the same manner that the Chinese used coins. The same source also mentions fairs in Yamato where one could barter. The Japanese annals too indicate the names of several fairs in certain regions of the country. These were probably temporary markets, established and controlled by local authorities, because free trade was still unknown at this time.

THE EIGHTH AND NINTH CENTURIES

The beginning of the eighth century was marked by an important event: the promulgation in 701 of the *Taihō Ritsuryō Code*, which laid the foundations for a state endowed with a central administration. The code was little more than a copy of China's "well-organized legal system," which E'nichi had recommended to his government in 623 (see n. 1), but the Chinese code had been adapted to Japanese sociocultural circumstances. The country thereafter was divided into sixty-eight provinces administered by provincial governors appointed by the court. This system had its capital at Fujiwara-kyō, south of modern Nara. The central administration, over which the emperor presided, consisted of the Council on Shrine Affairs and the Council of State—the latter comprised eight ministries and managed various aspects of court life, revenue, and the treasury.

The Japanese tax system, following the Chinese model, was based on the distribution of arable land (paddy fields) granted to all taxpayers for life, and taxes were levied on a per capita basis rather than on yield. Japan had three main forms of taxation: a land tax, payment in kind, and labor service (*corvée*). The land tax resulted in stores of rice, which for the most part remained in the storehouses of provincial administrations and were intended to cover expenditures. Payments in kind were sent by the provinces to the court. They consisted of: silk taffeta, silk floss, hemp cloth, iron, salt, seaweed, dried fish, and, for payment in lieu of *corvée*, plant materials, paper, wooden chests, and other items to which raw materials and handicrafts were later added. This tax constituted the revenue of the court and, in theory, covered its needs and those of its civil servants. Furthermore, many workshops attached to the court assured the production of items for the use of the aristocracy. The income of officials came from paddy fields, allocated according to their rank and post, and from semiannual allowances of plain-woven raw silk, silk floss, hemp cloth, and a quantity of hoes. Thus the economy was based on the transfer of goods from the provinces to the capital via taxes, but it did not take into account differentiated demand or the need for specific products by civil servants and religious establishments. This gap was filled by fairs.

Two markets were established in the eastern and western parts of the capital, following the example of those in the Chinese capital. They were managed by the Capital Bureau, which set prices and controlled weights, measures, and product quality. Markets were held in the afternoon. Noble families and religious establishments could sell products there to supplement their income and could purchase commodities they lacked. In 762 Tōdaiji, an official temple in Nara, for example, sold silk floss and hemp cloth received from the court treasury and bought 120 bolts of plain-woven raw silk, 7,600 sheets of paper, and 35 *koku* (3,000 liters) of rice. On other occasions Tōdaiji's agents purchased fabric, vegetables, grains, spices, oil, and even paper, writing brushes, and ink.

What then was the means of payment? Japan had used iron and copper coins for some time. Archaeological excavations have shown that mintage had been in use since the end of the seventh century, but written sources indicate it was not until 708 that the court established a workshop where the first official coins were minted. The 708 issue was minted in silver, but then, starting the following year, principally in copper. The introduction of this official coinage, inspired by the Chinese model, thus preceded the founding of the new capital of Nara. The issue of coins might have represented a supplementary source of court revenue to defray construction costs.

Following the issue of new coins, the court began to demand that a portion of the taxes from provinces in the vicinity of the capital be paid in cash and that cash be used in payment for certain temporary work projects. The government took progressive measures to stimulate circulation. It determined the price of grains and hemp cloth, then instituted a law that rewarded savings. Instead of travel provisions, it provided civil servants with money that circulated between the capital and the provinces. The court ordered that purchases of land be transacted in cash, it presented the ledgers of provincial resources in terms of coin, and it took even more measures during the eighth century. This course of action, however, resulted in the drainage of specie to the provinces. For instance, a 798 government decree noted that people in the provincial markets possessed large reserves of cash, while the population of the capital and its surrounding region lacked them.

Despite these efforts the government did not succeed in introducing a monetary economy, due to the devaluation of currency brought about in part by the appearance of counterfeit coins. The court repeatedly attempted to remedy the situation by issuing new coins—there were at least twelve official issues up to 958—but it could not prevent inflation. Currency played no more than a marginal role in this society, where it represented neither a source of revenue nor a medium of exchange. For several centuries rice and silk fabric were the standards of value. Moreover, silk was the predominant medium of exchange in official foreign relations.[25]

In the eighth century, official embassies came and went among Japan, Korea (Silla), and China. A fourth country then entered the scene. Parhae, situated north of Silla and constituted in part by a Tungusic tribe and in part by the former Koguryô nobility, became an independent kingdom circa 698. These four countries sent their representatives to pay visits to one another. In the eighth century, roughly seventy Japanese and foreign delegations crossed the ocean, the majority between Japan and Korea. These delegations brought to the foreign monarch tribute or official presents and in exchange received gifts; the delegates themselves also were rewarded by the court that welcomed them.[26]

EXCHANGES WITH KOREA

Of what then did tribute and presents consist? As far as Korea is concerned, the annals mention twenty-one missions to Japan in the eighth century, but in only two cases do they indicate the content of "special presents" accompanying tribute. In 719 an embassy presented a horse, a mare, and two mules, one male and one female.[27] In 732 another embassy brought two parrots, two dogs, two donkeys, and two mules.[28] A Japanese envoy received from the Korean court on behalf of his sovereign "a peacock and invaluable gifts" in 700.[29] Exotic animals therefore, as previously, were appreciated as "special gifts." As for Korean tribute itself, it probably consisted of silk fabric, precious metals, ginseng, and a few handicrafts, such as those found in the tribute sent to China.

In return, the Japanese court entrusted the Korean ambassadors with gifts for their sovereign. In 703 these consisted of 2 bolts (about 12 meters each) of brocade and 40 bolts of plain-woven raw silk;[30] six years later, 20 bolts of silk taffeta, 30 bolts of plain-woven raw silk from Mino Province, 200 skeins of silk thread, and 150 pounds of silk floss were given.[31] In 770, 25 bolts of plain-woven raw silk, 100 skeins of silk thread, and 250 pounds of silk floss were offered. Meanwhile, the envoys themselves were rewarded with plain-woven raw silk and silk floss.[32] The Korean annals also tell us that in 804 a Japanese embassy presented to the Silla king 300 ounces of gold—but it was a delega-tion appointed solely to search for a Japanese shipwreck.[33]

Aside from tribute, Korean missions to Japan were involved, more or less directly, in commercial transactions as well, as is attested for a delegation that arrived in 752: it included seven hundred persons led by a Korean prince, even though the letter from the Silla king mentioned only three hundred seventy embassy members.[34] One assumes that the others were traders. Indeed, approximately twenty "registers of products purchased from

Koreans" have been preserved in the archives, and one of these, dated 752, mentions the following products:[35]

Plant and animal-based substances used as medicines or perfumes: cloves, birthwort root (*Aristolochia debilis Sieb. et Zucc.*, or *Aristolochia contorta Bge*), frankincense (extract of *Boswellia carterii Birdw.*, a *Burseraceae*), nardostachys (*Nardostachys chinesis Batal.*), camphor, aloe wood, musk, fruit of Indian myrobalan (*Terminalia chebula Retz.*), rhubarb, ginseng, liquorice root (*Glycyrrhiza uralensis Fisch.*), honey, cinnamon, etc.;

Mineral and plant substances used in dyes: a lead-base white powder, a compound of sulfur and mercury, a resin-based yellow-red dye, orpiment (arsenic trisulfide), cinnabar, lapis lazuli, sapanwood, etc. (see appendix 8);

Everyday items: mirrors, felt rugs, folding screens, braziers of "white copper" (*sahari*, an alloy of copper with a scant percentage of tin and lead), censers, candelabras, and housewares such as bowls, basins, dishes, plates, bottles, spoons, mostly of white copper;

Ritual instruments and pilgrim walking sticks with metal rings;

Miscellaneous items: combs, belts, gold, bezoar (an antidote), packsaddles, fire prisms (crystals cut in the shape of a prism, used to ignite a flame with the help of the sun's rays).

Only a portion of these articles were produced in Korea: ginseng, bezoar, and some handicrafts—samples of which are preserved in Nara in the storehouses of the Shōsōin—which were sent to China as well. Plant substances, animals, and minerals essentially were Chinese or Middle Eastern products imported by Korea. China also exported these goods directly to Japan (see the next section).

We do not know if the Korean items were purchased by the court or by individuals (princes or high dignitaries). In 715 the court ordered the Kyūshū Headquarters (Dazaifu, which was the head of the provincial governments in Kyūshū) to give the Korean delegation upon their departure 5,450 pounds of silk floss and a boat, presumably as payment for merchandise.[36] In 768 the court appropriated to the heads of the Council on Shrine Affairs and the Council of State, a grand councillor, two ministers, and one princess silk floss from the storehouses of Kyūshū to permit them to "purchase Korean goods."[37] That year, however, there was no embassy from Korea—the dignitaries had to wait for the arrival the following year of an embassy comprising 187 full members and 31 accompanying persons, undoubtedly merchants.[38] One might surmise that Korean embassies from a certain point onward were laden with not only tribute but also trade goods.

Commerce, perhaps, was the main goal of official visits from Korea, because from a diplomatic standpoint, this country, traditionally Japan's closest partner, kept its distance starting about the middle of the eighth century. Relations between the two countries deteriorated as soon as the Koreans ceased to observe the etiquette of a "vassal" country as the Japanese court understood it. The Koreans, for example, simply termed "native products" what the Japanese considered tribute presented by the Korean king to the Japanese *tennō*.[39] Finally, in 779 the last Korean mission to Japan was dispatched by King Hyegong (r. 765–780), who was assassinated the following year. His successor stopped sending embassies. For its part Japan sent two final delegations in 779 and 799. Ties between the two countries from that time onward were continued through groups of Korean traders.

EXCHANGES WITH CHINA

Relations with China took place in a better diplomatic climate than those with Korea, although the number of delegations exchanged with China amounted to only one-quarter of those exchanged with Korea. Since the early eighth century, each Japanese sovereign (except Genshō, r. 715–724) until Kammu (r. 781–806) had sent an embassy to China, the final mission having gone in 838. The first in this series was appointed in 702, following a thirty-year interruption in official exchanges. That same year, the newly drafted *Taihō Ritsuryō Code* was promulgated. Ambassador Awata no Mahito, having been part of the commission that drafted the code, presumably had the task of introducing the new Japanese administration to the Chinese court, thus proving that the country had acquired the structure of an empire equal to China's. Was it merely coincidence that later, in 983, the first Japanese monk who departed for China after the advent of the Song Dynasty (960–1279) also brought with him a copy of a section of the Japanese code pertaining to the functions of government and a chronology of the Japanese sovereigns?[40] In any event, confirmation of Japan's diplomatic position was an essential objective of Japanese missions to China.

What was this tribute presented by these nine embassies to the Chinese court? Information on this subject is extremely scarce. We know only that in 734 the Japanese took plain-woven raw silk from Mino Province and wet-woven plain raw silk (*mizuori*), while in 838 they took pearls and silk.[41] A regulation issued in 927, however, may prove informative. It provides a list of products sent to China: 500 large ounces (21 kilograms) of silver, 200 bolts of wet-woven plain raw silk, 200 bolts of plain-woven raw silk from Mino Province, 300 bolts of fine plain-woven raw silk, 300 bolts of yellow plain-woven raw silk, 500 skeins of yellow silk thread, 1,000 pounds of high-quality silk floss, 200 bolts of colored silk cloth, 200 *chō* squares of silk floss (for padding), 200 pounds of compressed silk floss, 30 bolts of ramie (*karamushi*), 100 bolts of hemp cloth from Moda District, 100 *chō* of silk floss, 10 agates, 10 crystal fire prisms, 10 iron fire stones, 6 *to* of camellia oil (1 *to* corresponds to 8.5 liters), 6 *to* of Japanese Ivy juice and, finally, 4 *to* of Eleutherococcus oil (*koshiabura, Acanthopanax sciadophylloides Franch. et Sav.*).[42]

This list comes from the *Protocols of the Engi Era* (901–923) (*Engi shiki*), presented to the throne and published in 927, a time when there were no more missions. In principle, these regulations were founded on those previously drafted in 820 and 871. The products enumerated were not tribute items presented by the Japanese missions to the Chinese court, but rather items delivered to the Chinese delegates who came to Japan and intended for the Chinese emperor. The list helps us imagine the types of products that constituted tribute. Silk, including two kinds of plain-woven raw silk, corresponds to information from Chinese sources, and agates were mentioned previously in a Chinese report from 654. Silver was the most valuable item, but textiles—unpatterned, plain-woven silk or plant fiber-based fabrics, rather than brocades and twill damasks—made up the greatest number of tribute items.

In 760 the Chinese court ordered from Japan an article of a very different nature: horns. At that time, China was experiencing revolts fomented by one-time military officials who sought to seize power, and so the Chinese government requested, via a Japanese envoy, a supply of ox horns for the manufacture of bows and arrows. Consequently, the Japanese government taxed all of the provinces for the delivery of the horns, 7,800 pairs in total. The delegation that was to bring this tribute ran aground, however, and the horns surely did not reach their destination.[43]

Moreover, paper aroused the interest of the Chinese court. The official Chinese histories report that one of the Japanese envoys who came in 780 was a good calligrapher and that "the paper that he used was as soft as silk cocoons, the likes of which they had never known."[44] According to tradition, the Japanese learned Chinese paper-manufacturing techniques from a Korean monk who came to Japan in 610. Soon the Japanese began to make paper, and according to the code, a paper-making workshop with four paper specialists, ten makers of writing brushes, and four ink makers was attached to the court. Paper-making techniques were also transmitted to a few provinces, which from that time on became suppliers to the capital.

The Japanese later developed their own technique for making a soft yet sturdy paper. This technique was applied primarily from the ninth century onward, but already a Yamato Province (Nara Prefecture) register from the year 730 existed with this kind of paper. Was it this paper that inspired the admiration of the Chinese court in 780? An eighth-century Chinese author tells us in his collection of unusual events that Emperor Xuanzong (r. 712–756) used Japanese-made paper for a letter addressed to his brother. Paper can be considered the first Japanese product to be produced domestically with an imported technique and subsequently re-exported in an improved form. But in the eighth century, exports of this article certainly were minimal.[45]

Such were, according to extant documentation, the tribute articles sent to China. What then did Japanese ambassadors receive in exchange for tribute? The annals mention Chinese presents on only one occasion, in 805: these included brocade fabric, twill damask (*aya*), colored silk, perfumes, and medicines. These last items consisted of dried aromatic plant and animal substances, such as those purchased from the Koreans and later imported in large quantities. They were used as medicines, fragrances for the home or clothing, or incense for Buddhist celebrations. For some time fine fabrics, perfumes, and medicines were the exotic products most coveted by the Japanese aristocracy.[46]

Japanese delegates reported still more items. In 718 an ambassador received court garments from the Chinese court, one of which he wore the following year during his audience with the Japanese sovereign.[47] In 760 another envoy brought back soldier's paraphernalia complete with armor, helmet, sword, spear, and arrows, gifts from the Chinese court. The armor served as a model the following year, when nearly sixty thousand new sets were made for three provincial militia.[48] Another delegate presented a request to the Chinese court to obtain copies of the works of Laozi and other Chinese classics as well as Buddhist images. From his stay in China (717–735) the scholar Kibi Makibi brought back the following objects: a manual of court ceremonial protocol, a calendar with commentary, a foot-long iron ruler, a copper flute, twelve gongs, other types of flutes, a work concerning music, three bows with horn notches, and thirty bows of different kinds; he also drew up a list of the books (scrolls) brought back.[49]

Aside from gifts, the embassy members also had the opportunity to make purchases in Chinese coastal towns and the capital, and to do so, they were supplied with trade goods. Indeed, envoys of all ranks, about five hundred per embassy, received an allowance of plain-woven raw silk, silk floss, and hemp cloth prior to their departure. According to the *Protocols of the Engi Era*, the quantities amounted to a sum many times that of the semiannual salary allowances for officials of the same rank.[50] The ambassador received 70 bolts of plain-woven raw silk, for example, whereas his semiannual salary did not even amount to 8 bolts (figure from the code of 701). A calculation of the total quantity of fabric taken by the members of the first four ranks (i.e., the ambassador, the vice-ambassador, four councillors, and four ambassadorial secretaries), comes to 164 bolts of plain-woven raw silk, 650 pounds of silk floss, and 490 bolts of hemp cloth. Such figures could have doubled, depending on the number of students and monks accompanying the mission.

Besides their allowances the envoys of the highest ranks were supplied with special allocations of colored silk fabric and quality cloth. Considering that the costs of a journey to China were underwritten by the Chinese court, these allocations undoubtedly served as a medium of exchange. Furthermore, it seems that the delegates also used gold dust, that is, gold nuggets cleared of their coating by washing. In 701 a sizable mine was discovered in Mutsu, a northern province comprising the modern prefectures of Fukushima, Miyagi, Iwate, and Aomori; smaller mines existed in other regions of the country. In 776 the court, probably for the first time, awarded gold to one of its ambassadors who had been in China since 754; and from the end of the eighth century onward, it provided all ambassadors and vice-ambassadors with one to two hundred small ounces (1 ounce = 13.9 grams) of gold dust. Several monks also received one to three hundred small ounces for their voyage.[51]

Equipped with these means of exchange, the Japanese disembarked in China near the delta of the Yangzi river, if the winds were favorable, and from there first went to Yangzhou, a city of approximately five hundred thousand inhabitants—among whom were some thousand or so foreigners, particularly Arabs and Persians. The city markets offered tea and salt (government monopoly products), perfumes, medicines, and precious stones imported via Guangzhou (Canton), then the primary port for foreign trade. Yangzhou was also a center of trade for gold, arts and crafts, metalwork, weaving, and for manufacture of bronze mirrors. The Japanese could trade gold there for copper coins, gathered by the thousand on strings. In the period when the monk Ennin (794–864) was in China, from 839 to 845, the rate of exchange was 5,371 pieces per large ounce of gold (1 ounce = about 41.9 grams), and 1,700 pieces per small ounce. Currency then was in greater use in China than in Japan because China had moved toward a monetary economy in the eighth century, in particular through the codification in 780 of a system of taxes partly payable in cash. In his journal Ennin also provided a few references to prices: he commissioned a copy of a Buddhist image in mandala form for ten thousand coins; a vegetarian lunch, offered for an assembly of sixty monks, cost him six thousand coins.[52]

From Yangzhou, a small contingent of the Japanese delegation usually went on to Chang'an, then the Chinese capital, to present tribute to the court and attend an imperial audience with the representatives of other tributary countries who had arrived at the same time. The foreign guests were accommodated in official hostels, and the Japanese undoubtedly had the opportunity to encounter the envoys of other countries there—more than seventy countries, as we recall, regularly brought tribute to China. During their stay of several weeks, the Japanese could visit the city and its markets. Besides the Chinese, Chang'an, a metropolis of a million inhabitants within its walls and another million in the towns on its periphery, was inhabited by Arabs, Persians, Turks, Indians, as well as official envoys, students, monks, and merchants. The Japanese no doubt could barter with these foreigners and procure exotic items in the markets. The Chinese also established markets for trade with foreigners, presumably to allow them to purchase products that were in demand, especially, horses, camels, and other animals. The markets were subject to strict surveillance, and in some periods, the sale of certain articles was forbidden.

Following their stay in the capital, the Japanese returned to the coast to rejoin their companions and return home. One might imagine that their ship was laden with a quantity of exotic products, but the sources tell us nothing on this subject. The Shōsōin storehouses, still preserved in Nara today, however, can shed light on objects of continental origin that reached Japan.[53] Seven hundred artifacts and sixty medicines, bequests of Shōmu Tennō (r. 724–749) were deposited in these storehouses belonging to Tōdaiji temple from 756 to 758; and another collection of commonplace and ritual objects was transferred there in 950 from another Tōdaiji building. The collections included textiles of all kinds, court garments, musicians' and dancers' costumes, masks, glass vases, ornate golden goblets, stoneware, and spoons; furniture, such as tables, chairs, folding screens, shelves, chests, and boxes; musical instruments, such as flutes, tambourines, lutes, and zithers; ritual paraphernalia, including censers, banners, and images of divinities; writing cases, writing brushes, paper, and ink; mirrors; weapons, including bows, arrows, swords, and spears; dried plant and animal substances for medicinal use, and so forth. One finds among these artifacts a large variety of ornaments in Chinese, Indian, and Persian styles, including Byzantine glass, trays carved with motifs of clusters of grapes native to Greece, Persian-style ornamented vases, and dishes decorated in bas-relief depicting animals in the Scythian style. These objects were the products of Chinese, Korean, central Asian, and even Japanese artisans—in many cases, one cannot distinguish one from the other. The Shōsōin collection thus attests to the profusion and diversity of objects brought back by the missions sent to China as well as by those sent to, or that came from, Korea.

Besides handicrafts, Chinese books (scrolls) also were imported in large quantities. The Chinese writing system and literature were transmitted to Japan beginning in the fifth century or earlier. Thereafter, Chinese was the official written language of administration and education. A number of Chinese works are cited in the code of 701: nine classics, fourteen ancient commentaries on the classics, nine works concerning mathematics, seven titles pertaining to acupuncture, and five concerning medicine. Furthermore, the "Seventeen Article Constitution," a code of ethics for administration, attributed to Prince Shōtoku (564–622), had already mentioned, circa 604, approximately seven other Chinese literary titles.

At the beginning of the eighth century, therefore, the Japanese knew at least fifty or so Chinese works. In 757, during the revision of an educational program, some twenty titles dealing with astronomy, divination, calendar science, and history were added.[54] But these figures do not represent the total amount of Chinese books then available in Japan. Many other titles are mentioned in documents of the period, and they left their mark on Japanese literature and poetry.

In 831 a scholar completed the compilation of the first Japanese encyclopedia, titled "Inventory of the Court Storehouses" (*Hifuryaku*), mentioning a list of 1,500 Chinese works then at the Japanese court's disposal. This number represents about one-third of the literature hitherto produced in China. Another list, the "Catalog of Books Presently Existing in Japan" (*Nihonkoku genzaisho mokuroku*), compiled in 891, recorded 1,759 Chinese titles, itemized in forty categories, of which the main ones were classics and their commentaries; official histories, genealogies, poetic anthologies, administrative compendia, collections of tales, works on Confucianism and Daoism; and treatises concerning administration, military arts, rites, protocol, penal law, administrative law, history, music, medicine, divination, astronomy, and the calendar.[55] These works imparted knowledge of all aspects of public life and the sciences; they also served as models for the first Japanese works in these fields. These numerous books would not have reached Japan without the contribution of ambassadors to China, themselves scholarly men educated in the Chinese classics. The Chinese annals note that a Japanese envoy who came in 717 asked to study the classics under the supervision of a Confucian master, to whom he gave hemp cloth in gratitude, and that he used "all that he had received [from his government] to purchase books before departing for his country."[56]

Thanks to such purchases by ambassadors and the receipt of gifts in exchange for tribute, numerous continental goods reached Japan. The last Japanese embassy departed for China in 838. Another, appointed in 894, was canceled, probably because of revolts that ravaged China then and made travel dangerous. The departure of that delegation was to be postponed until such time as the country was restored to stability, but peace did not return to China, and the Tang Dynasty fell in 907. Nevertheless, from the ninth century onward, foreign merchants took over transport of exotic products to Japan, while tribute did not resume until much later, in the fifteenth century.

EXCHANGES WITH PARHAE

Relations with the kingdom of Parhae, which straddled what is modern North Korea and northeastern China (formerly Manchuria) today, had a commercial character, more so than those with China. Parhae sent fourteen delegations to Japan in the eighth century and twenty others up to as late as 926. The Japanese court dispatched twelve consecutive missions to Parhae, most of which accompanied Parhae embassies returning home. The last of these departed in 811. Tribute from Parhae normally consisted of animal furs. In 728 Parhae delegates brought 300 marten furs.[57] In 739 and 872 they presented 7 tiger furs, 7 bear furs, 6 leopard furs, and three and five *koku* (1 *koku* = 85 liters) of honey, respectively, together with 30 pounds of ginseng (1 pound, *kin*, weighed 670 grams) in 739.[58]

In exchange for these products, the Japanese court bestowed upon the envoys presents for their king consisting of, on average, 30 bolts of silk taffeta, 30 bolts of plain-woven raw silk, 150 skeins of silk thread, and 300 pounds of silk floss.[59] On one occasion, the court added to this 10 bolts of twill damask and 10 bolts of colored silk, most likely fabric previously received from Korea or China.[60] In 777, following the request of its envoy, the Japanese government granted the Parhae king 100 small ounces of gold, 100 large ounces of mercury, camellia oil, 4 agates, 10 fans made of palm leaves (of *Livistona subglobosa Martius*; Jp. *birō*), and Eleutherococcus oil.[61]

In 798 the Parhae king demanded that the dispatch of missions be regularized by stipulating a waiting period between visits (*nenki*), in accordance with the custom followed in China. He expected perhaps an interval of three years, like the one set for Korea in 732. But the Japanese court decided that delegations from Parhae should come only once every six years.[62] Then, in 824, the court noticed that the embassies from this country more closely resembled trade missions and were laden with treasures. It thereupon imposed a waiting period of twelve years between missions and limited the number of delegates to one hundred.[63]

Nevertheless, Parhae concerned itself very little with this regulation, and its missions returned to Japan as often as before. The Parhae king was compelled to accept only the return of some of those refused by the Japanese authorities. In 877, for example, an envoy attempted to present objects of curiosity and sake cups made of tortoiseshell, but these gifts were refused on the grounds that the waiting period had been violated. And this, even though a Japanese official declared that never before had he seen such marvelous objects, even in China.[64] Other missions from Parhae, however, had better luck and were welcomed to Japan, sometimes even before the waiting period had elapsed.

In the ninth century, the protocols for welcoming foreigners were as follows. Upon their arrival in the capital, visitors were lodged at a guest house; then came the official receipt of the sovereign missive and tribute. Later, near the guest house, a tent was set up where officials of the Ministry of the Treasury and the court storehouses proceeded, accompanied by warehousemen and assessors, to purchase trade goods that had been brought by the foreigners. According to the *Protocols of the Engi Era*, officials responsible for purchases had at their disposal 100 bolts of plain-woven raw silk from a northern province, 1,000 pounds of silk floss, and 30 strings (30,000 pieces) of cash from the Treasury.[65] Once the transactions were completed, officials drew up a list of products purchased, which they presented to the Council of State, after which they returned the sums not expended to the Ministry of the Treasury. The population of the capital then was authorized to purchase whatever remained from the foreigners, but all private trade was forbidden prior to the government's transactions.[66]

We have no information about the products sold by the Parhae delegations that continued to frequent Japan until 919. After this date, Parhae was occupied by the Khitans and fell under the control of the Liao Dynasty. Termination of official relations with Parhae signified in Japan the end of a period of several centuries marked by the sending and receipt of tribute.

CONCLUSION

What was the balance of official trade between Japan and foreign countries from the seventh to the ninth centuries? The question is impossible to assess in economic terms, but we can make a few observations. Material goods that reached Japan essentially consisted of fine fabric, perfumes, medicines, handicrafts, and books. Japanese articles taken as tribute or used as a medium of exchange mainly consisted of simple fabric (plain-woven raw silk or hemp cloth), and sometimes gold dust or amber, agates, and pearls. For Japan, at first glance, this trade meant the acquisition of luxury products, the consumption of which was limited to the high aristocracy, among whom such products played an important role (see chapter 3). Handicrafts undoubtedly also served as models for Japanese production. Although there are only rare reports on this subject—armor is one example—the similarity of Japanese and foreign objects, as seen among the artifacts preserved in the Shōsōin, suggests such manufacture based on a reproduction process. Moreover, books were a source of knowledge and permitted Japan to participate in the great progress of civilization.

From this standpoint, Japanese gains can be considered sizable, whereas the price paid by the Japanese, in contrast, seems moderate because it was only a matter of simply made articles or small quantities of metal and other valuable commodities. The Japanese government favored these exchanges and played a relatively active role until the early ninth century. But it stopped dispatching missions and limited the arrival of foreign delegations once Korean and Chinese merchants began to land in Japan. Exchanges thenceforth continued via trade.

CHAPTER 2

THE RUSH FOR FOREIGN GOODS
From the Ninth to the Twelfth Centuries

A group of Chinese traders arrived at the Kyūshū Headquarters. The Kyūshū officials were informed that it was forbidden for the messengers of families of princes and high dignitaries, as well as officials and civilians within the jurisdiction of Kyūshū, to propose price increases and to vie with one another to purchase imported products in a private capacity.[67]

By this decree, promulgated in 885, the Japanese government kept control over trade and asserted its right of preemption. This prohibition shows the keenness of court nobles and local officials to acquire Chinese goods for their personal use and, on the other hand, the eagerness of the government to secure the imports for the court in Heian. This stance seems to have characterized Japanese commercial relations with China and Korea from the middle of the ninth century onward. In order to analyze trade between these countries, we first should examine a few basic structural features of their respective economies.

THE CHINESE ECONOMY

The latter half of the eighth century ushered in significant changes in Chinese society that became increasingly important in the ensuing centuries. Economic and social power gradually passed from the aristocracy to the scholar-official elite and the emergent landlord and urban mercantile classes. Furthermore, the country's center of gravity—theretofore situated in the Wei River Valley, seat of the capital of Chang'an (modern X'ian)—shifted to the fertile lower Yangzi region (near the eastern coastal area of China), where Yangzhou and other mercantile cities experienced tremendous expansion. This transfer resulted in part from the military threat exerted by northern neighbors, the Khitans and Xixia, two powerful tribes who ultimately annexed part of China's territory. Another factor was the decline of the ancient commercial routes that linked

China and the kingdoms of central Asia, as well as the growth of maritime trade with Southeast Asia and the Middle East.

From the eighth century onward, agricultural production, especially the cultivation of rice in the lower Yangzi region, progressed considerably thanks to new techniques of planting and irrigation. Production, which hitherto had been enough for just the needs of the local population and the supply of taxes, yielded a tidy surplus that was marketed and distributed in other regions of the country. The same was true for the production of hemp and sericulture. In certain regions tea and lacquer plantations multiplied. Handicrafts, which had been merely a secondary occupation of the rural population, became an autonomous vocation. No longer were articles produced only for the payment of taxes; indeed, nearly as many commercial workshops were created as there were craftspeople to staff them. Thus ceramics, weaving, metalwork, papermaking, production of tea, salt, and alcohol, and wood-block printing of books (a typographic process invented in the eleventh century) flourished. These products circulated in the country's interior, both to the capital and interregionally. The waterways, the principal channel of transport, then comprised some fifty thousand kilometers of rivers and canals. In the cities numerous markets and commercial districts were created, and more and more individuals adopted commerce as their livelihood.

These developments were greatly encouraged by the government. Indeed, the supervision of prices and markets that had characterized trade in the Tang Dynasty (618–907) gave way to quasi- free trade under the Song Dynasty (960–1279). Gradually a new social structure emerged. Tang society was composed solely of a large population of peasants and a narrow stratum of aristocrats and officials. Under the Song, alongside them appeared new, primarily urban, landlord, merchant, and artisan classes. Consequently the consumption of agricultural and artisanal production was no longer limited to the court and the aristocracy but extended to all of urban society, which gave rise to an increase in demand and diversification of supply.

These structural changes were strongly linked to the system of taxation. Under the Sui (581–618) and Tang dynasties, the system was based on the allocation of lands for life: a household tax, rather than a land tax, was levied. But given the difficulties of registration, fraud, and progressive privatization of lands, in the eighth century an income-based tax was instituted, that is, on lands and harvests, and later taxes on commerce and handicrafts were imposed. In 780 cash accounting was introduced, and agricultural and artisanal products were assessed partially in cash: this was the first step toward a monetary economy. Furthermore, the State, in order to increase revenues, in quick succession instituted government monopolies on salt, alcohol, and tea. The profits derived from them were significant. In the eleventh century revenue from commercial taxes and monopolies amounted to half of the government's receipts; by the twelfth century, it surpassed income from agricultural levies.

Social and economic changes transformed the look of China's cities, as exemplified by the Tang- and Song-dynasty capitals. The Tang capital of Chang'an, dominated by the imperial palace in the northern part of the city, was principally an administrative metropolis, characterized by aristocratic life. It possessed two markets in the southern part of the city and a market for trade with foreigners, that is, with the official representatives of tributary countries. The markets were supervised by the government. The city of Kaifeng (known as Bianjing or Dongjing in Song times), situated farther east, in Henan, successively was the capital of four of the Five Dynasties (Liang, Jin, Han, and Zhou, 907–960) and of the Song until 1127. The first city walls dated from the year 781; a century later, the exterior streets in front of the city gates were occupied by boutiques, workshops, inns, and teahouses that escaped the control exerted within the city walls by the authorities. When Kaifeng became the capital, demographic growth forced the authorities to put up a second wall, and thereafter the administrative center mingled with the plebeian area of the city's outskirts. Markets multiplied in all the corners of the city, which ultimately was dominated by commercial activity. This was also the case in numerous other cities in the Song empire, such as Yangzhou, Chengdu in Sichuan, Hangzhou (the southern Song-dynasty capital from 1127 to 1279), and the large coastal cities.

Under the Tang Dynasty, the circulation of goods principally consisted of the supply of products for taxes and their redistribution by the State; but gradually this commerce was supplemented by quasi-free trade administered by professional, rather than occasional, merchants. In the Song Dynasty, the circulation of goods exceeded governmental parameters: the first step toward a market economy had been taken.

What then were the relations between China and foreign countries? They took place on an official level on the one hand, and a commercial level on the other. For centuries official relations with foreign peoples had to do with the receipt of tribute. Under the Song, numerous tributary countries continued to send their representatives to the Chinese court each year laden with tribute of local products, in exchange for which they received gifts constituting a kind of payment. The most-valued imports were horses, rhinoceros horn, tortoiseshell, ivory, and especially medicines and perfumes made from medicinal and aromatic plants.

The Chinese court bestowed upon the foreign representatives not only fine fabrics and handicrafts but also, above all, currency. An envoy of the Jurchen (a tribe from Manchuria), for example, in 1064 received 5,000 strings of 1,000 copper coins each on his sovereign's behalf, and a representative from Annam (Vietnam) who had brought rhinoceros horn was rewarded with 2,600 strings. One can imagine the expense that the annual visits from several dozen foreign missions entailed for the Chinese treasury. It was, however, inconceivable that China, a civilized country that by definition had to show its benevolence and generosity toward tributary countries, might reduce the gifts or the sums paid in exchange for tribute and thereby risk losing their allegiance. The Chinese court therefore took alternative measures. In 1016 the government proposed that missions arriving via the port of Canton present tribute to the city authorities without going to the capital, or, alternatively, that the number of envoys desiring to go to the capital be reduced to ten or twenty persons, depending on the country. This measure reduced the costs of reception, lodging, and rewards offered to visitors. Ten years later China did likewise with respect to the peoples of southern India, upon whom was imposed in addition an interval of two, then three years between missions. It was thus possible to reduce the number of foreign embassies. Later, the delegations from several Southeast Asian countries were welcomed at the frontier without being invited to come to the capital, while those of some other countries were limited to one visit every five years. Thus China took restrictive measures while maintaining the tributary tradition.[68]

With respect to foreign trade, however, the opposite occurred. Foreign merchants landed on the Chinese coast in large numbers from the eighth century onward. We know about the Chinese concept of foreign trade and the manner in which it was administered thanks to the economic treatise contained in the "Standard History of the Song Dynasty," chapter 186:

> In 971 the Office of Maritime Trade in Guangzhou [Canton] was restored, then, later, those of the cities of Hangzhou and Mingzhou [at Ningbo]. Merchants from the Islamic countries—Kalah [on the west coast of the Malacca peninsula], Java, Champa, Borneo, the Philippines, and Palembang [in Sumatra]—came to trade. They brought gold, silver, currency in coin and strings, tin, various kinds of silk fabric, and ceramics; and they sold perfumes, medicines, rhinoceros horn, ivory, coral, amber, pearls, precious steel (*bintie*), sea tortoise skin, tortoiseshell, agate, cheku-type shells, crystal, domestic fabrics, ebony wood, and sapanwood.[69]

This excerpt concisely describes the maritime trade that flourished between the Middle East and China (see appendix 8). In the seventh century, Arab troops subjugated and Islamized the Persian Sassanid Dynasty (224–651) along with other regimes in the region, eventually founding the Abbasid Dynasty (750–1258) at Baghdad. The main Abbasid port was Basra, situated at the interior extremity of the Persian Gulf. From the ports of Basra, Oman, and Siraf, ships rounded India, traversed the straits of Malacca, and stopped at Palembang, located on the northeast coast of the island of Sumatra (in Indonesia). Palembang then was the main port of call in Southeast Asia. From Palembang, ships reached the Chinese coast (see appendix 1).

A 1974 discovery provided evidence of this commercial activity.[70] Uncovered in Quanzhou Bay were the remains of a ship dating from the seventh or eighth century that measured 34.5 by 9.8 meters and had a capacity estimated at 374 tons. The vessel's thirteen holds contained the following merchandise: about 4,700 kilograms of aromatics, 9 kilograms of pepper, walnut areca, cinnabar, tortoiseshell, frankincense, and ambergris. Also found were approximately 100 wooden tablets inscribed with the names of merchandise, 500 coins, a wisteria-fiber hat, and lastly a Chinese chess piece. This ship corresponds to the junks used in China at that time for navigating the deep sea. Sources of the period refer to small-sized ships measuring thirty meters by nine meters with a capacity of approximately two hundred tons and to large junks of capacities of up to five hundred tons.[71]

Maritime trade was the subject of several Chinese works, of which the two most important featured detailed description of roughly forty countries and cities in Asia and the Middle East. These works refer to forty and one hundred fifty trade goods, respectively. The first, "Answers (to Questions) concerning Regions beyond the Mountain Range" (*Lingwai daida*), was written in 1178 by Zhou Qufei. The author drew his information from geographic treatises contained in the Chinese official histories and his own observations during a stay in Canton. The other, "Treatise on Barbarian Countries" (*Zhufan zhi*, 1225 C.E.), was authored by Zhao Rugua, who was Superintendent of Shipping in Quanzhou. The two works are invaluable sources of information. Below is a passage from the *Lingwai daida* chapter 3, "Barbarian Sailors":

> The coastal provinces and prefectures of our empire today
> stretch from the northeast to the southwest, as far as
> Qinzhou, and there maritime trade is conducted. In order to
> assure foreigners of a kind welcome, our government
> established offices for the supervision of maritime trade in
> Quanzhou and Guangzhou [Canton]. If foreign traders find
> themselves in trouble and wish to lodge a complaint, they
> should go to the Office of Supervision. Each year in the tenth
> lunar month [November], the office gives a large banquet in
> honor of foreign merchants before sending them off to their
> countries. Upon their arrival, after the summer solstice [June],
> the office assesses tariffs on imports and grants protection to
> the traders. Of all the wealthy barbarian countries, none
> possesses as great a variety of valuable products as the
> Islamic countries [the Abbasid Dynasty]. One may cite Java in
> the second tier, Palembang in the third, then many others.
> Palembang is a large port of call on the maritime routes
> between foreign countries and China.[72]

The Offices of Maritime Trade (*shibo si*) at issue in this paragraph are also referred to in the *Song shi* economic treatise cited above and were created in the eighth century, first in Canton, then in Quanzhou, Mingzhou (at Ningbo), Hangzhou, and other places. These offices had the task of inspecting cargo to prevent the import and export of forbidden products; and levying taxes in kind, which fluctuated, depending on the products and the period, between 10 and 40 percent. In the eleventh century merchants had to pay a 10 percent duty on pearls, camphor, and other products deemed of "high quality." The tariff imposed on tortoiseshell, sapanwood, and other articles considered of the second grade was 30 percent. Furthermore, the Offices of Maritime Trade purchased products that were subject to government monopoly, that is, medicines, perfumes, ivory, and sometimes other products. Later, other merchandise could be sold in the local markets. Finally, the offices lent protection to foreign merchants and encouraged their activities.

In the coastal cities communities of foreign residents were established. The foreign enclave in Canton was particularly sizable, comprising thousands of Arabs and Persians. Selected from among them was a head of foreign affairs endowed with jurisdictional and administrative authority. Foreigners had their own markets and their own places of worship: witness the mosques established in Canton, Quanzhou, and other cities.

The Song government greatly stimulated foreign trade, which permitted it to increase revenues through both customs duties and the sale of imported monopoly articles. Following the Song Dynasty's seizure of power, the government circa 978 dispatched eight imperial messengers to visit the countries of Southeast Asia and to invite their traders to come to China—they granted them a certain number of official permits to land in ports in Liangzhe Province, that is, in Mingzhou and Hangzhou.[73] In 1137 the government noticed that the number of traders arriving was insufficient; it thus directed the Superintendent of Shipping in Canton to stimulate more trade activity. It addressed him in the following edict excerpted from the "Important Regulations of the Song Dynasty" (*Song huiyao*): "The profit derived from foreign trade is considerable. If commerce is managed in a suitable way, one may count the receipts by the millions (of cash). Is this not better than imposing more taxes on our population? This is why we give so much attention to trade with foreign countries . . ."[74] These indications and many others contained in the sources reveal a constant concern on the part of the Chinese government with stimulation of foreign trade.

To understand the significance of foreign trade, let us examine some figures. Between the years 1049 and 1054, the annual receipts of taxes on imports of ivory, medicines, perfumes, rhinoceros horn, and pearls amounted to 530,000 strings of cash, and twenty years later to 540,000. Between 1076 and 1078 the state further realized an average annual profit of 300,000 strings of cash courtesy of its monopoly on imported products. If one considers that the government's annual receipts in cash (essentially domestic taxes and profits derived from the sale of domestic products subject to state monopoly) in the same period amounted to more than 7,000,000 strings, it is apparent that the profits derived from foreign trade represented about 12 percent of state cash revenue—though this was but a fraction of the state's gross receipts.[75]

THE JAPANESE ECONOMY

In Japan the situation was different, primarily due to the economic structure of the country, in which commerce played only a minor role. In 794 the Japanese court installed itself in Kyōto, then called Heian-kyō, which remained the capital until 1868. During the Heian Period (794–1185) this city was characterized by a preeminence of aristocracy in social life. No other city appeared in the course of this period.

From the early eighth century court revenue principally came from tax products sent from the provinces to the Nara court. They were supplied by peasants who worked distributed lands. Land taxes initially were calculated according to allotted acreage on a per capita basis, but as registration and supervision of land distribution became increasingly difficult, the authorities later adopted aggregate acreage as the basis of tax assessment and permitted local authorities more initiative. Furthermore, tax-in-kind products diversified, and speciality articles supplemented regular ones. Thus the provinces of Mutsu (in Tōhoku) and Tamba (Hyōgo Prefecture) sent paper, Wakasa (Fukui Prefecture) beechnut. Musashi (Tōkyō, Saitama and Kanagawa prefectures) supplied stirrups, and Mutsu also was renowned for breeding horses. Other specialities included foodstuffs, such as fish, rice cakes, millet, and fruit; or manufactured products, among which were boxes and chests, swords, sabers, baskets, combs, straw mats, ink, ceramic tablewares, and fabrics. As a general rule, production took place mainly in workshops tied to the court, sometimes in workshops managed by provincial administrations. According to the code promulgated in 701, all workshops and tools belonged to the state, and artisans were not free men but serfs or temporary workers from the provinces. The needs of the court thus, in theory, were satisfied by its own production and supplies from rents.[76] A new phenomenon emerged from the eighth century onward, however, the increase of private lands, called *shōen* (estates or manors). They originated partly from cleared lands—which the law sanctioned as private property—and partly from grants from the court in the name of merit or promotion consisting of a group of households (*fuko*) from which the beneficiary collected half the tax due to the government. Grants of households were quite common in the eleventh and twelfth centuries. Estates thus established enjoyed extensive exemption from taxation. Some also secured administrative immunity, which went so far as to forbid the entry of government agents. Estate owners generally were noble families or religious institutions (temples and shrines). Since they typically were absentee proprietors, they appointed estate officers who attended to the proprietor's supply of products and rents. The regent Fujiwara no Tadazane (1078–1162), for example, possessed approximately one hundred forty estates scattered throughout the country, from which he had the following products sent out: rice, silk, hemp cloth, paper, oil, salt, straw mats, melons, dried fruit, dried cooked rice cakes, fish, sake, Sweet Flag leaves (*shōbu*), cypress wood boxes, pine kernels (or pine wood), and shiia nuts. Rent items were stored by the central estate office. The noble owner, who resided in Kyōto, also had workshops at his disposal that fabricated and maintained items for his use. There was, therefore, no need to purchase handicrafts. So when Fujiwara no Sanesuke (957–1046), high dignitary of the court, in 1023 commissioned a decoration in gold lacquer for Chinese objects, he provided the artisans with raw materials and paid only for their labor.[77]

Aside from government taxes and estate rents, another category of goods circulated in the country: gifts and offerings. Gifts were exchanged between clients and patrons. Indeed, cliental bonds developed between provincial notables and court dignitaries in particular. Thus the regent Fujiwara no Michinaga (966–1027) in 1004 received approximately sixty horses from several governors and other provincial officials. He gave them out to his inferiors and to the Japanese royal house as a sign of favor, or as a reward for services. On other occasions Michinaga distributed rice and especially fabric. He frequently made gifts to the empresses and offerings to temples, often in exchange for religious services. Michinaga also sometimes favored officials with rewards that replaced the salaries normally paid by the government. The value of the gifts received by Michinaga from his clients seems quite considerable, because at times half of the court's receipts in fact went into Michinaga's storehouses. In return, half of the court's expenditures were assumed by the regent. What mattered were the bonds of generosity and obligation between superiors and clients. This practice went hand in hand, so it seems, with a certain disdain for mercantile activities. Textual evidence from the period implies that merchants were considered coarse people who amassed profits at the expense of others.

Whatever the form of these goods, gifts, taxes, or estate rents, they generally converged in the capital and satisfied the needs of the aristocracy; nobles did not have to resort to trade, except for specific products that could be procured at the fairs. In the Heian capital, the two official markets eventually lost their importance; whereas new markets were created at the intersection of avenues, like Shichijō (Seventh Avenue) which even today is the commercial center of Kyōto. There one found an array of boutique signs and displays filled with various products. A story in *the Tales of Times Now Past* (*Konjaku monogatarishū*), an early twelfth-century work, tells of a rich mercury dealer who each year sent his horses from Ise Province to the capital laden with silk and rice, among other goods. The same source notes that a Yamato (Nara Prefecture) merchant came to sell melons in Kyōto while a gold dust merchant hailed from Mutsu Province.[78]

Heian-period documents also refer to a certain number of provincial fairs, as evidenced in the following account dating from the 1130s. A merchant came to the Hoshikawa market, which was held in Ise on a Masuda house estate. He brought nine strings of sardines, about three kilograms of shelled rice, and thirteen sheaves of rice ears. When the guard demanded payment of a toll, the merchant began to shout and threatened him with a knife. The guard managed to take cover; the merchant was captured, and his merchandise was confiscated. Another fair was held on a Tōdaiji estate located in Nara. The temple received the following products from the estate: radish, burdock root, chestnuts, wild oranges, mackerel, bonito, horse mackerel, salt, Sweet Flag leaves, artemisia, glutinous rice, rice cakes wrapped in leaves, firewood, pine branches, and manufactured products, among which were straw mats, blinds, writing brushes, paper, and silk. In the 1170s the estate agent informed the temple that mackerel and horse mackerel had been purchased at the local fair, but that no bonito could be found there. The same was true of silk, but blinds were obtained at the Miwa fair. Provincial governors also had the opportunity to conduct business transactions, for they often bartered for products demanded by the court. The examples given illustrate the function of provincial fairs. They seem to have been controlled, or at least supervised, by the local authorities. The media of exchange were principally rice or fabric. Yet these fairs took place two or three times per month, and trade involving large quantities was still rare. Commerce was conducted as itinerant trade administered not by specialists but by occasional merchants, that is, peasants or their companions, who bartered some of their surplus production.[79]

One can notice a gap between the economical structures of the two countries. In China, a number of cities had permanent markets featuring an interregional exchange of goods through the hands of go-between merchants who dealt with various customers. In Japan, by contrast, goods would flow from the regions to the capital through extracommercial channels like taxes and other deliveries from the local allies of the Heian aristocrats. China had reached a market economy whereas Japan remained with a tax economy. A professional merchant class which generated wealth through investments was not yet born in Japan. The population of Kyōto at that time was 150,000 to 250,000, with a core of about 300 members of the high and middle aristocracy. They, along with the Buddhist temples and Shinto shrines, constituted the consumption center. The aristocracy and the religious institutions also were the sole clientele for products imported from the continent.

TRADE WITH FOREIGN COUNTRIES

The Japanese accounts relating to foreign trade date from the ninth century. At that time official relations with foreign countries were coming to an end. Embassies exchanged with Korea had been halted at the beginning of the century. China received one last Japanese mission in 836. Only the kingdom of Parhae continued to send official delegations to Japan up to the early tenth century. Apart from these contacts, trade provided the only link between Japan and the continent. The first Korean merchants came to Japan beginning in the 810s, but while nearly all declared that they had been carried by currents, this no doubt was a pretext to engage in trade. Two of these Koreans brought as presents four donkeys, seven goats, and two geese, respectively. The first Chinese merchants, so-called castaways themselves, were announced in the 820s. We do not know of all the transactions conducted with foreigners, but their merchandise seems to have aroused keen interest on the part of the Japanese, because in 831 a decree forbade noble families to compete with the court for the purchase of products imported from Korea.[80]

Chang Pogo, who had organized a trade venture from southern Korea, sent his delegates to Japan in 840 and 842. Upon their arrival in Kyūshū, they were ordered to return as soon as transactions were completed, but a Kyūshū provincial governor entrusted them with plain-woven raw silk and ordered Chinese products for his personal account. Another Kyūshū official procured books on behalf of the court, among which were titles from the celebrated Chinese poets Bo Juyi (772–846) and Yuan Zhen (779–831). This official was rewarded with a promotion in rank. It was around this time that the reputation of the Koreans went way down. They were suspected of espionage, and in official circles were fears of a Korean attack. This mistrust perhaps was aroused by Korean piracy, which had threatened the Japanese coast since the beginning of the century. In 842 the court decided Korean merchants should return as soon as transactions were completed, whereas the Chinese continued to be welcomed and lodged by the Kyūshū authorities.[81]

In 874 the Japanese government dispatched two low-ranking officials to purchase perfumes and medicines in China. They traveled aboard a foreign trade ship. These two individuals seem to have been the only Japanese civilians up to the eleventh century to go abroad under such conditions. This happening nevertheless reveals the court's demand for imported products.[82]

Thirty-five groups of foreign merchants, of between ten and sixty members, were reported in the sources for the ninth century, but the actual number probably was greater. Some of them took Japanese monks aboard their ships upon departing from Japan or returning from China. The port of disembarkation designated by the authorities was Hakata, located in northwestern Kyūshū. Trade with foreigners was administered by the Kyūshū Headquarters (Dazaifu), whose offices were located south of the port, near the modern city of Fukuoka. Officials of the Kyūshū Headquarters inspected the cargoes of incoming ships, even when they landed in other ports nearby, but did not levy any import taxes. This government agency was created in the seventh century. According to the

Taihō Ritsuryō Code, the Kyūshū Headquarters administered nine provinces and the three islands of Kyūshū, oversaw the departures and arrivals of official embassies, and accommodated delegates passing through in the foreign guest house. But from the ninth century onward, the Kyūshū Headquarters was also the court's agent for foreign trade. It reported to the court about foreign arrivals. Then, in accordance with a court edict, it gave traders lodging and food for the duration of their stay, in the guest house (*kōrōkan*) which had been used for official guests in former times. Foreign merchants, in particular the Chinese, thus theoretically were received in Japan like government guests; whereas in China and Korea merchants always had to finance the cost of their stay themselves. It must have been striking to a Chinese ship captain to receive such welcome, pay no taxes, and enjoy a free stay in a port with few or no other foreign ships at the same time; whereas in China, every port was crowded with dozens of foreign ships which all underwent strict controls and tax levies by the Chinese authorities. Yet it is unknown to what degree the Kyūshū Headquarters were able each time to provide lodging for a group of fifty to one hundred crew members who stayed there for several months or even more than a year.

It was also the Kyūshū Headquarters that was responsible for purchases. An 831 decree proclaimed that the court had the right of preemption and the prerogative of setting prices. The headquarters, therefore, first chose articles that interested the court and sent them to Kyōto. As a general rule, it paid traders in gold dust and then was reimbursed by the central government. Cui Duo, for example, who arrived in Japan in 877, received three hundred sixty ounces of gold dust in recompense for his products. From the late ninth century onward, purchases were made by messengers sent directly by the court, an official of middle rank and a disburser, both attached to the Chancellery.[83]

The nobles made enormous demands for imported products, however, and quite often they did not wait for the authorities to complete any transactions before sending their own messengers to Kyūshū as soon as they heard news of an arrival. They competed among themselves and exceeded fixed prices. The state took measures against these abuses in a decree promulgated in 831, which was reissued in 841, and again in 885. It seems that nobles turned a deaf ear, because the decree subsequently was repeated in 895 and 903. Here is an excerpt from the last of these decrees:

One hears these days that the moment Chinese traders arrive,
temples, sanctuaries, and the families of princes and high
dignitaries send their messengers to compete for purchases
before government emissaries have arrived. Rich families in
the capital greatly appreciate foreign products, and to obtain
them, inflate prices. For this reason, price levels are unstable.
This happens because provincial barrier officials do not
exercise sufficient control and officials of the Kyūshū
Headquarters neglect to make inspections. According to the
penal law, making purchases before the authorities have
completed their transactions falls into the category of the
offense of stealing and is punishable by three years of forced
labor.[84]

Through this decree and the previous edicts, the court reasserted its
rights to preempt goods and establish prices; it stated that purchases made hastily by dignitary families and religious establishments caused price instability and infringed upon government
prerogatives. These assertions rested on the administrative code of
701, even though the eighth-century statutes had not contemplated
trade with foreign ambassadors or traders.[85] These rules had
heretofore been followed, at least in exchanges with delegations
from the Parhae kingdom.[86] The court sought to maintain control
and thus ceaselessly repeated decrees forbidding infringements by
noble families. Moreover, maintenance of control was a general
concern of the ninth-century court, which feared a weakening of its
authority because of the progressive privatization of lands. As for
trade, one is tempted to think that state-controlled free trade, such
as existed in China, would have been more profitable for the
Japanese court. But such a system undoubtedly was unknown in
Japan, and the concept of marketing imported products seems a far
cry from the Heian standard of thinking that reduced the economy
to its fiscal aspects.

Given that imports increased and that it became difficult to
absorb them, the Japanese government found another solution. It
decided in 911 to impose a waiting period (*nenki*) of three years
between visits by foreign merchants. Waiting periods of this sort
had been enforced in China since the Tang Dynasty to avoid too-
frequent visits of embassies from certain countries; and Japan itself
previously had imposed an interval of six, then twelve years on

missions from Parhae.[87] Furthermore, in the tenth century, the Japanese government forbade its subjects to leave the country, or even to trade privately with the Chinese and Koreans. Through these measures the court claimed exclusive management of trade and limited its volume. Such policies did not derive from hostility toward foreign countries, but rather from an intent to assert or regain control and maintain the status quo. It can be assumed that these seemingly restrictive measures were designed to secure to the Heian court the priority in purchasing exotic products while avoiding excessive spending and at the same time prevent a flow of the precious merchandise to other private hands. In these days liberalization or privatization of trade was contrary to the court's principles.[88]

Hence commercial activities continued in the tenth century under considerable restrictions. Three groups of Chinese merchants landed in Kyūshū in 903, 909, and 919, bringing goats, geese, and peacocks as gifts for the Japanese court. At the time of the arrival of the second group, the court did not dispatch "an envoy in charge of Chinese products," no doubt for budgetary reasons, but it did put in an order to the Kyūshū Headquarters for imported articles. On the third visit a court messenger went to Kyūshū and brought back an exotic bird.[89] These traders came from the Wuyue kingdom, located in modern Zhejiang. At that time China was torn asunder: the northern part was ruled by five successive dynasties, and in the south ten kingdoms came and went. The Wuyue kingdom controlled the ports near the Yangzi delta and maintained relations with Japan and Korea.

In 922 and 929 individuals from a Korean kingdom, entrusted with a letter and presents from their king, landed on the Kyūshū coast. The court, however, refused to deal with them and ordered the Kyūshū Headquarters to send them back after giving them provisions. Kyūshū officials were instructed to write letters explaining that they did not have the authority to trade with foreigners or accept presents.[90] In 926 the monk Kanken, along with several disciples, received permission to depart on a pilgrimage to China aboard a foreign merchant ship. He received for his voyage one hundred small ounces of gold and was responsible for carrying four collections of works of renowned Japanese poets and a volume of calligraphed poems for the Chinese. This was one of the rare instances in which literary works were exported from Japan to China.[91]

A Chinese merchant came with goats as a present for the authorities in 935. He returned the following year and was welcomed in Kyūshū, although he had not observed the obligatory waiting period since his last visit. Moreover, the Regent Fujiwara no Tadahira (880–949) entrusted him with a letter addressed to the Wuyue king, probably in response to a letter from the king. The same merchant again landed in Kyūshū two years later. At that time, he received only hemp cloth in exchange for products because the official in charge of trade had died before making payments in gold dust.[92]

Korean traders arrived in 939 and 940, sent by the first king of the Koryô Dynasty, which had recently unified the Korean peninsula. These Koreans, however, were subjected to the same sort of treatment as their predecessors—they were sent back, and the presents from their king were refused. Three groups of Chinese merchants subsequently were welcomed in 940, 945, and 947, two of which presented a letter accompanied by gifts from their king. In response, the king received a letter from a Japanese minister and two hundred ounces of gold. Three other traders were sent to Japan by the Wuyue king in the course of the 950s, one of them laden with fine silk fabric. He was rewarded with a letter addressed to the Wuyue king. In fact two Japanese letters, written in 947 and 953 respectively, have survived. They were signed by ministers and not by *tennō* or the Council of State. They indicate that the government, in principle, did not maintain relations with foreign countries, but that, in consideration of the good intentions of the Chinese king, the authorities on occasion were willing to accept his presents. Nonetheless, it seems that this "exceptional" favor was often granted to Chinese merchants entrusted with presents from their sovereign. Thus one notices that the rules imposed at the beginning of the century concerning foreign relations were observed only vis-à-vis Korea. As far as China was concerned, violation of the obligatory waiting period between arrivals was tolerated, and several letters were honored with a response.[93]

Various collections of diaries of Heian high dignitaries as well as a thirteenth-century historical compilation, the "Hundredfold Polished Mirror" (*Hyakurenshō*), provide information on these exchanges. A visitor from Korea for instance, was reported for the year 972, when a commercial representative bearing a letter from the king arrived on Tsushima Island. The court dispatched a messenger, who brought back a horse with a dappled gray coat. The report notes contemptuously that this animal resembled an ordinary packsaddle horse and therefore could not constitute tribute from the king of Korea. In 960 the first emperor of the Song Dynasty, Taizu (r. 960–976), ascended the Chinese throne. Wishing to stimulate commerce, the emperor Taizu restored the Offices of Maritime Trade in the three ports of Guangzhou, Hangzhou, and Mingzhou. The last of these cities, modern Ningbo, played a pivotal role in trade with Japan. Traders from the Song empire began to disembark in Japan in the 970s. But soon difficulties in the regulation of accounts arose. It was stated in 982 that foreign merchants had not been paid for three years because of a shortage of gold dust. Mutsu Province, the sole producer of gold, suspended its supply and traders had to starve or return empty-handed. A similar case occurred a few years later when the Kyūshū Headquarters, while waiting for supplies of gold dust, could not pay a Chinese trader. In 983 the monk Chōnen (c. 938–1016) received authorization to depart for China. He returned in 986, and two years later sent to the emperor of China valuable gifts consisting of handicrafts, boxes, and writing cases decorated in gold lacquer and inlaid with mother-of-pearl.[94]

Several other arrivals in Japan were reported during and after this period. One of them was Zhu Rencong in 995. Instead of arriving in Kyūshū, this trader, accompanied by a group of seventy persons, landed in Wakasa Province (south of Fukui Prefecture), located on the Sea of Japan at the same longitude as Kyōto. When he was accused of a criminal offense against the governor of Wakasa Province, he was transferred to the neighboring province of Echizen (northern Fukui Prefecture), perhaps because it was close to the port of Tsuruga, formerly used in the eighth century by embassies from Parhae. At that time, there had been a foreign guest house, whether it still remained two centuries later is not known. Zhu reportedly traded with the empress' Household Office. When, at his request, Household Office agents wished to send him payment in gold dust, he had already left Echizen to go to Kyūshū, presumably on orders from the government. In Kyūshū he demanded anew that his accounts be paid and that the empress' Household Office once again send the gold. This time the sum remained in the hands of an official in charge of transactions in Kyūshū and did not reach its creditor. Following this incident, another messenger responsible for payment was dispatched, but the Kyūshū official again succeeded in intervening between the messenger and the trader and delivered to the trader only a portion of the sum, which occasioned a complaint from Zhu. This episode, which lasted several years, was not the only one that told about the malfeasance of Kyūshū officials.[95] A letter arrived from Korea in 997 but, considered a fake by the authorities, it did not receive a response. In the year 1000, another Chinese merchant named Zeng Lingwen must have struggled to obtain payment. The Kyūshū Headquarters decided to give him rice instead of gold dust, the official rate being one *koku* (eighty-five liters) of rice per ounce of gold; Zeng demanded a rate of three *koku*. The matter was reported to the court and was the subject of talks at the highest level. Minister Fujiwara no Michinaga personally set the rate at two *koku*. In the end, accounts were paid partly in rice and partly in silk taffeta.[96]

Another arrival was reported in 1003. A consultation of high dignitaries took place, as always, to decide whether to welcome the foreigner merchant. This time the Chinese was sent back because the waiting period of three years since his previous visit had not elapsed.[97] The following year the court purchased Chinese products for a price of three hundred ounces of gold. It acquired, among other things, a book of commentary on the "Anthology" (*Wenxuan*) a sixth-century poetic collection, and the works of Bo Juyi and Yuan Zhen. These items probably were brought by Zeng Lingwen, on his visit in 1000.[98] Zeng landed a third time the following year, in 1005. The advice of high dignitaries, in principle, should have been to send Zeng back for disregarding the obligatory waiting period, but this time some of them pointed out that numerous Chinese objects had been lost recently in a palace fire.[99] Minister Fujiwara no Michinaga (966–1027) "and two or three high officials conferred secretly"; three days later it was announced that the Chinese visitor would be welcomed.[100] Zeng subsequently presented to Fujiwara no Michinaga gifts of sapanwood, tea bowls, and literary works, in particular those titles that had been brought the previous year. In this instance one notices the pragmatism of Japanese leaders, who ignored trade regulations when it suited them—an attitude that no doubt explains the leniency shown toward foreign traders in numerous other cases. Furthermore, Zeng Lingwen conveyed to Minister Michinaga a letter from the monk Jakushō (964–1036), who had traveled to China in 1003. Subsequently, letters were exchanged several times between the minister and the monk.[101]

Another Chinese, Zhou Wenyi, acted as an intermediary in trade between Japan and China. He landed two times, in 1012 and in 1013. Just as Zeng Lingwen had done previously, Zhou brought letters from Jakushō and was accompanied by one of the monk's disciples. He thus was welcomed in Kyūshū, and brocade and twill damask fabric were purchased from him. In 1013 he brought yet another letter from Jakushō and offered peacocks to the court, and the birds were placed in the garden of one of Minister Michinaga's residences. The sources noted that eleven eggs soon were found, but that one hundred days later still no peacock babies had hatched. As for the letter from Jakushō, it informed the minister about the reconstruction of a temple on Mount Tiantai in China and requested a contribution from him.[102] Michinaga sent the following items: 6 rosaries made of stones from the fruit of a soapberry tree (*Sapindus sinesis*), 4 with amber ornaments and 2 with rock-crystal ornaments; a two-sectioned cabinet inlaid with mother-of-pearl as well as 2 boxes and a chest for clothing, all in gold lacquer; 6 screens the size of a folding screen; 3 ermines from Mutsu Province; a seven foot-long wig (2 meters), 100 ounces of gold dust, 5 large pearls, and 10 bolts of woven cloth with *tō* flower petals (a tree from Yunnan).[103] Minister Fujiwara no Sanesuke sent a lacquered wooden saddle inlaid with mother-of-pearl.[104]

The year 1019 was marked by an attack of pirates from the Jurchen tribe, a people living in Manchuria and Korea. A fleet of fifty ships came to attack first the eastern coast of Korea, then the islands of Tsushima and Iki, and last, Hakata Bay. The Japanese authorities had presumed that these were Korean pirates, but some months later the king of Korea sent a missive and repatriated two hundred Japanese prisoners captured by pirates. The Japanese court, for once, forgot its unfavorable prejudice toward Korea and sent a response via the Kyūshū Headquarters.[105]

An individual named Zhou Liangshi gained the favor of Grand Chancellor Fujiwara no Yorimichi (990–1074) in 1026. Zhou presented a genealogical document attesting that he had been born to a Chinese father and a Japanese mother, and he requested recognition as a Japanese subject. This request was accompanied by an offering of 300 bolts of silk fabric and a promise of other gifts of brocade and medicine. Yorimichi sent him 30 ounces of gold. The merchant returned to China, claiming to have been sent by the Kyūshū Headquarters with presents from the Japanese court. The Chinese emperor, however, refused the gifts, as the official letter from Japan was lacking. The gifts were purchased in the end by the Office of Maritime Trade at Mingzhou. Later, Zhou Liangshi returned again to Japan, but this time Kyūshū did not report it to the court. The official then in charge of trade in Kyūshū was Fujiwara no Korenori (963–1033). He was renowned for having accumulated considerable wealth during his term in Kyūshū, after he extracted goods both from the provinces and from Chinese merchants. Zhou Liangshi too complained about Korenori, accusing him of not having announced Zhou's arrival in Hakata and of confiscating his cargo.[106]

In 1028 Zhou Wenyi disembarked in Kyūshū a third time, and brought to Minister Fujiwara no Sanesuke the following gifts: 2 bolts of two different types of rare brocade, 3 bolts of white twill damask, 2 measures of musk, 50 ounces of cloves, 100 ounces of aloe wood, 20 ounces of frankincense, 10 Indian myrobalans, 30 ounces of lapis lazuli, 5 ounces of cinnabar, 200 rolls of various kinds of writing paper, and 3 pairs of sandals. But these gifts did not reach their destination via the Kyūshū Headquarters—rather they were sent through an official attached to Munakata shrine, which concurrently administered one of Minister Sanesuke's estates located near the port of Hakata. The estate administrator, on his own initiative, sent 10 pounds of sapanwood, 2 ounces of orpiment, 2 ounces of "purple gold" pigment, 48 ounces of verdigris, and Eleutherococcus oil. On the same date, the minister also received from the Satsuma (Kagoshima Prefecture) provincial government 10 bolts of silk taffeta, 10 pounds of sapanwood, 10 furs, tea bowls, an ink stone, and also 2 ounces of "purple gold" pigment, 30 Indian myrobalans, and 15 areca walnuts from a Kashiigū shrine administrator. Most of these items were imported from China, and one may assume that the senders had traded directly with Zhou Wenyi. Moreover, on other occasions in 1013 Fujiwara no Sanesuke also received furs, perfumes, and imported medicines from his Kyūshū estate.[107] These items represented the first recorded examples of private trade between estates and foreigners, which had formerly been considered illicit by the court, and such private trade subsequently multiplied. For the traders, direct transactions with private establishments presumably allowed them to profit from better prices and prompter payment.

Zhou Liangshi, the merchant born of a mixed marriage, paid another visit to Japan in 1034, and this time had particularly good fortune. He succeeded in making his way to the capital and even was received by the crown prince, the future *tennō* Gosuzaku (r. 1036–1045). One wonders whether this meeting was secretly arranged by Fujiwara no Korenori, who previously had traded with the Chinese in Kyūshū and now had returned to a post in the capital. The incident was noted in a manuscript fragment by the prince preserved in a private collection in Tokyo.[108]

Other traders arrived later in Japan: some were welcomed by the authorities, others were returned to their countries. Several claimed to have been brought by the currents, probably to avoid being sent back for violation of the waiting period between visits. A merchant traded with Hakozaki estate, located near the port of Hakata. Chinese merchants drew such interest among the Heian nobility that they generated various legends in literature.[109] In 1047 a resident of Hizen Province (Saga and Nagasaki prefectures) was arrested and punished for having illegally crossed the ocean; the products that he had imported were confiscated. This individual, perhaps, was acting on orders from an estate in the region or from a provincial official.[110] A Chinese man came in 1060 to the port of Tsuruga in Echizen Province claiming to have been shipwrecked. The council of high officials (*kugyō*) decided to send him back, but allowed him to wait for favorable winds "as in the time of Zhu Rencong in 995."[111]

In 1072 Korean annals heralded the arrival of two traders from Japan who brought to the Korean king the following gifts: a lacquered-wood saddle with mother-of-pearl inlay, a knife, a mirror case, a writing case, a comb case, a table, a painted folding screen, a censer, a bow with arrows, mercury, and mother-of-pearl shells. These Japanese were the first in a parade of merchants who landed in Korea over two decades. According to the Korean sources, they came from Tsushima, Iki, and the provinces of Satsuma (Kagoshima Prefecture) and Chikuzen (Fukuoka Prefecture); one might suppose that they were agents commissioned by an estate or a province. In 1087 one of the two traders brought pearls, mercury, and swords as well as oxen and horses. Two years later another presented pearls, mercury, swords, bows, and arrows to Korean authorities. In 1093 Korean officials confiscated the same items as well as sulfur and mother-of-pearl from another Japanese. These clandestine activities probably were not discovered by the Japanese government—the Japanese sources remain silent on the subject.[112]

In 1072 the monk Jōjin (1011–1081) embarked for China on a Chinese trading ship. He paid the Chinese for the crossing with 50 *koku* of rice, 100 bolts of silk taffeta, 2 robes, 4 small ounces of gold dust, 100 quires of superior-quality paper, 100 (units) of iron, and 180 ounces of mercury. The following year, several of Jōjin's disciples returned to Japan with a Chinese merchant named Sun Zhong. On behalf of the monk the disciples passed on a letter sent by the Chinese authorities to the Heian court, as well as a gift of twenty bolts of brocade and a copy of the Lotus Sutra written in golden characters.[113]

The letter and presents caused some embarrassment at the Japanese court. It had not maintained official contact with China for more than a century. Should it accept the presents, or not? Should it respond, and in what manner? These questions preoccupied the council of nobles for several years. When the court at last decided to reciprocate, it did not know whether to send a gift consisting fire prisms, mercury, silk taffeta from Mino Province (Gifu Prefecture), and pearls; or a gift of taffeta in long bolts, fine-quality hemp cloth, gold, and silver, with or without a Japanese zither. In 1077 it was finally decided to send to China a letter in a box inlaid with mother-of-pearl, two hundred long bolts of silk taffeta, and a quantity of mercury. It was Sun Zhong who delivered the gifts.[114] He returned two years later to the port of Tsuruga, this time entrusted with a letter from Mingzhou. After numerous discussions, which lasted two years, the letter was honored with a response.[115]

Another problem preoccupied the high dignitaries at court during this period: the receipt of a letter from the king of Koryô and official gifts consisting of 10 bolts of brocade, 20 bolts of twill damask, and 10 measures of musk. The king requested in his letter to the Japanese government that a renowned doctor be sent to treat him. The same request, when addressed to the Chinese court, had received favorable responses three times, and subsequently Chinese doctors visited the Korean court on several occasions. In Japan a similar request was declined in 1051, and this time it was also decided not to comply for fear of humiliation in the event of the Japanese doctor's failure.[116] The decision was conveyed in a letter addressed "to the king of a tributary country." Furthermore, the letter from Koryô had been transmitted by a Japanese upon his repatriation. This man, therefore, had previously crossed the ocean surreptitiously. When the regent asked the officials in charge whether other Japanese had gone to Korea, they responded, "The departures and arrivals are very frequent." It seems, however, that this lawbreaker was not brought to justice.[117]

Nonetheless, illegal trade was discovered and punished in 1093. A high official in the Kyūshū Headquarters, in collaboration with the governor of Tsushima island, had sent a monk to the Khitans, northern neighbors of China and Korea. The monk had sold the Khitans military equipment and arms, and had purchased exotic products. Following this incident, the Kyūshū official was relieved of his position, and the governor was deprived of his rank.[118] These measures show that the Heian court was still, then, maintaining its prohibition on all countrymen from leaving the country. Afterward, two letters from Mingzhou once again arrived in 1097 and 1116. The first received a response from the Kyūshū Headquarters, the second was the subject of talks that lasted five years and which finally remained unresolved.[119]

In this period other Chinese landed in Hakata or Echizen and Wakasa provinces, the majority of whom enjoyed the welcome of the authorities. For example, in 1133 a Chinese merchant came to Hakata.[120] Taira no Tadamori (1096–1153), administrator of an estate belonging to the retired *tennō*, soon sent messengers to Hakata to make purchases, claiming to be acting on orders from the retired *tennō*. In this case the Kyūshū Headquarters was reprimanded for having neglected its task and for having allowed private transactions—it received an order to report all arrivals to the court so that a decision could be made concerning the reception of the individual in question. Tadamori seems to have taken advantage of his position as a Kyūshū estate agent and as governor of several provinces. According to remarks by his contemporaries, he had accumulated innumerable riches by the end of his life. Furthermore in a journal entry dated 1134, a noble noted, "The storehouses of the former governor of Chikugo (Fukuoka Prefecture) contain seven jars filled with gold, seventy thousand ounces of silver and, in addition, innumerable Chinese and Japanese products."[121] In 1147 peacocks and parrots reached regent Fujiwara no Tadamichi (1097–1164) from his estate in Shimizu, the southern part of Kyūshū. This estate controlled the port of Bōnotsu, and the estate agent no doubt sometimes welcomed foreign merchants.[122]

About this time, a good number of Chinese traders settled in Kyūshū. Documents mention Chinese residents on Hirado Island to the west of Hakata circa 1150, noting that some of them maintained relations with the Munakata and Hakozaki shrines. According to one source, there may have been even a Chinese settlement comprising approximately one thousand six hundred families between Hakata and Hakozaki. In 1151 the Kyūshū Headquarters confiscated their goods because they had engaged in clandestine activities.[123]

In 1150 a Chinese trader came bringing twenty or so Chinese books for the Minister of the Left. This Chinese, having proven that he was born of a Japanese mother, requested to be recognized as a Japanese subject. The minister sent him thirty ounces of gold dust, referring to the precedent of Zhou Liangshi, who came in 1026, and put in another request for Chinese books. In 1168 Hizen and Higo provinces (in southwest Kyūshū) sent a present to the court, consisting of Chinese brocade, silver, sapanwood, alum, and red sandalwood. These products probably were obtained through private trade.[124]

An exceptional event occurred in 1170. A merchant came on behalf of Mingzhou bringing two letters and gifts intended for Taira no Kiyomori (1118–1181) and the retired *tennō*. Kiyomori was at that time the most important figure at court. Born to a family of warriors, he had inherited "innumerable riches" from his father Tadamori; alongside the *tennō*, he emerged the victor during quarrels over succession to the throne in 1156. He had assumed positions in Kyūshū, then named his brother and other close relatives to posts there, which permitted him to trade. He administered several estates in the provinces along the Inland Sea in this region and had the port of Ōwada rebuilt. Through a political marriage he had established relationships with the highest aristocracy of the court, thereby associating himself with the *tennō's* family. Later, in 1167, he had reached the highest post, that of Minister of State Affairs. The next year (1168) he retired as a monk and continued his political and economic activites at his residence at his Fukuhara domain near the Owada port. The letter and presents sent to him in 1170 are an indication of the relationships that he had entered into with foreigners. He invited the Chinese trader onto his estate in Fukuhara, located on the Inland Sea near the port of Ōwada, and even arranged an audience with the retired *tennō*. These activities ran counter to an ancient precedent laid down by Uda Tennō (r. 887–897), according to which the *tennō* could not have direct meetings with foreigners, a precedent which theretofore had been followed scrupulously. Criticism of Kiyomori's conduct was swift. A contemporary noted: "Not since the Engi era (901–923) have we seen such disaster inflicted by evil spirits!"[125] Furthermore, Kiyomori did not heed the rule that designated Hakata as the only port for the disembarkation of foreigners. Arrivals in other places had been allowed, but had never been officially approved.

Later, in 1173, Kiyomori personally sent a letter and gifts to the governor of Mingzhou, including a chest and a box in gold lacquer from the former *tennō* as well as a sword and a box of assorted contents. Later a court noble from the Nakahara family again criticized this initiative because Kiyomori had responded to a letter from China containing the phrase "various products sent to the king of Japan," an appellation that, for them, signified the ruler of a tributary country. Both letter and presents, in their opinion, should have been sent back. Finally, despite the illegality of exporting arms, Kiyomori added a sword to the gifts sent to China.[126]

Thus, for the first time, a public figure traded privately with foreign countries. Kiyomori, without changing the regulations, had broken with certain precedents that long had governed foreign trade. From 1175 onward Chinese sources mention arrivals in China of Japanese groups calling themselves castaways, but it was probably a question of agents sent by estates or provinces in Japan. Still, it would take several more decades before the liberalization of trade, which will be the subject of a later chapter.

CONCLUSION

Thus ended four centuries of trade with foreign countries. The principal players were Chinese merchants who came and went throughout this period. Roughly one hundred were reported in the written sources, but arrivals were noted on a nearly annual basis between the years 980 and 1020, a particularly well-documented period. An average of one boat per year also appears possible generally for the Heian Period, with an increase in the twelfth century. The Heian period thus had spurred many more exchanges with China than the earlier Nara Period during which only a total of twenty embassies had crossed the sea to Tang China in one and a half centuries. On the other hand Korean arrivals were rather sporadic from the tenth century onward, perhaps because they were received so badly. But in this era, even vis-à-vis other countries, Korea played a passive role—the Chinese went to Korea in droves, but few Koreans departed for China.

In Japan, foreign trade was controlled by the government: trade was managed by the Kyūshū Headquarters, Hakata was designated as the main port of entry for foreigners, the court claimed the right of preemption, the number of arrivals of merchants was restricted, and Japanese were prohibited from traveling abroad for trade. It was not a matter of explicit organization of trade or of a foreign trade policy that the court had elaborated at a specific moment, but rather of ad hoc measures (mainly prohibitions) adopted in response to concerns or immediate needs—measures that were based mainly on existing practices or ancient laws contained in the 701 code. The Japanese court did not create a new apparatus specifically responsible for foreign trade comparable to the Offices of Maritime Trade in China, but rather, entrusted this task to the Kyūshū Headquarters, which up to that time had dealt with official delegations.

As for foreign merchants, they enjoyed guest treatment in Japan. Some arrivals were the subject of high-level consultations at court, as if they were an event of the highest importance. When the government decided to welcome foreigners, it underwrote the costs of their stay. Besides, the waiting period imposed on visits of traders also was a practice appropriated to foreign embassies—it had been introduced in Japan for delegations from Korea and Parhae, and was used in China vis-à-vis embassies from the countries of Southeast Asia. The leniency of the Japanese toward violations of the waiting period paralleled the attitude that they had shown earlier toward guests from Parhae. Thus, in many respects, the Japanese government treated commercial trade as if it were the equal of official exchanges.

The import of exotica was so attractive that private trade emerged against the will of the government authorities. Initially it was characterized by private exchanges between estates or provincial agents and foreigners. Japanese traders also departed for Korea from the 1070s onward, and for China a century later. From this time onward certain individuals in the administration amassed great riches through trade. For its part, the Japanese government lost more and more of its hold over foreign affairs; thus the government control on foreign trade ultimately failed. Until roughly 1127 the court reminded foreigners to respect the stipulated waiting period between visits, and in 1133 it warned the Kyūshū Headquarters of its duty to maintain control. But this did not prevent the advance of private trade.

The Chinese government stimulated commerce in order to increase its revenues, whereas the Japanese court limited trade out of concern for maintaining its control over foreign affairs and prices.

This happened because Japan did not yet have a market economy and did not sense the economic benefits that foreign trade could bring. Also it did not impose tariffs on imports, and imported products were hardly commercialized. State-controlled free trade, such as in China, was inconceivable in Japan in an epoch when the power of the rich was expressed through material generosity. In Japan, neither the state nor the court nobles sold goods, they distributed them. Imported products then were hoarded as luxury goods or circulated as gifts. A domestic market for imported items emerged only several centuries later.

The attitude of Japanese authorities concerning foreign trade, therefore, was completely different from that of China. This stance perhaps can be explained by China's already having a market economy and a diversified domestic demand, predicated on emergent urban landlord, merchant, and artisan classes. In Japan, on the other hand, the circulation of goods still depended on a fiscal economy, at both the public and private estate levels, and the consumption of products in Japan was limited to an exclusive coterie of nobles and religious establishments. Given its economic structure and market situation, Japan was not yet ready for free commercial trade. Nevertheless, considering the growing demand for foreign products in Japan, it seems that protectionism had been maintained for too long, as evidenced by the birth and rapid expansion of private trade. In fact, the official control could not hinder the rush for foreign goods.

CHAPTER 3

TRADE COMMODITIES

Japanese homes are constructed of Korean pine, which today
is called the 'Luo tree' and produced domestically. The trees
are white and scented. All floorboards are of this sort. They
are coated with fragrance, and when one enters the rooms,
one is engulfed in scent. Since Japanese women smell
strongly, they cover themselves in perfumes. . . .

Furthermore, even during the warm season, they dress in
many-layered garments. Their garments have wide, short
sleeves; there are no belts. These robes are made of hemp,
sometimes of very fine quality. The Japanese send for twill
damask and other silks from China, and value them highly. . . .

Since their country does not produce aromatic plants, they
hold them very dear. For the manufacture of folding fans,
they use Japanese paper; and, for the blades, they use slender
carved rods. They decorate them with floral designs, colored
gold and silver, or with somewhat immoral images.[127]

This description, titled "Japanese Homes," comes from a collection
of Chinese anecdotes dating from about 1300. Its author, Zhou Mi
(1232–1308), lists the principal items exported to Japan such as
perfumes made from aromatic plants and fine silks from China. He
also mentions an export product, folding fans. The author seems
well informed about the role these items played in the life of the
Japanese court.

Before analyzing trade products, we will estimate the quantity
of goods imported and exported. No figures survive on this subject,
but the trade ships from China no doubt were similar to the 374-ton-
capacity junk discovered in 1974 off the coast of Quanzhou. To
imagine the volume of cargo, one may refer to another ship of later
vintage but in a better state of preservation, discovered near the
coast of Sinan in South Korea (see the section "Ventures Sponsored
by Temples" in chapter 4). The hold of this ship, of a capacity
estimated at between 150 and 200 tons, contained eighteen tons of

coins and eighteen thousand items (mainly ceramics). Three boxes were preserved, on average measuring 70 x 50 x 50 centimeters, each containing ten to twenty items. Since the other items originally were evenly packed in these boxes, the total number of boxes probably amounted to more than one thousand. One may thus imagine that each ship that landed in Japan from around the tenth and to twelfth centuries unloaded dozens of tons and hundreds of boxes of various products. On average, there was most likely one arrival per year, but from the late eleventh century onward, the Japanese themselves also left to trade abroad. We will analyze first the items imported into Japan, and then those exported overseas.

IMPORTS

In the previous chapter we gave lists of products that came from China in 1006, 1013, 1028, and 1168. They principally consisted of plant or mineral substances and textiles. This account is in agreement with another testament from the same epoch by the monk Jōjin. On the occasion of his audience with the emperor of China, Jōjin was asked: "For which Chinese products is there a demand in your country?" The monk replied: "Perfumes, medicines, tea bowls, brocade, and sapanwood."[128]

Another eleventh-century author provided additional details. In a work titled "The New Entertainments" (*Shinsarugakuki*), he described a Japanese merchant and enumerated his trade goods. Among them were forty-five "Chinese items":

Aloe wood, musk, a blend of incense (*ehi*), cloves, nardostachys, frankincense, birthwort root, camphor, white sandalwood, cloves of a different type than the first, white sandalwood of another sort, red sandalwood, bishopwood [*Bischofia javanica Blume*], sapanwood, alum, "red snow," "crimson snow," two kinds of cinnabar-based ointments, a "purple gold" pigment, croton, orpiment, Indian myrobalans, areca nut, a resin-based yellow red pigment, a cochineal-based pigment, verdigris, a copper ore-based medicine, cinnabar, another type of cinnabar, a lead-based white powder, leopard and tiger furs, wisteria-patterned tea bowls, bamboo boxes, rhinoceros horn, buffalo horn *nyoi* [a Buddhist ritual scepter], a belt adorned with agates, glass jars, twill damask, brocade and silk gauze of different kinds, *kuretake* and *kanchiku* bamboo, and blown glass pearls.[129]

Perfumes and medicines

More than half of the products on this list were raw materials—
items that the monk Jōjin and his contemporaries designated as
perfumes and medicines. Indeed, they were used in the
manufacture of medicines, incense, perfumes, cosmetics, and dyes.
One finds listed here products that China itself imported from the
countries of Southeast Asia and the Middle East (see chapter 2),
most of which consisted of medicinal or aromatic plants. The only
animal substances were musk and a scarlet pigment derived from
the cochineal insect. The list also includes ten mineral materials,
among them alum (aluminum potassium sulfate), "purple gold"
(possibly an alloy of tin, zinc, iron, and arsenic), verdigris (copper
acetate), and orpiment (arsenic trisulfide).

All of these materials were used in various ways, foremost in
medicine. Medicine was one of the court's standard concerns. There
was, at least in the ninth century, a medicinal herb garden in the
capital, and the court probably conducted workshops for the
preparation of medicines. Plants and medicines also were produced
in many provinces and were furnished to the court in the guise of
taxes. Apart from medicines produced in Japan, imported medicinal
plants included the following: nardostachys (an aromatic plant from
India or Yunnan), frankincense (Boswellia extract), camphor,
birthwort root, Indian myrobalans (a very tall tree indigenous to
South China and Malaya), areca nut, and croton (a small shrub
whose seeds contain a toxic oil). Birthwort seems to have been the
one plant also grown in Japan; it was a component of the tax
products sent in from three provinces at the beginning of the tenth
century. Mineral-based medicinal substances comprised "purple
gold," two sorts of cinnabar-based ointments, a material derived
from copper ore (probably alum), and powdered medicines, called
"red snow" and "crimson snow"—the former being composed of
sodium sulfate, mercuric sulfide, antelope horn, ginseng, and other
plants.

In 1091 an official made a gift of sugar to a high dignitary of
the Fujiwara family, explaining that it was said to be a sweetener
from China; the use of sugar, however, did not spread to Japan until
the fourteenth century. Finally, given that Japanese flora
encompassed a large variety of medicinal plants different from
those mentioned above—more than fifty species are enumerated in
the regulations of the early tenth century—one could think that

Japanese medicine did not depend on imports to a very high degree.[130]

For incense, the situation was different. It was indispensable for Buddhist rites, and each rite was celebrated with an incense particular to it. We know the composition of incense for four rites of the period. In all of them one finds cloves, white sandalwood, and frankincense; two of them contained camphor. Other ingredients included aloe, red sandalwood, and nardostachys. The four kinds of incense were composed of 50 to 75 percent imported materials derived from plants that did not grow in Japan. This is why incense and perfumes (designated in Japanese by the single term *kō*) appear on nearly every one of our lists of imported products. Thus, when trade was briefly interrupted in 1281 on account of battles with the Mongols, at one point the Japanese court experienced such a shortage of aromatic plants that it had great difficulty in celebrating a religious rite intended to mitigate natural disasters.[131]

Plants were used also in the manufacture of beauty products, to which the Japanese of the period attached great importance. Indeed, Heian society was characterized by what might be called "the cult of beauty." More than virtue, it was good taste that mattered in the lives of gentlemen and ladies of the court. Court members appreciated the way in which a lady combined the colors of her garments, or the fragrance that persisted after such a gentlewoman passed by, or even the aroma that engulfed an individual's residence. Descriptions of such appreciation abound in the literature of the Heian Period. Furthermore, the aristocrats of this era did not often have the opportunity to bathe, and their complicated garments were difficult to clean. So men and women perfumed their hair and clothing and powdered their faces. Perfumes were prepared according to individual taste, and an individual put all his or her artistry into them. Indeed, "the perfume game" was a competition that was enjoyed thoroughly by the courtiers. Murasaki Shikibu provided an account in her *Tale of Genji* (*Genji monogatari*), written the early eleventh century:

> The prince decided that among the autumn scents, the "chamberlain's perfumes," as they are called, Genji's had an intimacy which however did not insist upon itself. Of Murasaki's three, the plum or the spring perfume was especially bright and original, with a tartness that was rather daring. "Nothing goes better with a spring breeze than a

plum blossom," said the prince. Observing the competition
from her summer quarter, the lady of the orange blossoms
was characteristically reticent, as inconspicuous as a wisp of
smoke from a censer. She finally submitted a single perfume,
a summer lotus-leaf blend with a pungency that was gentle
but firm. In the winter quarter the Akashi lady had as little
confidence that she could hold her own in such competition.
She finally submitted a "hundred pace" sachet from an
adaptation of Minamoto Kintada's formula by the earlier
Suzaku monarch, of very great delicacy and refinement. The
prince announced that each of the perfumes was obviously
the result of careful thought and that each had much to
recommend it. "A harmless sort of conclusion," said Genji.[132]

There were five participants in this competition, and their perfumes
were made up of, among other ingredients, aloe, frankincense,
sandalwood, musk, nardostachys, cloves, and cinnamon. Musk, in
particular, seems to have been highly esteemed. When the monk
Jōjin, then in China, sent his disciple back to Japan, he told him to
buy "thirteen measures of superior quality musk" for 2,500 coins,
and he remarked that this purchase was worth 500 *koku* (42,500
liters) of rice in Japan.[133]

Imported cosmetics were compounded mostly of mineral
substances: lead-based white powder, with which men and women
powdered their faces; cinnabar, which was probably used as
lipstick; orpiment, which yellowed the complexion; verdigris; and,
last, a resin-based yellow red pigment. One wonders what effect
these substances had on the health of the courtiers' skin! All these
products played an important role in the lives of nobles, which
explains why aristocrats so coveted fragrances and medicines, and
ceaselessly competed to purchase these items brought by Chinese
traders.

Textiles

Another category of imported items consisted of valuable fabrics.
The author of "The New Entertainments" cited twill damask (*aya*),
brocade (*nishiki*), silk gauze (*ra*), and granulated-design gauze
(*kome*). Fabric manufacturing, from the eighth century onward, was
under the control of the government and managed by the central
and provincial administrations. Hemp cloth, of which there were
several grades, was the fabric generally used for clothing, and also

as a medium of exchange. The use of silk certainly was reserved for the nobility. As a rule, fine fabrics and simple silk taffeta were woven in the workshops belonging to the state, situated around the capital and in certain provinces. Compared to hemp material, these silk fabrics were manufactured in relatively small quantities until the tenth century. If one adds up the tax products recorded in the *Protocols of the Engi Era*, for example, one arrives at a figure of slightly more than 150,000 bolts of hemp cloth, and about 30,000 bolts of silk that were supplied annually to the capital. Among the silks, one finds only 700 bolts of twill damask and 55 bolts of brocade, with the rest made up of taffeta.[134] Production of fine silk, however, must have increased from the tenth century onward.

Heian courtiers, who attached the utmost importance to clothing, were crazy about rare fabrics. To illustrate this point, here is an excerpt from the "Diary of Murasaki Shikibu" (*Murasaki Shikibu nikki*):

> The Empress was dressed in red as usual. Her inner *kimono* was purple and red with pale and dark green and two shades of yellow. His Majesty's outer dress was grape-coloured brocade, and his inner garment white and green, all rare and modern both in design and colour. . . . The Nurse . . . wore grape-coloured *uchigi* and patternless *karaginu* of white and old rose. That day all did their utmost to adorn themselves. One had a little fault in the colour combination at the wrist opening. When she went before the Royal presence to fetch something, the nobles and high officials noticed it.
> Afterwards, Lady Saishō regretted it deeply. It was not so bad; only one colour was a little too pale. Lady Kotaiyu [sic] wore a crimson unlined dress and over it an *uchigi* of deep and pale plum colour bordered with folds. Her *karaginu* was white and old rose. Lady Gen-Shikibu appears to have been wearing a red and purple figured silk. Some said it was unsuitable because it was not brocade.[135]

We note here the significance attached to colors. Dyes consisted of pigments derived almost exclusively from Japanese plants such as indigo, madder, lithospermum, silver grass, saffron hybrid, and gardenia. Only one plant, which was indispensable for the production of red maroon, was not grown in Japan: sapanwood,

Caesalpinia sappan L., a tree of the Caesalpinia family, grown in Southeast Asia and India (alt. sapanwood or Indian brazilwood). Sapanwood often appeared among imported products, and Jōjin mentioned it when he was questioned by the Chinese court.

As for fabrics, twill damask and brocade are mentioned frequently in the literature of the period. The *Tale of Genji*, for example, noted:

> The plans for the Third Princess's initiation were so grand that it seemed likely to oust all other such affairs from the history books. The west room of the Oak Pavilion was fitted out for the ceremonies. Only the most resplendent imported brocades were used for hangings and cushions, and the results would have pleased a Chinese empress.[136]

Furthermore, Chinese brocades were mentioned by Sei Shōnagon at the top of a list of "Exquisite Things" contained in the *Pillow Book* (*Makura no sōshi*).[137] And the "Tale of Utsubo" (*Utsubo monogatari*) described the manner in which the court procured these fabrics:

> Upon each Chinese arrival, the officials of the monarch's private Chancellery [*kurōdo dokoro*] go to purchase "Chinese things," and they return with their trunks full of twill damask and brocade—the two rarest sorts of fabric—and with other trunks full of excellent-quality perfumes of their choice.
> . . . In the private Chancellery's ten trunks are twill damask, brocade, twill with floral motifs, and various sorts of perfumes, among them musk, aloe, and cloves. Musk and aloe fill the trunks upon each arrival of Chinese.[138]

According to the tales of Genji, Utsubo, and Eiga, Chinese twill damask (*kara-aya*) was used only on rare occasions: it graced the ceremonial dress of the highest-ranking ladies during the celebration of certain ceremonies before high dignitaries. This fabric does not seem to have been used for men's clothing, except rarely for Buddhist religious garments. Chinese brocade and twill also adorned luxury furniture, for example, the borders of a folding screen or blinds. Aside from these exceptional cases, clothing and decor for court ceremonies were made of textiles woven in Japan; nobles' ordinary garments were made of silk taffeta or hemp.

Perhaps Heian authors also referred to Japanese twill with Chinese designs as *kara-aya*, like those that decorate the fabrics in the Shōsōin. Only twenty or so Japanese fragments from the Heian Period and some rare bolts of contemporary imported fabric exist today. Seven fragments of imported twill were discovered in 1953 inside a Buddhist statue that the monk Chōnen had brought back from China in 986. They are preserved at Seiryōji temple in Kyōto. A robe brought back by Kūkai in 806 still exists at Tōji. One ascertains that the techniques of weaving twill are the same in China and Japan. This is why modern specialists, especially the Japanese working on the Heian Period, distinguish the origins of textiles with difficulty. In this case, the pattern serves as a point of reference, but we know that the Japanese sometimes adorned their fabric with Chinese motifs, although this was no longer as fashionable it had been in the eighth century.

In the late twelfth and early thirteenth centuries, a new textile was introduced from China: satin damask (*donsu*). It seems that this fabric too was called *kara-aya*. Indeed, a high dignitary noted in his diary in 1229: "In recent years, weavers . . . in the capital have begun to make *kara-aya*." Three years later, at the time of the initiation ceremony of a princess, a weaver named Tamemune was put in charge of providing fabric for ceremonial dress, among which was pale red *kara-aya*.[139] These are the only references to this subject. A legend claiming that "Chinese weaving" (*kara-ori*), widespread in Japan beginning in the sixteenth century, dated back to the Heian Period cannot be confirmed because that fabric was very different, an embroidered brocade used later for Nō theater costumes.

Yet another kind of imported fabric was mentioned in an eleventh-century correspondence manual. In a letter that presumably was addressed to the court treasury, a Kyūshū provincial governor confirmed that he had received an order for "damascene-type" brocade (*zōgan*), and that he would send the Treasury the pear-and-black-colored fabric. The governor further declared that he had also found purple gauze and red brocade, and that among the fine fabrics from Shu recently brought by a Chinese trader was a type of twill called "bamboo tuft" (*sōchiku*). The Shu region, located in modern Sichuan, was renowned for its brocades, which in certain eras contained gold thread. Several fragments of this fabric are preserved in the warehouses of the Shōsōin, but it is still not known whether they are of Chinese or Japanese manufacture. From the thirteenth century onward, Japanese army generals who had received special authorization wore Shu brocade under their armor, and later this fabric was used for the ceremonial dress of ladies of the warrior society.[140]

Furthermore, the monk Jōjin as well as the author of "The New Entertainments" mention tea bowls (*chawan*, pronounced *sakan* in that era), which also came from China. Indeed, one finds them among the items imported in 1005 and 1028. They consisted of ceramic bowls or cups that were served for drinking tea in China, but probably in Japan were used for rice or cereal, because the use of tea had not yet spread widely there. Thus the word *chawan* is absent from the "Encyclopedia of Japanese Words" (*Wamyō ruijushō*), which was completed in the 930s by Minamoto no Shitagō (911–983). In fact, one might imagine that the word *chawan* was introduced to Japan by the monks who had noticed the tea bowls during their travels in China, and that in practice the word denoted ceramics in general.

Ceramics

From this period onward, ceramics were a principal Chinese export item. Archaeological excavations have unearthed numerous pieces from the Song (960–1279) and the Yuan (1279–1368) dynasties in more than twenty countries in Asia, the Middle East, and even Africa, for example, in the Philippines, Indonesia, India, Ceylon, Saudi Arabia, Egypt, Pakistan, Ethiopia, and Somalia. Chinese ceramics had reached a degree of perfection that specialists consider unique in the world. The most renowned were celadon pieces, which reached their high point in the twelfth century, and the celebrated blue-and-white porcelains of the Ming Dynasty (1368–1644), which enjoyed great prestige, even in Europe.

Japan began to import Chinese ceramics in about the seventh century. In that era they consisted of "three-colored" stoneware (*sansai*, green, yellow/ochre, and white), numerous pieces of which have been preserved in the warehouses of the Shōsōin and served as models for the production of similar pieces in Japan. Furthermore, excavations have unearthed Song- and Yuan-dynasty ceramics in numerous regions of Japan: on the coasts of Aomori and Akita prefectures, at Hiraizumi (Iwate Prefecture), in Kamakura, Kyōto, Ichijōdani (Fukui Prefecture), Kusado-sengen near Fukuyama (Hiroshima Prefecture), Fukuoka, and in Okinawa.

A spectacular discovery was made during construction work on a subway in Hakata (Fukuoka) in 1978. On the site of the ancient port of foreign trade were thirty-five thousand Japanese and Chinese ceramic fragments. The fragments of Chinese origin consisted of white ceramics and Yuezhou celadons from the ninth and tenth centuries, and especially post-eleventh-century ceramics, including white pieces from the kilns of Jingdezhen and Fujian; Jizhou and Cizhou ceramics decorated with designs in ferrous oxide beneath a transparent glaze; celadons from Longquan and Tong'an; pale green Jingdezhen celadons; and finally some pieces and fragments in ferrous oxide-colored brown black glaze originating from the Jian kilns, called *tenmoku* by the Japanese. All these kilns (except Cizhou) were located in Chinese coastal prefectures.

One also finds among the excavated ceramics stoneware incised with peony and garland designs that were characteristic of the period. Without doubt it was these designs to which the author of "The New Entertainments" alluded when he spoke of wisteria adornments. Furthermore, a certain number of pieces bear brush inscriptions on the bottom, from which one can decipher the Chinese name "Commander Zhang" and "Commander Zheng." No doubt these were the names of the owners of cargo shares.

Unlike silks, perfumes, and medicines, imported ceramic crockery was not highly praised in literature of the Heian Period. Did it not enjoy the same favor among the courtiers? And yet nobles certainly enjoyed white stoneware from Yuezhou and mentioned it under the poetic Chinese name of "forbidden items" (*hisoku*), recalling that in times past its use was reserved for the emperor's family and forbidden to commoners.

Indeed it seems that the Heian nobility preferred lacquerware and, perhaps to a lesser degree, "white copper" plates and spoons (*sahari* metal) that were imported from Korea from the eighth century onward. Approximately one thousand of these metal pieces are preserved in the Shōsōin. As for ceramics, they were produced in abundance in Japan, but their quality was quite inferior to Chinese ceramics. They consisted of reddish pottery fired out in the open, called *hajiki*; and *sueki*, hard gray, unglazed and clear-coated pottery. Japanese ceramists also began to produce celadons and white stoneware copied from Chinese models, but in that period, they had not yet developed new techniques. Ceramic housewares seem to have been used in daily life, but they did not attract much attention from nobles, writers, and poets. They were similarly neglected in administrative documents, in particular in the registers of products provided by the estates of Tōdaiji and Tōji temples, even though pottery was produced there. It is difficult to explain why one finds relatively few Chinese pieces from the eleventh century in excavations, particularly since the importation of ceramics expanded considerably, especially from the twelfth century onward.[141]

Until now we have spoken only of products imported from China, because information about Korean products is quite scarce for this period. It was increasingly rare for Korean merchants to come to Japan, and we do not know what the Japanese who departed for Korea from the eleventh century onward brought back from their travels. Nevertheless, the list of Chinese products in "The New Entertainments" has much in common with those items imported from Korea in the eighth century (see the section "Exchanges with Korea" in chapter 1). Moreover, we know of the gifts that accompanied a letter from the king of Korea in 1080. They consisted of 10 bolts of brocade, 10 bolts of twill damask, and 10 measures of musk—all products that Korea itself apparently obtained through trade with China.[142]

Indeed, silks and medicinal substances were the primary products of Chinese origin imported into Korea, meaning that Korea practiced a type of transit commerce. Japanese sources typically did not mention Korean products, such as those exported by Korea to China, namely ginseng, pine nuts, ramie cloth, copper, lacquer items, and more rarely ceramics, paper, and fans. One is especially struck that Japanese archaeologists have discovered relatively few Korean ceramics in Japan, even though these were of very good quality. Korean celadons with incised designs were developed in Korea in the twelfth century and remain celebrated even to this day. Did the Japanese not value Korean ceramics, or was their trade of so little importance? These questions still remain unanswered.

Chinese books

Although seldom mentioned in the lists of goods cited above, in the era of diplomacy, Chinese books were brought back in great number by embassies. About one-third of all extant Chinese literature had reached Japan by the mid-ninth century.[143] Some new titles subsequently came to be added, especially works by the great poets Bo Juyi (772–846) and Yuan Zhen (779–831); they were purchased by a Kyūshū official for the first time about 840 from a Chinese trader.[144] We have proof that collections by these poets were still being imported into Japan in 1004 and that Bo Juyi's verse appeared among the imports of 1006. In two later instances, these verse works were accompanied by the "Five Tang Ministers' Commentary on the 'Selections of Refined Literature'" (*Wuchen zhu wenxuan*) and the "Anthology" (*Wenxuan*), a sixth-century Chinese poetic anthology long known in Japan. Several copies of the *Wenxuan* commentary were already in Japan at that date because the court leader Fujiwara no Michinaga about 1004 had received gifts of this work three times; the empress, his daughter, also offered it to the *tennō*.[145] In 1010 Michinaga made a present to the *tennō* of "copies printed in China of commentaries on the 'Anthology' and the collection [of Bo Juyi]."[146]

Furthermore, calendars were brought from China on two occasions. In 937 the Kyūshū Headquarters received an order to copy a Tang calendar that had just arrived.[147] And in 1048 a Song calendar was imported, at which time it was ascertained that there was no difference between the Chinese and Japanese calendars, except for the twelfth lunar month. Other books were sent to Japan from the Wuyue kingdom in the middle of the tenth century, but their titles are not known.[148]

In 986 the monk Chōnen brought back from China the first printed books: an edition of the Buddhist canon. The imperially commissioned xylographic printing of this collection had been completed in Chengdu in 983 after twelve years of work. Chōnen also brought back 286 scrolls of sutras newly translated from Sanskrit into Chinese. The monk had traveled on board the ship of a certain Zheng Rende.[149] In an eleventh-century manual, "Correspondence from Izumo" (*Unshu shosoku*) by Fujiwara no Akihira (?–1066), there was a letter from a high Kyūshū official mentioning an order for literary works: "Given that our country venerates the way of literature, the list of titles that we request is very long."[150]

Nevertheless, the importation of books does not seem to have satisfied the demand of Japanese authorities. In a letter addressed in 1008 to the monk Jakushō, who was then staying in China, a high dignitary regretted that for quite some time traders no longer brought books because they preferred to transport merchandise that was lighter and yielded better profits (aromatic plants for example). Five years later Jakushō responded to this request and sent books to Japan, among them "a printed collection," no doubt of works by Bo Juyi, as well as a picture of Mount Tiantai. During his audience before the Chinese emperor, Jakushō took the opportunity to boast of the wealth and level of civilization of his country while enumerating the titles of Japanese literature and the many Chinese books that were found in Japan. He was referring mainly to ancient Chinese classics that had been known in Japan for several centuries, however, and included only a few more recent works, such as a Bo Juyi collection, the poems of Jiang Fang (early ninth century), the "Comprehensive Records of Affairs within and outside of the Court" (*Chaoye qianzai*) by Zhang Zhuo (late seventh century), and the "Record of Drunken Land" (*Zuixiangji*) by Wang Ji (585–644).[151]

In 1073 the monk Jōjin sent his disciples back to Japan laden with fine fabrics and a gilt-lettered copy of the Lotus Sutra—gifts from the emperor of China—as well as other newly translated sutras. One wonders whether other works, particularly secular literature, would have been of more interest to the Japanese court. It was only much later, in 1151 according to our information, that secular works again reached the government. At that time a minister received as a present from a Chinese two volumes of the works of Su Shi (1036–1101), the "New Standard History of the Five Dynasties" (*Xin wudai shi*) by Ouyang Xiu (1007–1072), and the "New Standard History of the Tang Dynasty" (*Xin tang shu*) by the same author. These, perhaps, were printed books. The Japanese minister, delighted, gave the trader thirty ounces of gold dust and transmitted to him an order for other books.[152]

In the 1040s, four centuries before Gutenberg, the Chinese invented typographic printing; nevertheless, wood-block editions predominated. The Japanese were fascinated by these printed books. When a minister borrowed from the empress-mother a commented edition of the "Book of Rites" (*Liji*) in 1143, he exclaimed: "This has greater value than the income from ten thousand households." Another official, having succeeded in procuring an ancient commentary on the "Book of Changes" (*Zhouyi*, alt. *Yijing*), declared: "My joy is greater than if I had received one thousand ounces of gold."[153]

About 1179 one of the great Song-dynasty Chinese works reached Japan, the encyclopedia the "Imperial Digest of the Taiping Reign Period" (*Taiping yulan*), completed in 983 by Li Fang (925–996); at that time, however, one could obtain only three hundred of the one thousand volumes of this work. The encyclopedia subsequently was imported several more times and enjoyed a certain popularity among the courtiers.[154] One wonders, however, why it took two centuries to introduce this important work into Japan and why neither traders, nor even the three Japanese monks who had made long stays in China, were able to obtain this encyclopedia for the Heian court. One reason, perhaps, was that in China it figured among of the titles forbidden for export.

In spite of the embargo Chinese traders repeatedly exported quantities of books overseas and were paid handsomely, especially by the Koreans. Numerous decrees of prohibition—coupled with punishment for disobedience—promulgated by the Chinese court in the eleventh century attest to this clandestine trade. In 1091 the Chinese government even transmitted to Korea via an ambassador a list of Chinese books it wanted back, knowing that numerous titles had reached that country. From about 1080 onward the Koryô king attempted to acquire the *Taiping yulan*. Twenty years later, on his third request, he received authorization from the Chinese government. In the 1090s the Koreans also succeeded in procuring the great collection of documents and poems, "Finest Flowers of the Preserve of Letters" (*Wenyuan yinghua*) completed in 987, and the historical encyclopedia "Tortoise Shells for Divining from the Imperial Archives" (*Cefu yuangui*), completed in 1013, as well as the "Comprehensive Mirror for Aid in Government" (*Zizhi tongjian*), the major historical chronology completed in 1084 under the direction of Sima Guang. There was nothing like them in Japan. Indeed these works and many other great Song-dynasty titles were not mentioned by Jakushō in his list of Chinese works or by the authors of diaries of the period. Nor did they appear in the request of 1151, a request that included more than one hundred Chinese titles, mainly different versions of, and commentaries on, the classics.[155]

If one takes into account the volume and diversity of works imported into Japan up to the tenth century, the proportion in the subsequent period seems quite small. This can be attributed not only to the hazards of trade, but also to a lack of diligence and pursuit on the part of monks and Japanese officials. The latter seemed to marvel at printed books, even when they were ancient classics that were not novel to the Japanese. Nevertheless, this lack of interest is comprehensible. Admiration and emulation of Chinese literature had indeed been eclipsed by composition of Japanese-language poetry and tales. Moreover, Japanese literature had become sufficiently rich, even in regard to administrative matters, that one no longer resorted so frequently to Chinese precedents. Chinese books no longer were considered indispensable reference works, but merely objects of curiosity. One had to wait for the warrior age before seeing numerous great Song titles arrive in Japan.

Furs, bamboo, and exotic animals

Several other imported goods were less often cited, such as leopard and tiger furs. They were frequently brought by delegations from Parhae before the tenth century. In Japan itself, furs of wild boar, oxen, horses, and stags were produced, mainly for the manufacture of armor, shields, sheaths, and lacquer boxes.

In 1088 a Chinese merchant brought back bamboo and dogs. According to "The New Entertainments," the two species of imported bamboo were known as *kuretake* and *kanchiku*. *Kuretake* probably denoted the bamboo variety used to make flutes. *Kanchiku* was the first Japanized name, according to ancient dictionaries.[156] In 1150 a flute made of *kanchiku* bamboo amazed several court personalities. The prince to whom this instrument belonged clarified that the bamboo had been obtained by a Chinese trader two years before, and he remarked with some regret that the importation of bamboo had dwindled in recent years.[157] In the warehouses of the Shōsōin are six harmonicas, three of which are in *kuretake*, three in *kanchiku*, and a transverse flute in *kuretake* bamboo. According to some legends, the Japanese paid exorbitant prices to purchase this kind of instrument.[158]

Since the sixth century, exotic birds and quadrupeds had been brought to Japan as "special presents" accompanying tribute or merchandise—peacocks, parrots, geese, goats, donkeys, mules, and dogs in particular. All were considered objects of curiosity. With the exception of dogs, none of these animals was native. The Japanese did not consume meat or milk; they did not use the furs of goats (or sheep) nor did they know about the weaving of wool. Birds graced the gardens of the palace and the residences of high dignitaries. Parrots were brought to Japan by merchants in 1066, 1082, and 1148, and enjoyed the particular favor of courtiers.[159] Sei Shōnagon wrote about them in her *Pillow Book*: "Parrots are altogether charming, even though they come from abroad. They repeat everything men say."[160]

Other items appeared sporadically among the imported products: sandals, paper, ink, and ink stones, i.e., flat stones used for grinding ink sticks, for example. Other products are cited in the list appearing in "The New Entertainments." And a new item appeared in the middle of the twelfth century: Chinese coins. They soon became a prime import (see the section "Chinese Currency" in chapter 4). Up to that time, however, the products in greatest demand without any doubt were perfumes, medicines, and textiles.

EXPORTS

Gold, metals, sulfur

What products were exported by Japan in exchange for imported items? The sources indicate payments to foreign traders in gold dust (see chapter 2), citing quantities of 20 to 30 ounces (1 small ounce of gold being equivalent to 13.9 grams). In the case of the merchant Cui Duo, who came in 877, however, the value of purchases made by the Kyūshū Headquarters seems to have amounted to 360 ounces (5 kilograms).[161] In 1004 the court spent 300 ounces to purchase Chinese products.[162] The Japanese monks, and before them the ambassadors sent to China, also allocated for themselves a quantity of gold dust of between 100 and 200 ounces.

The first gold mine was worked by the Japanese court in 749. It was located in Mutsu Province, in the modern region of Tōhoku. From then on that region became the primary provider of gold until the fourteenth century. Other lesser mines were developed in the provinces of Suruga (Shizuoka Prefecture), Shimotsuke (Tochigi Prefecture) and, from the twelfth century onward, on Sado Island. Gold was extracted by the process of washing, which rid the nuggets of their coating. It was used as a means of payment until the modern era, mainly in its natural form of nuggets or dust. Gold coins were not minted, with the exception of a single issue in 760. In addition, gold was used to decorate luxury items used by the high nobility and the temples. The techniques of veneer, repoussage, gold lacquer, gold inlay, and later that of painting on gold backgrounds were also utilized.

In 749 Mutsu Province sent in a tax consisting of 900 ounces (12.5 kilograms) of gold. This tax most likely was intended for the construction of the Nara Great Buddha, the gilding of which required 58 kilograms in total. Furthermore, in 1187 another special levy of 30,000 ounces of gold (417 kilograms) was demanded from the province for reconstructing the same statue.[163] One may thus estimate that from the eighth century onward, the exploitation of gold was sufficient for the needs of the Japanese and even allowed them to make payments abroad.

As for China, its gold resources were never plentiful. There were deposits in Yunnan, Lingnan (modern Guangdong and Guangxi), and Annam. This last region, which corresponds to Vietnam and Cambodia, however, achieved independence in the tenth century. Gold was imported into China in all periods, either as payments or in the form of manufactured items. It is estimated that gold was worth seven times as much as silver in China and that its value nearly doubled in the twelfth and thirteenth centuries, while in Japan, gold was only four times as valuable as silver. Japanese gold probably seemed like a bargain to Chinese traders.

As far as other metals are concerned, a silver deposit was worked on Tsushima Island until the fourteenth century; thereafter, silver had to be imported from the continent. The gold and silver mines of Mutsu and Tsushima were known to the Chinese. The monk Chōnen had stated as much to the Chinese court in 983, as was noted in the "Standard History of the Song Dynasty" (*Song shi*) and the "Treatise on Barbarian Countries" (*Zhufan zhi*) of 1225. Deposits of copper and iron also were worked in Japan from the late seventh century onward. Prior to that date, these metals were imported from Korea.[164]

In addition to precious metals, foreign merchants also purchased other products in Japan. According to Jōjin's travel journal, one merchant with whom the monk made the crossing had purchased great quantities of mercury and sulfur in Japan. Also among the articles paid by Jōjin for his passage were 180 ounces of mercury. During his stay in Hangzhou, he entrusted 3 small ounces of gold (41.7 grams) and 100 large ounces of mercury (1 large ounce = 41.9 grams) to the proprietor of his guest house to obtain coins in exchange. Ten days later, the innkeeper returned to him 13 strings (13,000 pieces) of cash. Moreover, the monk's companions in China sold 200 pearls for medicinal use for 800 coins.[165] Mercury, sulfur, and pearls also appeared among the items exported by the Japanese to Korea in the 1080s and 1090s. In 1084 for instance, the prefect of Mingzhou issued an order to ten commercial enterprises for a total amount of 500,000 pounds of sulfur from Japan.[166]

Mercury was obtained in Japan from the early eighth century onward in Ise Province (Mie Prefecture). Until the seventeenth century, this region remained the primary source of this metal that was extracted from cinnabar ore. Mercury was an indispensable element for gilding, which required five parts of mercury for every one of gold. More rarely, mercury was also found in the alloys of certain smelted items. In China mercury was used as a medicinal substance. In particular, alchemists prescribed an ointment made of silver, lead, and mercury as a stimulant for the heart and the spirit, and they accorded cinnabar the power of prolonging life.

Sulfur was extracted from mountainous regions in Japan, in particular in Shinano (Nagano Prefecture), Shimotsuke (Tochigi Prefecture), Satsuma (Kagoshima Prefecture) in southern Kyūshū, and on "Sulfur Island" (Iōjima). But sulfur is mentioned only rarely in Japanese documents. This material no doubt was used as an igniter and as a pigment for dyeing. In China sulfur was used as a pharmaceutical component in medicine and alchemy and, since the beginning of the common era, sulfur spring baths were known there as a treatment for skin diseases. Medicinal virtues were also attributed to sulfur. Sulfur had been imported to China for some time from the kingdoms of Southeast Asia, and Japan became a new supplier with a growing volume of exports—by the fifteenth century, exports of sulfur from Japan amounted to hundreds of thousands of pounds.

Pearls

In China pearls were the theme of numerous legends; they symbolized wealth, beauty, and supernatural powers. The harvesting of pearls was practiced from the first centuries of the common era on the southern coast of Guangdong. But Chinese pearls were of an inferior quality compared to those of other countries, and they soon became a typical import item from Southeast Asian and Arab sources. According to an account from the thirteenth century, the merchants of these countries concealed pearls in the linings of their clothes and the handles of their umbrellas to avoid taxes. Pearls were used in China in the decoration of ceremonial furniture and as jewels for men's and women's fashions; in particular, they adorned the headdresses of emperors. But they did not escape the crushers of doctors and alchemists, who treated cataracts and other diseases of the eye with amalgams of powdered pearls, because pearls were round like the eyes and luminous as the full moon. Taoists also considered them to have the power to prolong life.

The shipment of pearls from Japan to China as tribute was reported in 654 and 838. Pearls were harvested in Japan on the western coast of Honshū (Shimane Prefecture), Tsushima Island, and in Ise, which is still renowned for the cultivation of pearls. The pearl trade no doubt was profitable. An account from the thirteenth century reported that a Japanese merchant bought a precious pearl for sixty bolts of silk fabric and that he resold it in China for five thousand pieces of twill damask. Furthermore, in the middle of the eleventh century, a Kyūshū official informed the governor of Ise that a Chinese person had just arrived on a quest for "pearls as bright as the moon."[167]

According to these sources, the principal exported items were gold, mercury, sulfur, and pearls. These products and others were enumerated in a Chinese text from the thirteenth century, the "Treatise of Siming [Mingzhou] of the Baoqing Era" (*Baoqing Siming zhi*):

> Japan, that is, Yamato, is situated in the far east, near the place where the sun rises. The trees of this country are of the very finest quality, having formed rings over the course of many years. Normally, the Japanese are skilled manufacturers of paper in five colors and, using gold leaf, they decorate it with orchids and other flowers in a manner still unmatched by the Chinese. They mainly use this paper for copying sutras. Their bronze craft also is more refined than that of China. Their trade ships arrive on our shores by a northeasterly wind, and they bring us all sorts of merchandise: products of high value—gold leaf, gold dust, decorative pearls, pearls for medicinal use, mercury, stag horn, and dichrocephala [*dichrocephala latifolia DC.*, a medicinal plant grown in southern Japan]; and second-class products—sulfur, mother-of-pearl shells, rush mats, pine wood, cryptomeria wood, and planks of Luo tree wood.[168]

Paper

This account first describes a certain type of paper from Japan. Paper of Japanese manufacture was already noted for its excellent quality in the eighth century (see the section "Exchanges with China" in chapter 1), and the refinement of paper and ink was even praised by a Chinese writer in 1008 when he received a letter from a Japanese high dignitary. The monk Jōjin was also provided with paper for his travels and distributed it to the Chinese as gifts or payments.[169]

What were the characteristics of Japanese paper? Chinese paper, such as that imported into Japan, was made with hemp fibers and paper mulberry. Then, refined and diluted paper pulp was poured onto a screen, drained, and allowed to dry. The Japanese are credited with having discovered the use of the fibers of a daphne-like plant, *Wikstroemia sikokiana Franch. et Sav.* (*gampi*), the use of which soon spread throughout Asia. In the Heian Period, hemp was abandoned, and more often a mixture of paper mulberry and *Wikstroemia* was used. Furthermore, Japanese manufacturers turned toward a new method of production. The paper paste was not poured directly onto screens, but into a vat. The dipper then plunged the screen into the liquid and took it out while slowly shaking it in order to spread the pulp evenly. The thickness of the layer depended on the skill of the dipper. The sheet then was detached from the screen and dried. This technique, necessitating great skill on the part of the dipper, facilitated the production of finer qualities of paper. The Japanese also developed gelatinous plant-based glues mixed with pulp. Subsequently, Japanese paper underwent further improvements and its renown persisted abroad. In 1428 the king of Korea charged one of his envoys to Japan to inquire about the Japanese technique with an order thus worded: "As Japanese paper is of a solid and soft quality, we should learn the method of manufacture to introduce it at home"[170]—this even though Korean paper itself also had a good reputation. The Chinese thirteenth-century account cited above mentioned "a five-colored paper." It likely consisted of rolls made of differently colored juxtaposed sheets. Several sutras written on this type of paper have been preserved, in particular at Saikyōji temple in Ōtsu. They are flecked with gold leaf but do not have floral decorations, such as those described by our Chinese author.

Construction wood and mother-of-pearl gifts

Furthermore, the list of products exported to China reveals several new Japanese export items, among them construction wood: pine (*matsu*), cryptomeria (*sugi*), and Luo tree. The last was mentioned in two other Chinese texts, "Japanese Homes" (see the beginning of this chapter) and the "Treatise on Barbarian Countries" (*Zhufan zhi*). The latter reported:

> [The Japanese] grow a lot of cryptomeria and Luo trees,
> which reach heights of fourteen to fifteen *zhang* [41 to 44
> meters] and up to four feet [1.2 meters] in diameter. The
> inhabitants of the regions concerned cut them into
> rectangular planks and load them into large vessels to sell
> them in Quanzhou. The men of Quanzhou go to Japan only
> rarely.[171]

One can assume that the Luo tree was the Japanese cypress (*hinoki*), a conifer used as construction wood and today considered much more valuable than cryptomeria. This is the tree that makes up the great forests of Honshū, Shikoku, and Kyūshū. No documents concerning the wood trade survive from the Heian Period, but we know that in the thirteenth century the monks Myōan Yōsai, Chōgen, and Enni sent wood to certain temples in China to assist them in their repair work. From that period on, construction wood must have been loaded often onto Japanese ships leaving for China.[172]

As for fabrics, such as silk taffeta and hemp cloth, they vanished from lists of exports, even though they had occupied an important place therein up to the ninth century. Japanese fabrics probably did not present anything of interest for China, whose textile industry was highly developed.

Other goods produced in Japan were transported to the continent through extracommercial channels as private or official presents. We know about the gifts sent to China in 1015, 1078, and 1173, as well as those sent to Korea in 1072, 1087, and 1089 (see chapter 2). There is still one more list of gifts sent by the monk Chōnen to the emperor of China in 988 that detailed such offerings as a sutra placed in a box of aristolochia wood; 3 rosaries variously decorated with amber pearls, blue, red and white crystals, and red and black soapberry fruit stones, all nestled in a flat, flower-shaped box ornamented with mother-of-pearl inlay; a leather trunk trimmed with fur, containing 2 shell cups; a wicker trunk containing 2 conch shells and 20 dyed skins; a gold- and silver-lacquered box containing 2 artificial floral bouquets for use in religious services; a gold- and silver-lacquered box holding two scrolls of calligraphy by Fujiwara no Sukemasa (944–998), a volume of offering texts, and a book of letters; a gold-and-silver-lacquered writing case with an ink stone for gold ink, a stag bristle brush, pine soot-based ink, a small bronze water bottle, and an iron knife; a gold-and-silver-lacquered fan box with 20 fans made of cypress wood blades, as well as 2 paper fans; a pair of comb boxes inlaid with mother-of-pearl, one containing 270 red sandalwood combs, the other, 10 pieces of mammoth bone; a lectern and bookstand, both inlaid with mother-of-pearl; a flat box lacquered in gold and silver containing 5 bolts of fine white hemp cloth; a stag-leather trunk containing an ermine; a wooden saddle inlaid with mother-of-pearl and a bit; iron and bronze stirrups, and a croupier braided in red thread; a screen; a Japanese-style painted folding screen; and finally 700 pounds of sulfur.[173]

Among the numerous objects noted here and in the preceding lists, several attract our attention, as they did in China, where they were imported in increasing quantities. Foremost were wooden objects inlaid with mother-of-pearl. In the eighth century, specimens of this craft of continental origin had been introduced to Japan. Some twenty pieces—tables, musical instruments, boxes, and chests—are preserved in the Shōsōin. They were attributed to Chinese artisans and were made mostly of sandalwood inlaid with mother-of-pearl, but extant pieces also incorporate tortoiseshell, amber, and glass. Subsequently, this technique of ornamentation developed rapidly in Japan, even though it declined in China. From the tenth century onward, the Japanese also used lacquer backgrounds, which brought out more of the mother-of-pearl's brilliance. Japanese craftsmanship, in turn, seems to have aroused the admiration of the Chinese. Toward the end of the eleventh century, a Chinese author noted: "Mother-of-pearl ornaments originally came from Japan. Their fashioning and variety show great skill. These objects are quite different from those that merchants sell at home."[174] Thus, the Japanese had attained such mastery that the author had forgotten its Chinese origin. Mother-of-pearl inlay was one of many techniques of lacquer ornamentation in this period. Others included gold and silver foil inlay and several techniques of painting with mineral or vegetable-based pigments mixed with fixatives. All these techniques were of continental origin and they are represented in the objects in the Shōsōin.

From the ninth century onward, Japan developed a new technique that prospered for many centuries, gold lacquer (*makie*). The earliest gold-sprinkled lacquer preserved in Japan is the sheath of a Chinese sword held in the Shōsōin, and a fragment unearthed in Nara in 1986. There are, however, only a few such artifacts in China, and indeed the history of gold lacquer techniques is not yet well known.

The Japanese concentrated, in particular, on the following processes: a design painted with still-liquid lacquer on a dried-lacquer object was then sprinkled with fine gold or silver powder so that the powder adhered to the design's outline. Afterward, the parts sprinkled with gold powder were dried and covered with a new layer of lacquer. The embellishment thus was in bas-relief (*hira-makie*). A second process consisted of polishing the entire piece and the decorated portion several times with the aid of charcoal, horn meal, and various oils, until the decoration was level with the background (*togidashi-makie*). This process was standard until the twelfth century. A third process consisted of first mixing lacquer, used for painting the design on the piece, with charcoal powder and grinding stone powder, which created a high-relief decoration (*taka-makie*). Besides these decoration techniques, the Japanese also elaborated several processes for gold backgrounds. The art of gold lacquer was highly appreciated by the nobility during the Heian and subsequent periods. Artifacts of this refined craft also appeared among the gifts sent to China and Korea over several centuries.[175]

Fans

Another Japanese creation enjoyed great success among foreigners: the folding fan. It was invented in Japan in the eighth or ninth century, when only round and fixed (*uchiwa*) fans made of palm leaves were known—their usage had spread throughout China in antiquity. Two types of folding fans developed: one was made of cypress-wood blades bound by a thread (*hiōgi*); the other had a frame with fewer blades which was covered in Japanese paper and folded in a zigzag pattern (*kawahori-ōgi*).[176]

Fans had wide ceremonial and practical usage in aristocratic circles: as part of certain court ceremonies, and as an obligatory accessory, on certain occasions, for men's and women's wardrobes. In addition to paper fans, there were also so-called summer fans, which created an agreeable breath of air on warm days. For ladies, fans were also objects of pleasure, because they were decorated with painted images; whereas fans for men had two plain sides.

The paper fan was described by a thirteenth-century Chinese author (see the beginning of this chapter), but well before that date Chōnen had offered twenty wooden-bladed fans and two paper fans to the emperor of China. Furthermore, in 1123 a Chinese ambassador had the opportunity during his visit to the Korean court to admire "Japanese cryptomeria fans and folding fans decorated with pictures, showing landscapes, men with their horses, and women."[177] In turn, Korean envoys presented fans imported from Japan among the tribute items to China. Although the Chinese had encountered this item courtesy of trade with Japan and Korea, they continued to use round, fixed fans; the use of the folding fan did not become widespread in China until the fifteenth century. The admiration of foreigners for this exotic item however was also expressed early on by a Chinese author who gave the following description:

At the end of the Xining era (1068–1078), during my walks to the Xiangguo temple (market), I saw people selling fans from Japan. Made of deep crimson paper, mounted on lacquered blades . . . they were used to make wind. Flat, distant landscapes were painted upon them with the aid of a refined powder, delicately applied in five colors. On this side of the shore, the seagulls stood between the cold reed stems and the fragile knotweed sprays. This resembled a landscape of the eighth or ninth lunar month. A fisherman, covered in his straw cloak, was fishing there, seated in his attached small boat. In the background, the sky grew dark, there were little clouds and the birds flew off. The ambition of the artist was profound, and his brush of a delicate vigor. No doubt, even the good Chinese painters cannot do as well. The prices that were asked for these fans were extremely high. At that time I was poor, and I regretted each time I passed that I could not buy myself one. When I later returned, there were no more fans in any of the town's markets.[178]

From this text it is evident that the Chinese author was especially charmed by the picture that decorated the fan. Some rare copies of these items have survived at Itsukushima shrine, near Hiroshima. One sees there, for example, a young nobleman wearing his headdress and a lady of the court, garbed in her layered robes, sitting under a pine tree, painted in the Japanese style of *Yamato-e* on a mauve background enhanced with gold leaf. The figures dressed in Heian fashion and the delicate execution, with its glints of gold, would indeed have aroused a certain curiosity abroad, where this style and technique were not practiced. Later, another Chinese author pointed out that "they paint scenes of everyday life and landscapes of their country in richly applied colors, making great use of gold leaf."[179]

This type of painting decorated folding screens as well. A painted folding screen was brought to China by Chōnen in 983, and another appeared among the presents sent to the king of Korea in 1072. In the same period the Chinese court also preserved a Japanese painting exhibiting a seascape, and two others containing popular scenes in its storehouses. In the fifteenth century Japanese fans became models for the Korean production of imitation items destined for export to China. It seems, however, that these replicas were worth only one-tenth the price of the Japanese originals. Fans then enjoyed great popularity among the Chinese elites of the Ming Period (1368–1644), by which time they had become a favorite imported item.[180]

Swords

Other manufactured items that assumed growing importance in Japanese foreign trade were swords. They were privately exported to Korea by Japanese merchants in the late eleventh century, and in 1173 Taira Kiyomori sent a sword, among other gifts, to the Chinese authorities. Traders no doubt had brought them to China on other occasions, because the Japanese sword was already known there in the middle of the eleventh century (see hereafter). Since the Tang Period (618–907), China had stocked up on blades from the foundries of Sichuan, located near the Yangzi River gorges, but it also imported Korean swords, Manchurian blades, and quality steel (*bintie*) from Persia and India. Nevertheless, the market for blades gradually passed into the hands of the Japanese.

Since antiquity Japan had known the use of bronze weapons. In about the fourth century Korean immigrants probably introduced iron weapons: large swords, halberds, and daggers. At that time iron swords were of the *chokutō* type, with a straight blade. Several specimens from the seventh and eighth centuries are preserved in the Shōsōin. Ancient documents from the Shōsōin archives distinguish "Chinese swords" from "Chinese-style swords." From about the tenth century manufacture of swords in Japan took a turn and differentiated itself from the ancient Chinese school.

In the ensuing centuries, the shape of the blade, that is, its curvature and length, underwent modifications. From the tenth to the twelfth centuries, the Japanese sword had a relatively large pommel, was curved near the handle, and became straightened toward the point: it was approximately eighty centimeters long. Sword-making reached its highest point in the late Kamakura Period (1185–1333). The Kamakura sword was larger, but uniformly so, from handle to point; its curvature, less marked than that of the previous period, was placed toward the middle of the blade. The principal types then were broad swords (*tachi*, hereafter "short sword") and daggers equipped with hilts (*tantō*). In the fourteenth century, a very long sword of more than one meter was created, and an ancient model concurrently reappeared: the medium-size sword (*uchigatana*), approximately sixty centimeters long, which curved toward the point, thus permitting rapid unsheathing. The medium-size sword became standard in the fifteenth century, a period that was marked by incessant warfare in Japan. Consequently, during this time the activity of blacksmiths was intense, at times tantamount to mass production of swords. These weapons were also exported in great number to China.

Japanese blacksmiths also devised especially innovative blade-making techniques. Originally straight swords were made with the same piece of steel, obtained by folding and repeated refashioning of the metal. A maximum-strength steel sword kept its cutting edge a long time, but risked breaking, whereas a soft steel sword became dull and bent easily. The Japanese focused on a combination of different steels: a soft steel core blade (achieved through about five folds of the metal), more elastic sides (for example, seven folds), and a hard steel cutting edge (ranging from fifty to several hundred folds). The forging was followed by filing, tempering, and finally polishing. Japanese artisans polished haphazardly, leaving traces of forging and patterns produced by tempering, which gave the blade a certain gleam. The Japanese sword thus was characterized by its curvature, complex structure, and residual gleam. From the thirteenth century onward these qualities improved and incomparable mastery of craftsmanship was achieved.[181]

In the Heian Period swords still were not exported in large quantities, and they most likely were dress arms rather than combat weapons. The beauty of these swords was appreciated by the Chinese from the eleventh century onward. In the following ballad (which has been attributed to both Ouyang Xiu and Sima Guang), the author, using swords as a pretext, expresses at once his admiration for the skill of foreigners and his regret that certain techniques would be lost in his own country thereafter:

The Kun barbarians no longer come, the route is distant.[182] It is said that they (were gifted at) the casting of swords; who still is able to do it? These days precious swords come from Japan, the traders of Yue [Zhejiang] obtain them to the east of the ocean. The sheaths of perfumed wood are decorated with fish-scale inlay and brass mingled with white copper. They were introduced at great expense by afficionados; those who wear them at the waist will be safe from evil spells. One hears that this country is located on a large island with fertile ground and civilized customs. In times past, Xu Fu deceived the people of Qin.[183] (He departed for a distant country) to gather herbs of immortality; he remained there, and (one after another) the children, their heads covered by bonnets, ended up growing old. In this country [Japan],[184] the one hundred artisans (who arrived with him) are settled and the five grains are grown; to this day, the items that they make are all excellent. In previous reigns, they frequently came to present tribute and the literati were continually engaged in the composition of poems and of prose. Since the time of Xu Fu, the classics have not been burned[185] and the one hundred volumes of the "Histories" that were lost in our country have survived there. They adamantly forbid the transmission of the classics to China, and in our entire country nobody knows ancient literature anymore. The great works of the previous dynasties have since been preserved among the northern barbarians. The eastern ocean is immense, and nothing links the harbors (on the opposite shores). This distresses us and we are left to shed tears. Of what importance in comparison to this are several rusty daggers.[186]

The beauty of the Japanese swo rd reminds the a uthor of how many things had been lost in China, and he deplores the lack of erudition of his compatriots. The judgment that the Chinese author passes on the quality of Japanese craftsmanship is significant. Even if the poet's pen carries him away in its praise, what he says is not without foundation. Indeed, various authors in different periods have lavished the same praise. We have read, in particular, admiring testimonials of the Chinese for Japanese paper, mother-of-pearl ornaments, and fans, as well as compliments with regard to paintings and golden decorations. These manufactures were fruits of the elaboration and development of new techniques by the Japanese, and overseas fascination with the refinement of their work was well founded. One has the impression that the renown of the quality of Japanese products was thenceforth established. Highly finished products, once sent as presents to foreign countries, gradually gained ground in foreign trade. Indeed, they appeared among the principal items exported back to China by Japanese from the fourteenth century onward. It was thus in the Heian Period that the structure of Japanese exports emerged.

CHAPTER 4

FREE TRADE

From the Twelfth to the Fourteenth Centuries

"Lined up stern to bow, the Japanese cross the stormy sea and come to sell their merchandise."[187] This remark, made by a Chinese author in his 1259 geographic treatise on the Mingzhou region, is emblematic of developments in the thirteenth and fourteenth centuries. Although the sortie of Japanese ships abroad had been prohibited by the Heian court in former times, agents commissioned by estates and provinces in Kyūshū had gone out to Korea since the late eleventh century. Then, from 1175 onward, the arrival of Japanese boats on the Chinese coast was heralded. This phenomenon, ignored by the Japanese sources, was reported in the "Standard History of the Song Dynasty" (*Song shi*).

In 1175 a crew member of a Japanese ship murdered a Chinese person, and by imperial order, his penalty was entrusted to his commander. Indeed, sentences for offenses committed by foreigners—for exam-ple, Arabs and Persians residing in Canton—had been determined according to the law of the native country of the accused since the Tang Period. In 1176 Japanese landed at Mingzhou, claiming to have run adrift and to be without provisions. A hundred or so of them went as far as the capital of Lin'anfu (Hangzhou), and pursuant to a government edict, they were granted a daily ration of two *shō* (1 *shō*=0.85 liters) of rice and fifty coins while waiting to be able to set off again with another ship from Japan. In 1183 a group of seventy-three Japanese, also claiming to be castaways, arrived in Zhejiang and were given rice and coins from the prefectural reserves. In all likelihood the Japanese in question were less impoverished than they claimed. They probably came to find out about the Chinese coastal ports and commerce, with which they still were not so familiar as with the Korean coast, and then brought back informa-tion and products to their sponsors.

These cases presumably were not the only voyages to China in this period, because starting in 1179 a Japanese court dignitary complained about the negative repercussions on the Kyōto market caused by currency imported from China; however this currency could also have reached Japan in part through Chinese traders. In

1180 one of them disembarked at the port of Ōwada and sold medicines to the representative of a Kyōto high dignitary.[188]

Taira no Kiyomori did important reconstruction work at the port of Ōwada (later called Hyōgo), located on the Inland Sea coast near modern Kōbe. Until Kiyomori came to power, foreign traders had been welcomed only in Hakata or other ports of Kyūshū. In 1170, however, Kiyomori, on his own initiative, invited a Chinese merchant to come as far as Ōwada and even arranged an audience with the retired *tennō* for him. Private trade thus was inaugurated by a public figure, but without the sanction of the Japanese court.

In late twelfth century the power structure in Japan underwent considerable changes that greatly affected foreign trade. Mid-century quarrels surrounding the succession to the throne and control of government affairs had set the Fujiwara, imperial princes, and the retired emperors, who called on the military forces of the Taira and Minamoto families, against one another. The Taira achieved victories in 1156 and 1159; Taira no Kiyomori subsequently was vested with tax authority over some thirty provinces and ceded the rights to several hundred estates located in southern Japan and along the Inland Sea. At the same time he held key government posts, and in 1168 his heirs succeeded him when he retired to become a monk, all the while continuing to manage his business.

The Taira withstood repeated clashes with the Minamoto, who decisively defeated them in 1185 in a battle at Dannoura Bay in northern Kyūshū. Minamoto no Yoritomo (1147-1199) meanwhile had seized control of part of the Kantō region in northern Japan, and in 1180 had set himself up at Kamakura, a village in Sagami Province (Kanagawa Prefecture). A close associate of the ex-monarch Goshirakawa (r. 1155-1168), Yoritomo obtained from the court administrative and tax rights over nine northern provinces in 1183. Minamoto no Yoshinaka (1154-1184) and the Taira then divided the rest of the country among themselves. But they were soon pushed back by Yoritomo's forces.

In 1185 following the victory over the Taira, Minamoto no Yoritomo bestowed upon himself the authority to appoint constables (*shugo*) in all the provinces, who had charge of military forces and policing authority; he also named estate stewards (*jitō*) who exercised control over taxes and rents from the provinces and estates. Yoritomo appointed his vassals to these posts and established a Kamakura-based "military government" called Bakufu, which managed the affairs of warriors and administration of provinces and estates within his domain. Finally, in 1192 he was named shogun by the court—that is, "great general in charge of subduing the barbarians" *(seiitaishōgun)*—and thus was accorded military, but not administrative, power at a national level. Somewhat later, however, administrative and judicial power over regions controlled by the military government passed de facto into the hands of the Hōjō family, who held posts as shogunate regents *(shikken)*.

In Japan provincial forces did not usurp the throne, nor did they overthrow imperial power, as was often the case with dynastic changes in China. On the contrary, they sought legitimation of their rights by the throne, even though they later expanded their power at the expense of the court. In this way, the military government and the *tennō's* court coexisted during the Kamakura Period (1185-1333) and up until 1868.

This new distribution of power had consequences for Japan's economy and foreign trade. The redistribution of revenue, consisting of taxes and estate rents, diversified the economy. In addition to the traditional centers of collection, namely Kyōto and the religious establishments of Nara, there emerged a third, the Kamakura Bakufu. The transportation system expanded, and fairs multiplied in the provinces and at the three main centers of collection and consumption. New markets were created near exchange points, ports, local administrative seats, and temple ports. These markets or fairs were held periodically, approximately three times per month, and were managed by temples, local administrators, or estate stewards, who collected tolls. Exchanges thus were conducted as itinerant trade. The foundation of the fiscal and estate economy had not undergone any fundamental modification.

The new power structure affected foreign trade inasmuch as it gradually induced commercial liberalism because the control of the different power centers was weak. Thereafter, the arrival of foreigners in any port was accepted de facto, and three-year waiting periods between arrivals and bans on Japanese departing for foreign countries were unheard of. This result, however, came from the inability of the court to impose its will and not necessarily from a more favorable stance toward trade. For its part, the Bakufu, the military government, that is, certainly had an interest in foreign trade, but because it was less established in Kyūshū than the Taira formerly had been, several decades elapsed before it was able to assume an active role—as is evident from the following series of events.

After the victory at Dannoura in 1185, Minamoto no Yoritomo's younger brother—Minamoto no Yoshitsune—brought back from Kyūshū 10 bolts of brocade, 110 bolts of twill damask, silk gauze, and taffeta, 10 ink sticks, 20 tea bowls, and 50 mats all as presents for the retired *tennō* Goshirakawa. For Yoritomo and his wife, he brought brocade, twill damask, and silk taffeta, all of which had been imported from China.[189]

During this period many Japanese agents, that is, those commissioned by investors, seem to have circulated between Japan and China. An administrator from a Chinese coastal prefecture, in an article concerning the currency situation, stated that since Emperor Xiaozong's reign (1163-1190) trade ships from Japan and Korea had landed every year in Mingzhou. He explained that these traders had always bartered before, but that recently they required payment in Chinese currency, which had given rise to a monetary influx into Japan.

A curious incident occurred about 1186: Minamoto no Yoritomo nominated one of his vassals to the post of Kyūshū commissioner (*chinzei bugyō*), whose task consisted of commanding the region's provincial constables. When a Chinese vessel arrived at the southern Kyūshū port of Bōnotsu in Satsuma (Kagoshima Prefecture), located on an estate belonging to the Konoe noble family of Kyōto, Kyūshū Headquarters officials attempted to seize the merchandise, following regulations previously estab-lished by the court. Whereupon the estate official, a Konoe family representative, lodged a complaint against the Kyūshū Head-quarters. A letter then was addressed to the Kamakura Bakufu by the Konoe family stating that its estate had always managed trade in this port and that the action of the Dazaifu violated precedent. The Bakufu accepted these arguments and informed the Kyūshū Headquarters accordingly. Thus the Konoe estate validated a customary prerogative that would have the Bakufu sanction its private trade, a trade that formerly had been declared illegal by the court. In this instance, the court appears not to have intervened.[190] This case demonstrates that the jurisdictions of the head of the Kyūshū Headquarters (an official named by the *tennō*) and the Kyūshū commissioner (appointed by the military government) overlapped. Their respective spheres of responsibility would be demarcated only later.

Traders continued to come and go without regard for the authorities. Arrivals of Chinese ships were reported in the years 1191, 1200, and 1211: the first landed on Hirado Island and the second in Iwami Province (Shimane Prefecture) on the Japan Sea. Yang, head of the first ship's crew, and his companion Chen were fugitives sought by the Chinese authorities. In a letter, Chinese authorities asked that the Kyūshū Headquarters penalize these two individuals who had caused trouble in China since Yang claimed to have been born in Japan and thus fell under Japanese jurisdiction. Kyūshū requested a decision on this matter from the court in Kyōto. Furthermore, arrivals of vessels from Japan were recorded in Chinese sources. In 1193 so-called castaways landed in Taizhou (in Jiangsu) and Xiuzhou (in Zhejiang) prefectures and were supplied with provisions by the Chinese authorities. The same was done for other Japanese in 1200 and 1202. Remarkably, the identity of one of the Japanese agents is also known: he was named Shōjiro.[191]

For this period when trade with China flourished, there is no information on relations with Korea. But in 1223, "Japanese plundered the coast of Kumju" in Korea, and two years later two ships piloted by Japanese pirates landed in southern Korea and incited unrest.[192] In 1226 a fleet of ten pirate ships arrived from Japan to pillage and burn Korean homes in the same region. Korean guards successfully seized some of the plunderers; the others took flight.[193] These were the first episodes of so-called Japanese pirate activity, which worsened in the fourteenth century.

Who were these pirates (called *waegu* in the Korean sources from the fourteenth century onward, and in Japanese *wakō*)? They came from Tsushima Island and from the Matsura region (northern Nagasaki Prefecture). In Matsura, located in far western Kyūshū in Hizen Province, were families who presumably were involved in local administration. Hizen Province supplied seafood as taxes to the Kyūshū Headquarters, but gradually some families detached themselves from the central administrative network. One way to do so was to open rice fields, over which openers' families assumed the right of exploitation. Thus they became local landlords.

As a defensive measure, and also in a quest for adventure, these local landlords assembled troops of warriors and even a flotilla. These actions were spurred by, among others, the Taira in the midst of their struggles against the Minamoto in the 1180s. After the defeat of the Taira, some Matsura families became Minamoto vassals; others affiliated with the provincial constable or with estates in the region; still others did not submit to any hierarchy. These families did not form permanent confederations, they merely formed ad hoc alliances. This seems to have been the case at the time of their 1226 expedition to Korea, and the Japanese sources then referred to them as Matsura leagues (*Matsura-tō*). The court openly deplored their activities; a high dignitary stated that deterioration of relations with Korea would harm Sino-Japanese trade, especially where aid was needed for ships that became stranded in Korea. On this occasion, the court did not consider Korea a commercial partner.

Nevertheless, the pirates' exploits did not end there. In 1227 two armed ships again accosted the Kumju coast. A complaint was lodged forthwith. A Korean prefectural commissioner denounced the pirates' activities in a letter addressed to the Kyūshū Headquarters. According to this letter, for years "Japanese from Tsushima Island" had come to bring presents to Korea and had always been accommodated in a special hotel; the Korean commissioner noted that it would be regrettable to put an end to this "system of exchanging courtesy gifts." The head of the Kyūshū Headquarters sent copies of the letter from Korea to the court and the Bakufu, without waiting for a decision from his superiors, however, he had ninety Japanese pirates executed in the presence of the Korean envoy and wrote a letter of apology to the Korean commissioner. The Japanese court sharply criticized the Kyūshū official; it deemed his actions "shameful," and the writing of the letter improper.[194]

As an official of the court, the head of the the Kyūshū Headquarters was to obey the court's orders. How could he have acted on his own initiative yet escaped punishment? The reason was that the individual in question, Mutō Sukeyori (1160-1228), was a Minamoto vassal, faithful to the Kamakura military government. The Bakufu had gradually consolidated its position in the southern provinces, especially since a failed attempt by the court to overthrow its power—the court had raised troops against the Kamakura Bakufu and suffered a total defeat in 1221. The Bakufu then exiled the *tennō* and the ex-monarch Gotoba, confiscated many court estates, and installed deputies (*tandai*) at the Rokuhara Office in Kyōto. In 1226 the Bakufu made Mutō Sukeyori, head (*daini*) of the the Kyūshū Headquarters. Thus the military government de facto controlled relations with foreign countries insofar as it had jurisdiction over the Kyūshū Headquarters.

In 1232 the Bakufu dealt with the subject of piracy in its new "Code of Judicial Protocols" issued to its vassals, the *Goseibai shikimoku*. Article 3 stated that the punishment of pirates, thieves, and brigands fell within the competence of provincial constables.[195] That same year, there was an opportunity to apply this provision when a Matsura landlord led an attack on Korea.

More pleasant events were reported in 1243 and 1244: Japan repatriated Korean castaways, and sent gifts for the Korean authorities back with them. One can assume that it was the Kyūshū Headquarters or a representative from Tsushima Island who took action out of concern for establishing or improving commercial relations with Korea. Moreover, a Korean official was tried by his government for mistreating Japanese traders who had brought silks, silver, and pearls.[196]

The attacks, however, soon resumed. In 1251 Korea fortified the Kumju coast to ward off pirate attacks, yet they still occurred several times in the 1260s. Again the Korean authorities complained. They pointed out in a letter that piracy harmed neighborly relations and trade between the two countries, trade that previously had been regulated. The letter also cited courtesy delegations— consisting of two ships—that came annually from Japan, which leads us to think that the head of the Kyūshū Headquarters, or a representative from Hizen or Tsushima Island, would have established commercial relations with Korea and endeavored to curtail piracy. We have no information on this subject, however.[197]

As for China, texts concerning Japanese monks who made voyages to this country provide evidence of constant comings-and-goings between the two countries in the thirteenth century. More than seventy monks in all likelihood traveled overseas, mostly aboard ships of Japanese agents. Furthermore, there were also Chinese residents in Kyūshū who were engaged in business. These families conceivably had been settled in Japan since the previous century. We know that one of these Chinese living in Hakata helped the monk Enni (1202-1280) construct a temple in Chikuzen Province (Fukuoka Prefecture).

In the mid-thirteenth century, a Chinese financial inspector observed that forty to fifty Japanese ships landed each year on the Chinese coast and took away Chinese currency. In 1242 Saionji Kintsune (1171-1244) commissioned trade ships to sail to China. Kintsune had taken Minamoto no Yoritomo's niece as a wife and occupied key posts at the court. He thus maintained close ties with both the court and the Bakufu. Kintsune filled his boats with enough cypress wood for a whole pavilion, intended for the emperor of China, but this gift is not mentioned in the Chinese sources. The crew returned in the seventh lunar month (August) with 100 thousand strings of cash and exotic products, including a buffalo and a parrot. The sum of 100 million coins seems disproportionate at first glance, but it is confirmed by other figures cited below. Given that such a cargo weighed approximately three hundred tons, one envisions a flotilla, because the capacity of boats then in use in Japan for deep-sea navigation did not exceed a hundred-or-so tons.[198]

CHINESE CURRENCY

Importation of Chinese currency, which began in the mid-twelfth century, was a new element in Sino-Japanese trade. In 1179 a Kyōto dignitary complained of a disruption in market prices due to currency from China.[199] In the same period, a Chinese official noted with dissatisfaction the progressive drainage of Chinese currency to Japan and Korea. In 1199 a Chinese edict proclaimed "a ban on Korean and Japanese merchants purchasing our currency."[200] But Korea and Japan were not the only countries concerned. The flight of Chinese money was a universal phenomenon in progress since the tenth century. Decrees forbidding the export of currency had been proclaimed in China in the early Song Period (960-1279) and were frequently repeated from the middle of the twelfth century onward.[201] Measures were then taken to inspect ships when they left the Chinese coast.

Moreover, difficulties were encountered in minting coins because copper deposits, principally located in Yunnan and Guangdong, gradually were exhausted. Thus in 1158 the Chinese court had to call for the seizure of metal tableware and copper goods throughout the country in order to use them for minting coinage. Then, in 1219 it arranged to use fine silks, silk taffeta, ceramics, and lacquerware, instead of currency, as means of payment in foreign trade. But no measures could stop the flight of money, and China was forced to rely on the issue of convertible notes similar to modern bank notes. Convertible notes were the primary tender in domestic trade under the Yuan Dynasty (1279-1368).

It seems that Chinese currency was used also in several other countries. Excavations have unearthed Song-dynasty copper coins in Singapore, Java, Malabar, southern India, and even in Africa, in Somalia and Zanzibar. One therefore cannot be surprised to read the declaration of an eleventh-century Chinese official: "Coins were originally an invaluable means of payment to China, but today they are in circulation among the barbarians of all four directions."[202]

Japan was among these countries. The first comment concerning the importation of currency dates from 1092: a Chinese trader who came from the Khitan Liao kingdom brought currency to Japan; these were silver coins, however.[203] In 1171 the first grievance with regard to Japan was heard by a Chinese official. The complaint deplored the monetary flight toward the south, north, and east of China, citing Korea and Japan, and recommended that the government introduce punishments for those who attempted to leave China with ships loaded with Chinese currency. The Chinese court, from 1199 onward, forbade the exportation of Chinese coins to Korea and Japan. This prohibition was repeated in 1214, but to no avail.

We have established that in 1242 the vessels sponsored by Saionji Kintsune brought back to Japan 100,000 strings of cash, that is, 100 million copper coins. Furthermore, in 1249 guards at a watch post on the Chinese coast reported Japanese ships anchored near Mingzhou (then called Qingyuan); their cargoes consisted of 200,000 strings in total. At this time, an investigation conducted by a coastal region inspector revealed illegal purchases of currency by the Japanese. The inspector remarked that forty or fifty ships from Japan, each including one hundred-or-so crew members, landed every year in Taizhou and Wenzhou (in Zhejiang) prefec-tures and at the ports of Fujian and Guangdong, where there were no Offices of Maritime Trade. The Japanese sold construction wood, mother-of-pearl, and sulfur and were paid in cash. They escaped inspection either through bribery, or by hiding the coins in double-bottomed boats, or even by keeping them on small boats or small islands from which they later recovered them.[204]

Even if the figures are exaggerated, or there was not always a clear distinction between Japanese and Koreans, this account contains an element of truth and is supported by archaeological research conducted in Japan. Indeed, excavations conducted by four teams of researchers in forty sites from Hokkaidō to Kyūshū unearthed approximately 1.3 million coins, of which more than 75 percent were from the Northern Song Dynasty (960-1127).

How did Chinese money penetrate the Japanese market? According to written records, twelve issues of Japanese currency had been minted between 708 and 958. Eighth-century measures to stimulate their use failed, leaving the circulation of currency very weak. Exchanges then were transacted principally in rice and fabric. No more coins were minted in Japan until the institution of private minting in certain fiefs in the late sixteenth century and also during the official issue under Toyotomi Hideyoshi (1536-1598).

The first written evidence of utilization of Chinese currency in Japan dates from the years 1150, 1162, and 1179, and pertained to property transactions. In 1150 land located near Tōdaiji temple in Nara was sold for 27 strings of cash.[205] In 1179 an estate plot near Kyōto belonging to the Tachibana family was purchased for a sum of fifty strings.[206] Later, beginning in the mid-thirteenth century, land deals were transacted more often in cash than in rice. With regard to the price of land, one can only imagine how many parcels were valued at hundreds of thousands of strings imported from China.[207]

The court observed this development with distrust. An official noted in 1179: "These days an epidemic reigns throughout our country, it is called 'the currency epidemic.'"[208] The council of senior nobles recommended that the circulation of currency be forbidden; violations of this order were subject to the same sentence as that for minting of counterfeit coins. This prohibition was reiterated for Mikawa Province (Aichi Prefecture) in 1187, and similar ordinances were promulgated in 1192 and 1193. The last of these ordinances said, "An order intended to arrest the circulation of Chinese currency. The Minister of the Right and the Minister of the Left decree: . . . If we do not halt currency exchanges, people may compete with one another and set their own prices at the time of transactions. This is why it is ordered that the Police (*kebiishi*) and Capital Office (*saukyōshiki*) put a stop to the use of currency forever starting today."[209]

The reason for the prohibition, therefore, was that the use of currency caused price disruption. According to the regulations governing the organization of markets in the capital, prices were set by the government, and fluctuations due to movements in supply and demand were not permitted. The regulation of prices also had been the great concern of the court when it had limited foreign trade in the early tenth century. Neither then nor in 1193, however, was there any consideration of economic matters, only concern for the maintenance of control over commerce. The court opposed the circulation of currency even though it had been integrated into the system of equivalences, which also existed for rice and fabric: the value of a string of cash had been fixed at one *koku* (eighty-five liters) of rice. The court thus remained faithful to its centuries-old principles and did not attempt any reform.

Thus the repetition of prohibitions pertaining to the circulation of currency proves that there were repeated violations. We know, for example, of a private trade between a seller and a buyer who was a shrinemember involving currency. The persons were denounced by Mount Hiei monastery near Kyōto, even though the local chief of the police bureau himself had attempted to conceal this affair.[210]

From the late twelfth or early thirteenth century onward, currency also played a part in the payment of rents. It could then replace certain items supplied by the estates. For example, in 1221 an estate in Iyo Province (Ehime Prefecture) paid 480 strings of cash in rent to the proprietor, a high dignitary in Kyōto. Furthermore, a Yamashiro (Kyōto Prefecture) estate substituted 200 copper coins for its lamp oil quota. Finally, in 1226 the Bakufu decided to collect rents from then on in cash instead of hemp cloth.[211] The military government, unlike the court, thus favored the circulation of currency; as a rule its directive applied only to the provinces under its control, however.

Thereafter, payment of rent in cash became more commonplace. Whereas only six cases prior to 1250 are known, the sources reported thirty cases in the latter half of the thirteenth century, and triple that number in the first half of the fourteenth century. Remittance in cash indeed simplified the transport of rent income and was especially advantageous in cases where the products were not consumed as such by the beneficiary but, rather, exchanged in local fairs.[212]

Soon the military government had to confront the circulation of counterfeit Chinese coins. In 1239, it issued a writ of prohibition on these coins, which was repeated in 1263.[213] Counterfeit coins multiplied in the fourteenth century. One wonders why the Japanese themselves were not minting coins officially, or even clandestinely. In theory, their copper resources were sufficient. There were deposits in the provinces of Tamba (Kyōto and Hyōgo prefectures) and Bitchū (Okayama Prefecture). But importation of coins probably sufficed to meet the demand, or seemed more convenient than a domestic issue.

Thus trade with China resulted in the circulation of Chinese currency to Japan. But currency still did not represent a standard of value, even after the establishment of an equivalence with rice, because its convertibility was still limited and its circulation was not yet widespread. Nevertheless, as circulation broadened, Japan increasingly depended on the importation of this currency and, therefore, on trade with China.[214]

From the mid-thirteenth century onward, trade with China was marked by diverse events. In 1254 the Bakufu dispatched two directives to Chikuzen Province (Fukuoka Prefecture), where the seat of the Kyūshū Headquarters was located. One concerned the duties of estate stewards in that region, the other, ships departing for China. The Bakufu proscribed "leaving more than five boats anchored" (in the port of Hakata) and ordered the destruction of all surplus ships.[215] Ten years later, the military government ordered that the Kyūshū Headquarters stop sending ships to China commissioned by provinces within the jurisdiction of the Bakufu, that is, the nine provinces in northern Japan administered since 1183.[216] It is very difficult to interpret these two ordinances because there are almost no sources concerning trade in this period. Perhaps there had been some abuses. In any case, the ordinances seem to have had only limited effect, because twenty years later, the military government itself sponsored the arming of merchant ships.

In 1268 Japan received distressing news. A Korean envoy came bearing a letter from Khubilai Khan (1215-1294) demanding that Japan submit to Mongol authority. This was the first confrontation of the Japanese authorities with the events that had transpired on the continent since the beginning of the century. From his headquarters at Karakorum in Mongolia, Ghengis Khan (1167-1227) had launched attacks in northern Asia and Mongolia. He had successively occupied the Jin-dynasty capital of Beijing, the kingdom of the Uighur in Xinjiang, and that of the Xixia in Inner Mongolia, and had conducted campaigns in the Caucasus, the Ukraine, and even Poland. His successors had continued these offensives and established an immense Mongol empire that stretched from Hungary to Korea and from Moscow to the Persian Gulf. This empire was controlled by four khans, one of whom was Khubilai Khan. Khubilai had established his capital at Beijing and launched attacks against Korea, which succumbed in 1259. He and his successors had taken Chinese-style imperial names and later the appellation of the Yuan Dynasty.

In 1266 Khubilai Khan, who reigned as Emperor Shizu (r. 1260-1294), had sent to Japan his first messenger, who had returned, however, without having fulfilled his mission. His second envoy had disembarked in Kyūshū in 1268. The commissioner and the head of the Kyūshū Headquarters immediately conveyed the two letters to Kamakura, one from the khan and another from the king of Korea, bypassing Kyōto. The court and the military government understood the gravity of the situation. Then, four Korean messengers dispatched by the Mongol emperor arrived in Japan, one after the other. The Japanese court, panic-stricken, had rites celebrated throughout the country; the Bakufu ordered preparations for war in Kyūshū.

Since none of the envoys had reported Japan's response, Khubilai Khan took measures to launch an attack via Korea. In 1274 a fleet of more than 30,000 Mongol and Korean warriors invaded Kyūshū. The continental army enjoyed some success, but on the return route, a typhoon caused the total loss of the fleet. Furthermore, the khan continued to conduct offensives in China and he sequentially occupied Xiangyang, the Chinese capital of Lin'anfu (Hangzhou), and Canton. In 1279 the Song empire fell under Mongol dominion. The Mongols became the masters of China for nearly a century.[217]

Meanwhile, new messengers arrived in Japan: two were put to death upon their arrival in Kyūshū. In 1281 Khublai launched a second attack on Kyūshū. The fleet was again destroyed by a typhoon. In the "Right Lineages of the Heavenly Sovereigns" (*Jinnō shōtōki*), a treatise from the fourteenth century, this typhoon was called "the divine wind," (*kamikaze*). It was thus "due to the help of the gods" that Japan escaped occupation by foreign forces.[218] Other ambassadors came from the Mongol empire, and the troops in Kyūshū remained on alert, but plans to invade Japan apparently were abandoned after the death of Khubilai Khan in 1294.

During the entire period of hostilities, commercial activities continued on and even were stimulated by the policies of the Mongol sovereign. Immediately following the occupation of the Chinese capital, he reestablished the Office of Maritime Trade in three ports: Qingyuan (Mingzhou, modern Ningbo), Ganpu (located on the northern shore of Hangzhou Bay), and Quanzhou. Then he ordered that foreign traders be treated with care. Khubilai Khan thus perpetuated the favorable policy toward foreign exchange enacted in the Song Dynasty. In 1277 Japanese were authorized to disembark in China to sell gold and purchase currency. The following year, an edict was addressed by the Mongol administration to officials in maritime prefectures with the intent of stimulating trade with Japan. Another Japanese ship that left for China, however, returned without having been able to complete its dealings. The commander of that ship was the first to inform the Kyūshū Headquarters of the fall of the Song empire and its occupation by the Mongols. But then, in 1279, four vessels with two thousand Japanese aboard landed in Qingyuan and were authorized to trade.[219]

Moreover, monks continued their voyages to China. Hōjō Tokimune (1251-1284) then was the head of the military government in Kamakura. A fervent Buddhist, he dispatched two monks to China in 1271 and 1277, that is, between the Mongol invasions. The second time, he entrusted the monks with a letter of invitation for a Chinese monk. Thanks to this invitation the Chinese monk Mugaku Sogen (Wuxue Zuyan, 1226-1286) arrived and, under Hōjō Tokimune's patronage, founded Engakuji temple in Kamakura.[220]

VENTURES SPONSORED BY TEMPLES

The following information can shed light on several Japanese foreign trade procedures. In 1287 the government of Tsushima Island addressed to the court a document containing several petitions, one of which concerned the boats returning from China. The governor deplored the encroachment of the island provincial constable on his position, which entailed collecting tariffs on the ships that landed there.[221] That is to say the provincial constable had attempted to levy taxes on his own initiative. Undoubtedly, this was a sort of toll, comparable to those collected at the fairs.

Three years later, on the occasion of the founding of Sennyoji temple on Mount Kaminari in Chikuzen, it was decided to dispatch a commercial team to China, with the intent of later allocating the trade goods to construction work on the temple. The Bakufu then gave the order to the provincial constable of Chikuzen to allocate "fixed sums, previously collected on the boats that departed for China" for the construction of a trade ship.[222] It is not clear whether these were sums collected from tolls or imported currency that for some reason or other had been confiscated by the Chikuzen authorities.

Another documented episode occurred in the year 1298. A vessel left an island located on the Gotō archipelago, west of Kyūshū and opposite the village of Aokata, bound for China. It was, however, cast onto another island several leagues from the first, and thieves who lived there seized a significant portion of the cargo. The Kyūshū commissioner and the Tsushima Island governor then ordered their vassal who controlled Hizen province, including the Gotō archipelago, to recover the seized goods. Although we do not know the outcome, the public documents published in this case contain exceptional information on the proprietors of the cargo and its contents.

The ship was under the supervision of Tōtarō, called Nin'e, his religious name. He was accompanied by other monks, one of whom was a representative of the Bakufu. From among the goods in the monk's charge the thieves seized 137 measures (*kiri*) of gold dust, 200 measures of gold nuggets, mercury, silver-plated swords, and white cloth. Another monk on board the ship came from Jōchiji, a Kamakura temple founded by members of the Hōjō family. He himself was relieved of 124 measures and 5 ounces of gold dust and nuggets, 10 silver-plated swords with sheaths decorated in gold lacquer, pearls, and mercury worth 40 strings of cash. Finally, two other monks had been delegated by two Hōjō family noble women. One was entrusted with 35 measures of gold dust, 93 measures of gold nuggets, 17 vials filled with mercury, 5 silver-plated swords, 29 bolts of white cloth, 2 white hats, monk's robes made of Chinese (*sha*) gauze, and another robe. The other monk brought with him 240 ounces of gold dust, 60 measures of gold nuggets, 103 bolts of silk taffeta, 2 vials of mercury, a cuirass, a breastplate, a sword and two daggers with handles inlaid with gold, tea cups, small buckets, 8 writing cases, and shelves on which to store containers holding powdered tea—the last 4 items were in *nashiji*-type gold lacquer—a writing case in *makie* gold lacquer, nightgowns (known as *tonoimono*), and four kimonos with wide, short sleeves.[223]

These three episodes allow us to make several observations. Tsushima Island and Hizen Province, along with the Gotō archipelago, played a part in the passage of boats, and the local authorities collected tolls. But the jurisdictions were not clearly delineated between local leaders attached to the court and those delegated by the military government; there was no institution responsible for managing all foreign trade affairs. On the other hand, the head of the Kyūshū Headquarters and the inspector-general represented the interests of the Bakufu and issued directives to local leaders. The position of the Kyūshū commissioner was strengthened during the Mongol invasions, when an army made up of troops from the provinces and estates of the region was established. Moreover, in 1286 the Bakufu installed a sort of court of justice for adjudicating estate affairs in Kyūshū.

As for investors and owners of trade ships, they are not mentioned in the documents. In 1242 Saionji Kintsune played the role of principal, but he probably was neither an entrepreneur nor a ship owner. At the time of the undertaking in 1298, one might suspect that the ship or ships belonged to Tōtarō and that the venture benefited from a joint investment on the part of Hōjō Sadatoki (1271-1311), regent and head of the Bakufu, Hōjō Morotoki (1275–1311), founder of Jōchiji temple, the two ladies of the Hōjō family, and perhaps other unknown investors. These individuals provided the merchandise and sent their agents with it.

In the same period, the Mongol administration of the Yuan Dynasty took measures to tighten control over foreign trade because of fraud and abuses committed as much by Chinese officials as by foreign merchants. In 1293 the Mongol government issued twenty-two regulations concerning trade. According to these ordinances, seven ports were designated for transactions with foreigners, consisting of the three named above as well as Wenzhou, Hangzhou, and Canton. Duties on imports were set at 10 percent for products of high value, and at 6 2/3 percent for second-level items. This tariff was lower than the one previously imposed by the Song Dynasty.[224]

Boat commanders thereafter were provided with an official document, a duplicate of which was retained by port authorities. The document indicated the boat's specifications; the names of the commanders, the proprietor, and the crew members; the country of destination, and the contents of the cargo. The traders were required to come back to the port of embarkation upon their return. These official documents were granted to foreigners as well as Chinese. The regulations also prescribed all sorts of punishments for tax fraud and for abuses of officials when they tried to collude with merchants. The products prohibited for export were precious metals, currency, and slaves.

Furthermore a special guard was installed in Qingyuan (Ningbo) in 1292 because weapons concealed in the bottom of a Japanese boat had been discovered there. The same year, a Korean messenger went to Japan on Khubilai Khan's orders bearing a letter demanding allegiance to the Mongol empire, but the letter went unanswered. Perhaps, at the time of the discovery of concealed weapons, the Chinese officials feared an attack from Japan. Trade, however, seems to have been conducted peacefully. In any event the documents do not mention any incidents up to 1304, when a watch post was installed in Dinghai, north of Qingyuan in Hangzhou Bay, which assumed control over Japanese ships.[225] The following year, a boat from Japan initially was refused permission to land, and then a higher-than-normal tariff was imposed upon it.[226]

In 1306 a commercial crew came bringing gold and armor as gifts for the Mongol sovereign. These items could have come only from a Kamakura or Kyōto family. Perhaps it was the ship cited in a Hōjō family document that was sent to China to raise funds for repairs to Shōmyōji temple in Musashi (Yokohama), belonging to a Hōjō estate.[227]

In 1307, however, difficulties arose. During a quarrel with Chinese officials, Japanese traders began to burn and pillage several homes in the locale where they had landed. The same thing happened again two years later. The Japanese then used sulfur intended for sale to set fire to a guard post and a Chinese customs office. In 1311 the Zhejiang provincial administration took measures concerning the treatment of foreigners and the struggle against piracy, and a council also met to decide how to suppress Japanese acts of violence. The Japanese, however, were not the only ones to incite unrest. Consequently, the Yuan administration abolished and reestablished the Offices of Maritime Trade several times and even prohibited foreign trade for brief periods.[228]

As for the Japanese, they continued to come and go nearly every year, even when the Offices of Maritime Trade were abolished, if one can believe the biographies and documents concerning monks who made voyages to China.[229] Among the many ships were some filled with items for sale, supplied by the Hōjō family. We have in hand a document from the year 1326, preserved in the archives of the Hishijima family of Satsuma Province in southern Kyūshū: an order addressed by the representative of the provincial constable of Satsuma to Hishijima Tadanori, estate steward in the same province, asking that the latter have a guard accompany as far as Kyōto "merchandise from ships returned from China allotted for the construction of Shōchōjuin and Kenchōji temples."[230] These two temples had been founded in Kamakura by Minamoto no Yoritomo and Hōjō Tokiyori (in 1251), respectively, and they had suffered several fires. Part of the profit from trade ships, therefore, was allocated to reconstruction work on these temples.

Furthermore, a letter written about 1329 by the shogunal regent Hōjō Sadaaki (1278-1333) mentions "a boat that left for China to collect funds for the construction of a gigantic statue of the Buddha in the Kantō."[231] This bronze statue, more than fifteen meters tall, still exists in Kamakura, but the temple in which it was located has been destroyed. Plans for this statue were put forward for the first time in 1238, but the casting work began only in 1252.

In 1332 the departure for China of a trade ship in conjunction with work on Sumiyoshi Shrine in Settsu Province (Ōsaka, Hyōgo Prefecture) was reported. This millennia-old shrine was dedicated to patron deities of the state, of navigation, and of Japanese poetry. Trade profits were needed to finance the repair work. It seems that this undertaking was launched by the Godaigo Tennō (r. 1318-1339).[232]

More detailed information has survived regarding a commercial venture launched on the occasion of the construction of Tenryūji temple in Kyōto, a temple that was founded in 1339 by Ashikaga Takauji (1305-1358). Takauji had become the premier political figure after having fomented an attack against the Hōjō family, overthrown the power of Kamakura, and founded a new Bakufu, whose headquarters were located in Kyōto's Muromachi quarter. In 1338 Ashikaga Takauji was named by the court "great shōgun charged with maintaining peace in the country," in the same manner that Minamoto Yoritomo formerly had been invested by the court with the post of shōgun. The Muromachi Bakufu held military power until 1573.

In the aftermath of Godaigo's death in 1339, and as commemoration for his afterlife, Takauji undertook the founding of Tenryūji. Two years later, his younger brother, Ashikaga Tadayoshi (1306-1352), addressed a document to the first abbot of the temple permitting him to dispatch two boats to China to subsidize the construction in progress and asking him to appoint a commander. Tadayoshi pointed out that this decision had been made following many discussions, given that it was the first venture conducted by the new Bakufu. The abbot suggested first dispatching a single boat, and nominated the monk Shibon for commander. Two days after writing to the abbot, Tadayoshi sent a directive to Shibon. The latter replied the same day; he proposed to provide the temple 5,000 strings of cash upon his return, even without knowing whether his deal would be profitable. It appears, therefore, that Shibon was both the crew commander and the shipowner.

Considering that Saionji Kintsune's expedition to China in 1242 had brought back 100,000 strings of cash, and that other ships had brought back from China 200,000, Shibon's proposal surely did not entail much risk. Indeed, the sum of 5,000 strings for a temple probably represented only a minute portion of the anticipated profits. Did the profits go to the Bakufu, into the pockets of the commander, or into the account of an unknown investor? There is no answer to this question in the sources. We also do not know who financed the construction of the boat, who hired it, and who provided the export items. We can only speculate that the work on Tenryūji was not the only rationale for the venture; otherwise, why would someone not have thought of it two years earlier, at the beginning of construction?

Be that as it may, the ship arrived near the Qingyuan coast in the winter of 1342, but it had great difficulty in obtaining permission to land. The Chinese authorities mistook the Japanese for pirates and had the boat guarded offshore for several weeks before allowing it to land. Even then, they authorized only part of the crew to disembark to conduct their business. Nevertheless, the transactions seem to have been successful. An author noted thirty years later in an article concerning Tenryūji temple: "The profits from transactions amounted to one hundred times [the investment]."[233]

About 1323 another boat left for China, this time in connection with Tōfukuji temple in Kyōto. This temple had been founded in 1236, and from the 1330s onward was among the five great Zen monasteries (*gozan*) in Kyōto. The ship in question is known thanks to archaeological research, although it was not mentioned in any document. The vessel was discovered in 1976 submerged off the coast of Todôko in Sinan, South Korea. Work conducted by the Korean government over a six-year period unearthed numerous objects stored on a vessel 28 meters long and 6.8 meters wide with a capacity estimated at 150 to 200 tons.

In the vessel's hold were 18 tons of Song-period coins bound in strings and assembled in lots. These were labeled with wooden tablets inscribed in Chinese characters. Above the coins were chests containing the rest of the cargo, but only three chests were intact. Eighteen thousand cargo items were discovered, among them 16,800 ceramic items, 600 pieces of metal tableware and bronze artifacts. More than half of the ceramic items were celadons from the Longquan kilns, while those of pale green color came from Jingdezhen; one-third consisted of fine white ceramics. The rest were earthenware pieces decorated with ferrous oxide, and black-glazed tea bowls, known as *tenmoku*. Most of these pieces came from the same kilns as the numerous fragments unearthed in Hakata in 1978 (see "Imports" section in chapter 3). In the entire cargo, only three pieces came from Korea; several earthen-ware items, bronze mirrors, lacquer bowls, and sword hilts came from Japan.

The merchandise was divided haphazardly into chests: that is, objects of different types were combined in each chest, which then was marked in ink with names and symbols. One of the chests, however, was filled entirely with pepper. In addition, a Chinese scale, batches of medicinal plants, red sandalwood, Japanese chess pieces (*shōgi*), and a pair of *geta* sandals were found. These latter objects are an indication that at least a part of the crew was Japanese.

Several inscriptions on the lots of coins and the chests could be deciphered. Most of them were marked "commander" (*gōshi, kangsi*), using the same term by which the monk Shibon had been designated. Other inscriptions read *kanjin-hijiri*, signifying the post of a monk in charge of raising construction funds, "objects belonging to Tōfukuji"; "Hakozaki's coins," Hakozaki being a shrine near Hakata; and "Chōjakuan," the name of a Shōtenzenji temple shrine located in Hakata within Shōtenzenji and affiliated with Tōfukuji. Also decipherable were twenty or so names of monks, ten or so names of laymen, and finally a group of "objects for the official use of the *shuaifu*"—that is, the Duyuan *shuaifu*, a guard headquarters installed in Qingyuan in 1292 when the Chinese had discovered concealed weapons in a Japanese boat. The discovery of items inscribed with the title "*shuaifu*" aboard a 1323 vessel suggests that this headquarters had put the Japanese in charge of transactions for its own benefit. Thus the interested parties in this undertaking were a commander and shipowner, the Tōfukuji and

Shōtenzenji temples, the Hakozaki shrine, and perhaps other religious establishments whose agents' names appear on the tablets, as well as the Qingyuan guard headquarters. Among the indecipherable names also were perhaps representatives of the court or the Bakufu.[234]

In this period, particularly from the 1350s onward, Japanese pirate attacks on Korea again were being reported after a century-long respite. This time, the pirate bands made nearly annual expeditions aboard several dozen ships. The incursions into Korea worsened until the end of the century, causing considerable discord in the relations between the Japanese and Korean governments. As far as commercial trade was concerned, the sources make no mention of it after 1263, the year in which a Korean letter reported the arrival of annual courtesy visits from Kyūshū or Tsushima Island. One cannot, however, rule out the possibility that such activities were pursued on the fringes of the two countries' governmental institutions.[235]

Our chronological discussion will end with the following episode: in 1367 Tajima Michitada, a doctor and monk entertaining plans to construct a hospital in Kyōto, proposed (to the Bakufu or the court) that a special tax of ten coins be levied on the households in that city to construct a ship. It would enable him to conduct business in China, from which the profits would be allocated for the erection of the hospital. In this case it was a venture launched by an individual and proposed to the authorities. If the population of Kyōto numbered ten thousand households, the doctor could have counted on the receipt of one hundred strings of cash to construct a ship. Given this modest investment, one can imagine how lucrative the deal seemed to him. We do not know who was supposed to provide the export goods.[236]

Whether or not this plan was implemented, it was the last instance of trade with China under the Yuan Dynasty. The following year, the Mongols were overthrown and China was returned to native sovereignty. The first emperor of the new Ming Dynasty (1368-1644) established official relations with monarchs of numerous countries, among them Japan. Thereafter, trade once more was conducted under the auspices of official relations, and this meant the end of semiprivate trade sponsored by the Bakufu and the Japanese court.

EXPORT AND IMPORT PRODUCTS

What were the trade goods of the thirteenth and fourteenth centuries? From the standpoint of value, the primary product exported from Japan was gold. We know that gold was sent to China in 1277, that it constituted part of the cargo of the ship led by Tōtarō in 1298, and that it was given as a gift to the Chinese authorities in 1306. During this period Marco Polo resided in China for several years as a guest at the court of Khubilai Khan. The Venetian authored the legend about the inexhaustible wealth of gold in Japan. Europeans read of it in his travel account, written after his return to Italy. Here is an excerpt:

> And I can tell you the quantity of gold they have is endless; for they find it in their own Islands, [and the King does not allow it to be exported. Moreover,] few merchants visit the country because it is so far from the mainland, and thus it comes to pass that their gold is abundant beyond all measure [internal citation omitted]. I will tell you a wonderful thing about the Palace of the Lord of that Island. You must know that he hath a great Palace which is entirely roofed with fine gold, just as our churches are roofed with lead, insomuch that it would scarcely be possible to estimate its value. Moreover, all the pavement of the Palace, and the floors of its chambers are entirely of gold, in plates like slabs of stone, a good two fingers thick; and the windows are also of gold, so that altogether the richness of this Palace is past all bounds and belief [internal citation omitted]. They have also pearls in abundance, which are of a rose colour, and quite as valuable as the white ones.[237]

Aside from gold, Tōtarō also transported mercury, pearls, and refined handicrafts, that is, ceremonial weapons, armor, and gold-lacquered artifacts. In 1367 the Japanese also delivered to a Korean envoy the same type of items: 3 swords, 2 suits of armor, 10 saddles, 300 fans, twill damask, and silk taffeta. It seems likely that these luxury items appeared also among the merchandise of Bakufu-sponsored ships that departed for China in conjunction with the construction of temples.[238]

In addition to vessels sponsored by the Bakufu, numerous other Japanese ships went to China on a nearly annual basis. If the

Chinese authorities had observed dozens of them each year in the mid-thirteenth century, surely not all of these ships were sponsored by the court or the military government, rather they must have been commissioned by provincial leaders or estate managers in southern Japan. These investors undoubtedly did not have at their disposal luxury handicrafts for export, the production of which was limited and distribution concentrated in the circles of the high nobility and warrior aristocracy. Therefore, they could entrust their vessels only with raw materials and items of simple manufacture, products native to the region that were sold in local markets.

Chinese documents report that the Japanese came to sell gold, lumber, and sulfur. This information was also attested by a treatise on the Siming region written in the Zhizheng era (1341-1368) which contained a long list of approximately 276 products that were traded in Mingzhou. On this list we find Japanese products—designated by the prefix Yamato (*Wo*)—and other products which, without the origin specified, probably also came from Japan. The following Japanese items were classified as "high value": gold, silver, pearls, mercury, stag wood, and dichrocephala. Those in the "second class" category were lumber, iron, Lu (Luo tree?), mother-of-pearl, and sulfur.[239] This information agrees with to that provided by a treatise on the same region written around 1226.

As for what the imported items actually were, the discovery of a ship sunken off the Korean coast provides undeniable evidence. The primary ones were currency and ceramics, although until the late twelfth century what principally had been purchased were fine silks and aromatic plants. Thereafter, written sources do not allude to the importation of fabric, and even the manuscripts of the Hōjō family do not mention it. Nonetheless, they do document many other products from China, among them musk and aloe wood. Given the scarcity of documents concerning this period and the fragility of textiles, it is difficult for us to draw definite conclusions concerning the importation of fine fabrics.

In addition, the Japanese purchased numerous books in China. In 1260 a member of the Fujiwara family procured the one thousand-volume *Taiping yulan* encyclopedia for the sum of thirty strings of cash. This amount roughly corresponds to prices paid a century earlier for plots of land near Kyōto and Nara. The *Taiping yulan* had also been part of an exchange of gifts between two court officials in 1247. This work, completed in 983 by Li Fang (925-996), had been printed in the eleventh century. Two printed editions imported in the Kamakura Period are preserved to this day at Tōfukuji temple in Kyōto and at the Imperial Household Agency in Tōkyō.[240]

Many other books have survived thanks to the Kanazawa Bunko archives in Yokohama. These archives originally constituted the library belonging to Hōjō Sanetoki (1224-1276) at his Musashi Province estate in modern Kanagawa Prefecture. Grandson and cousin of the Kamakura regents, Sanetoki had the opportunity to obtain imported works, and his collection was completed by his successors down to his grandson. The Kanazawa archives have preserved 235 Chinese works related to Buddhism and 89 titles of secular literature, all from the pre-Yuan period. Half of these works are manuscript editions, the other half are printed books.

Among the secular titles one finds classics from antiquity and works of ancient Chinese history that the Japanese had long known. There were also sixty-six works from the Song Period. In particular these included the geographic treatise on China and foreign countries "World Geograpy Composed in the Taiping Era" (*Taiping huanyuji*), completed in 979 by Yue Shi; "Finest Flowers of the Preserve of Letters" (*Wenyuan yinghua*, 987), an anthology of poems by sixth- to tenth-century authors and compiled by Li Fang; a collection of tales, "Extensive Gleanings of the Reign of Great Tranquility" (*Taiping guangji*, 978), by the same compiler; and three collections of works by the celebrated poets and authors Ouyang Xiu, "Collected Writings of Ouyang Xiu" (*Ouyang wenzhonggong ji*, 1007-1072); Su Shi, "Complete Collection of Su Dongpo" (*Su Dongpo quanji*, 1036-1101); and Wang Anshi, "Collected Writings of Wang Anshi" (*Wang wengong wenji*, 1021-1086). Another title attracts our attention: the "Anthology of Political Doctrines" (*Qunshu zhiyao*), an encyclopedic work dealing with administration, which was comprised of articles drawn from the Chinese classics and various pre-seventh-century works. It was completed in 631 by Wei Zheng. This work was lost in China after the Song Period—only a single copy survived in the Kanazawa archives. It was edited and printed under the direction of Tokugawa Ieyasu in 1616, then reexported to China in the seventeenth century. And finally, the Confucian classics along with their commentaries, as well as the "Brief Treatise on Philology" (*Xiaoxue*) written by a disciple of Zhu Xi (1130-1200) in 1187, were imported in this period.[241]

The monks of Kyōto and Kamakura were the bearers and transmitters of these works. We know the names of about three hundred monks who departed for China since the twelfth century, and twenty or so monks from China who came to establish themselves in Japan. Some of them enjoyed the high regard of the court or the Bakufu. They founded great monasteries and played the role of religious masters to sovereigns and regents. Zen Buddhism received particular attention from the Kamakura regents starting with the period of Hōjō Tokiyori. Thus began the propagation in Japan of the philosophical, artistic, and material culture of Zen. We must credit the monasteries as the mediators of Chinese culture in Japan during this period.

An innovation of great significance for imports from China was the introduction of the use of tea. Although this beverage had been known somewhat in Japan, it was the monk Myōan Yōsai (1141-1215), founder of the Rinzai Zen sect in Japan, who, after his return from China, taught monks to drink tea during long meditation sessions. Tea drinking soon transcended the religious setting; it gave rise to the popular fashion of tea gatherings.

Tea gatherings took place following a well-defined protocol. To begin, light dishes composed of Chinese specialties, filled balls, rice and wheat-flour cakes, noodles and vermicelli of all sorts, soy pâté, fermented beans (*nattō*), pine nuts and other edible grains, jujubes, and exotic fruits, were served. Then came the sampling of tea: one served many kinds of Japanese and Chinese teas, and guests loved to organize competitions to guess the names of the different varieties. This game was sometimes accompanied by betting, so much so that at times the sums wagered were so exorbitant that it was necessary to forbid tea gatherings. The sampling of tea was followed by a traditional-style banquet celebrated with sake and accompanied by music.

These pleasurable gatherings were supposed to take place in a two-story pavilion with a garden view. Thus architecture and landscape art came into play. Moreover, interior decoration had to follow certain rules: the principal wall was decorated with an image of a Buddhist deity, before which was set a vase, a censer, and a candelabra; on the other walls were hung Chinese paintings of landscapes, floral and bird motifs, or portraits; in a corner near the principal host were placed a jar, tea bowls, small basins containing powdered tea and other items, which were arrayed before a screen.[242]

These tea sessions, precursors of the tea ceremony, were very much in vogue from the late thirteenth century onward in warrior circles, and they gave the host the convenient opportunity to display the exotic objects that he possessed. Indeed, snobbery dictated that the paintings, bowls, other items, and tea all be of Chinese origin. Sasaki Takauji (1306-1373), constable of many provinces and a great landowner, was known for loving to flaunt his collection of Chinese pieces during tea gatherings. He belonged to a new class of lords who gave themselves over to luxury entertainments.[243]

Invaluable information is also found in the manuscripts of Hōjō Sadaaki (alias Kanesawa Sadaaki, 1278-1333), grandson of Sanetoki, who founded the Kanazawa archives. In a letter Sadaaki noted that objects from China were valued highly because tea was so popular, and in another document he alluded to the practice of exhibiting collections of Chinese pieces. He even pointed out that people fought over imported items as soon as cargoes of ships that had come back from China were unloaded in Kamakura, and that the town had abounded in Chinese products since the return of a group that had left for China during the construction of the Shōmyōji temple. The items mentioned in Sadaaki's manuscripts, all of Chinese origin, included *tenmoku* bowls (in black glaze from the kilns of Jian) and other tea bowls, vases, paper, scales, straw hats (*kasa*), paintings, writing brushes, ink stones, wood rosaries, musk, aloe, and, finally, fermented beans.[244]

A list of treasures preserved in a pavilion attached to Engakuji provides still other details. This catalog documents more than 150 items, a large number of which were imported from China. At the top of the list were 47 portraits of Chinese monks and sages, followed by 43 Chinese paintings, some with indications of painters' names, of whom one was Muqi (1232-1279). Another category comprised 17 panels of Chinese calligraphy and 20 panels of Japanese calligraphy. One finds, lastly, an enumeration of monks' robes; ceramic crockery, in particular celadons and *tenmoku*; metal housewares; 10-or-so pieces of Chinese lacquerware; Chinese mats; and 30 wooden bowls.[245]

Currency, ceramics, items of curiosity used for entertaining, books, raw materials for incense, and perhaps textiles accounted for the balance of imports. Yoshida Kenkō, an individual affiliated with the court, however, considered the taste of his contemporaries for exotic things senseless:

As far as Chinese things are concerned, we do not lack for much if we do not import them, with the exception of medicines and pigments. Chinese books are already widespread in our country, and they can be copied easily. What a vain enterprise is that of loading the ships with useless merchandise and bringing them here, risking a hazardous voyage. The ancient texts say, "Do not value as treasures the objects of distant countries," and even, "Do not overvalue things solely because they are difficult to obtain."[246]

But let us remember that in addition to the importation of material goods, there was the introduction of invisible goods—knowledge and techniques. One can cite the Chinese styles of architecture, called *daibutsuyō* and *zenshūyō* in Japan, for example, which were transmitted by monks during the reconstruction of Tōdaiji in Nara in 1195 and the founding of Engakuji in Kamakura in 1282.

The study of Chinese Buddhist literature in Japan kindled a revival of writing in Chinese, especially by monk-authors from the great Zen monasteries known as the *gozan*. The introduction of Chinese painting resulted in a new Japanese style, that of monochrome painting. Chinese ceramics greatly influenced the manufacture of celadons in the Seto kilns. A new carved-lacquer technique transmitted from China inspired the creation of lacquered carved wood (*kamakura-bori*). And, finally, printing technology spread. All these new techniques were applied in Japan, especially from the fourteenth century onward, and they contributed to the blossoming of Ashikaga culture. Thus the importation of "invisible goods" especially benefited the rulers of the post-Kamakura era.

One of the characteristics of the period considered in this chapter has been the paucity of sources, or more particularly the scarcity of documents that furnish information on trade with foreign countries. While the diaries kept by Heian dignitaries were relatively explicit sources of such information up to the twelfth century, their relevance for our purposes diminished when the court no longer had ascendancy over trade affairs. Warriors did not adopt the habit of keeping such diaries, recording the events of the passing months and years; and the documents of the regents' family, which surely contained important testimony, have nearly all disappeared, with the exception of several letters by Hōjō Sadaaki.

The two chronicles known as the "Hundredfold Polished Mirror" (*Hyakurenshō*) and "Mirror of the Eastern Provinces" (*Azuma kagami*), written under the direction of the court and the Bakufu respectively, have survived; but both conclude their entries in the mid-thirteenth century. Therefore the chronology of events outlined above contains gaps, sometimes spanning several decades.

Nevertheless, some general features can be distilled. While control over trade eluded court officials on the one hand, the military government did not yet have sufficiently extensive power to impose its will on southern Japan on the other. Thus the local leaders of Kyūshū provinces acquired a certain independence in administering trade. They made full use of it and sent to China numerous commercial missions nearly every year from the thirteenth century onward. On the other hand, the arrival of Chinese traders in Japan was no longer reported after the middle of the century. It seems that the Japanese agents took over. This was confirmed by the "Treatise on Barbarians" in 1225, which reports that "the people of Quanzhou only rarely depart for Japan," and by Marco Polo's comment that the merchants of the continent hardly ever went to Japan because it was too far away and abounded in all things. The Kamakura government also joined investors and participated in sending commercial missions to China. Each time the purported official goal was the gathering of funds intended for the construction of temples or shrines, but profits far surpassed what was needed for temple buildling, thus facilitating the importation of thousands of handicrafts and millions of coins.

As for Korea, where Japanese agents had disembarked since the late eleventh century, it seems to have maintained regular commercial relations with certain families or local leaders from Kyūshū and Tsushima Island. Korea was besieged by Japanese pirates (*wakō*), led by, among others, petty landlords from Matsura and the islands of western Kyūshū. Piracy was a growing cause of disruption in Japan's trade with its neighbors.

But in this period, Korea was not considered a commercial partner by the two Japanese ruling authorities. The court cared about Korea only because it gave assistance to passing ships that had departed for China but ran adrift on the Korean coast. The Bakufu moreover never contemplated sponsoring a commercial venture to this country. One reason was probably that the Japanese valued Chinese products more, especially currency. The importation of Chinese currency marked the first step toward the influence of foreign trade on the domestic economy. While imported items previously were merely "nonmercantile goods," which were hoarded or used in their original form as luxury items, currency was a standard of value. Currency permitted the purchase of land and goods in the domestic market and the payment of a portion of taxes and rents in cash. It seems that even other imported items, ceramics for example, were also sold in the domestic fairs from this point forward. So we see for the first time the commercialization of products imported from foreign countries.

CHAPTER 5

GROWING EXPORTS
From the Late Fourteenth to the Sixteenth Centuries

A Letter Addressed to His Majesty the Emperor of the Great Ming Dynasty:

Ever since its foundation, the country of Japan has never
ceased to communicate with Your respected land. By good
luck I am holding the reins of government, and throughout
the land there is nothing to worry about. In accordance with
the regulations of olden times, I am especially sending Soa,
accompanied by Koitsumi, to establish friendly relations and
to offer as native products one thousand liang of gold, ten
head of horses, one thousand jō of fine paper, one hundred
fans, three pairs of folding screens, one suit of armor, one
breast-plate, ten double-edged swords, one long sword, one
inkslab with box, and one book stand. I have sought out a
number of [Chinese] who have drifted to these islands, and I
am returning them herewith. In real fear and dread and
kneeling again and again, I respectfully state this.[247]

This letter was addressed to the emperor of China in 1401 by the
third leader of the military government of Kyōto, Ashikaga
Yoshimitsu (1358–1408). Yoshimitsu thus unveiled a new era in
Japanese foreign trade, marked by the sending of missions to China
and Korea. The restoration of official relations was preceded by
many attempts that were complicated by political instability that
reigned in the three countries concerned.

Korea was continually besieged by attacks led by large bands
of pirates from southwestern Japan. Furthermore, after having
succeeded in recapturing a portion of Korean territory from the
Mongols, the Koryô Dynasty suffered serious internal dissension,
which led to its downfall and to the advent in 1392 of the new Yi
Dynasty (which remained in place until 1910). In China, rebellions
against the administration of the occupying Mongols broke out in
many parts of the country. One of the leaders of insurgent troops
conquered the country region by region, and in 1368 occupied the
Mongol capital of Beijing, proclaiming himself emperor and
founding the Ming Dynasty. The new emperor, known by the name

of Hongwu (r. 1368–1399), established his capital in Nanjing (Nanking).

During this period, Japan had two courts. Godaigo Tennō (r. 1318–1339) made attempts to restore monarchial power and obtained the support of several vassals, among them Ashikaga Takauji. The latter overthrew the Kamakura military government in 1333 and established his new headquarters in Kyōto. In 1336, however, he enthroned another *tennō*, Kōmyō (r. 1336–1348); two years later, Takauji was appointed shogun. Godaigo fled Kyōto with his adherents and founded a rival court in Yoshino, south of Nara. The ensuing period was marked by civil wars sustained by the dynastic rivalry, internal quarrels of the Ashikaga clan, and struggles between the shogun and provincial leaders. A provisional peace was reinstated in 1392 when the third shogun, Ashikaga Yoshimitsu, succeeded in negotiating the reunification of the two dynastic lines. The Ashikaga leaders, however, never attained the level of dominion over the provinces that the Kamakura military government had.

The fourteenth and fifteenth centuries were also characterized by changes in the social and economic structure of the country. The *shugo*, who initially had been vested with the power of military surveillance in the provinces of their jurisdictions, assumed more extensive administrative authority and even levied taxes, at the expense of estate stewards (*jitō*), who were supposed to represent the interests of proprietors. This development was facilitated by temporary wartime conferral to provincial constables (*shugo*) of the authority to collect fifty percent of the rents (*hanzei*) so that they could maintain troops of warriors. But the *shugo* (hereafter called provincial military governor) soon monopolized most of the estate revenues, which permitted them to assemble followers and organize a provincial vassalage.

One saw therefore a slow decentralization of power that gradually led to changes in the trade system. A vertical structure still prevailed, characterized by the supply of taxes from the provinces to the centers of collection, principally Kyōto and Nara, especially since several provincial military governors also resided in the capital of Kyōto. Gradually, horizontally structured trade within and between provinces advanced, particularly in regions far away from the capital, mainly Kyūshū. Commercial activity was not stifled by the civil wars of the fourteenth century; on the contrary, it was stimulated, because the fighting waged in various regions fostered progress in the transport of men and goods. Moreover, the system of double-cropping (alternating the planting of rice and non-irrigated grains) each year spread, enabling the agricultural surplus to be sold.

A principal feature of the Ashikaga Period economy was the rapid expansion of services, namely, transportation, storage of merchandise, wholesale trade, exchange, and credit. Wholesale trade initially was conducted by the agents of estate proprietors and provincial military governors, who collected rent goods and income at crossroads, usually near ports. Gradually, certain surplus products were marketed. The agents occasionally acted on behalf of several proprietors and also engaged in trade, because a portion of the rents was delivered in cash that sometimes was sent in the form of a letter of exchange. Storage, mainly purveyed in Kyōto and other towns, developed similarly. The warehouses, which often belonged to religious establishments, became involved in credit dealings. They were joined in this enterprise by the sake wholesalers. In 1426 in Kyōto, for example, there were 347 sake houses engaged in credit brokerage.

One saw therefore considerable commercial specialization, favoring the growth of a merchant class. The same was true in the handicraft sector. Trade and artisanal production were no longer intermittent avocations of farmers and serfs working for estate proprietors. Itinerant trade still prevailed, but the number of markets grew and the frequency of fairs increased. Furthermore, manufacturers and trade guilds gained importance. Guilds generally operated under the supervision of noble or warrior families, or even religious establishments, which granted them protection in exchange for payment of fees. In the middle of the fourteenth century, for example, the Gion Shrine in Kyōto collected a duty of 200 coins per year from the silk floss merchant guild, then numbering 64 members, and was supposed to protect their monopoly on sales in the city of Kyōto.

Even the *tennō*'s household and the Ashikaga military government in Kyōto were obliged to participate in certain commercial activities because traditional revenues drawn from estates were no longer sufficient. The Bakufu required certain religious establishments and noble families to yield to it a portion of the rents supplied by their estates, assessed a tax on wholesale houses as well as a storage tax, and from the mid-fifteenth century onward also collected tolls at many roadblocks. Foreign trade was also an important source of revenue in the fifteenth century. The commercial activities of the Bakufu astonished a Korean envoy, who noted during his visit to Kyōto in 1420 that "the government's storehouses are empty and its resources depend on the support of rich merchants."[248]

Many Japanese towns formed around commercial activities. Yamaguchi—a village in southern Honshū that had prospered thanks to foreign trade—and Fuchū (Shizuoka) in the Kantō were the respective headquarters of the Ōuchi and Imagawa families, military governors of provinces in these regions. But above all it was harbor activity that attracted population growth. Alongside the old ports of Hakata and Bōnotsu in Kyūshū, Hyōgo (Kobe, formerly Ōwada) on the Inland Sea, and Tsuruga (Fukui Prefecture) on the Sea of Japan, several new ports appeared. One was Obama in the vicinity of Tsuruga, a port initially used by the Yamana family, who held the military governorship of the region; Obama was a center for fairs from time to time and for wholesale houses. The new villages on the Inland Sea coast were particularly numerous: Murotsu (Hyōgo Prefecture), Onomichi (Hiroshima Prefecture), another port exploited by the Yamana, and above all Sakai, which played an important role in trade with China.

Sakai, situated astride the provinces of Settsu and Izumi, (modern Ōsaka), consisted of two estates, which passed into the hands of different proprietors, namely Tōji and Shōkokuji temples of Kyōto and Sumiyoshi Shrine in Settsu Province (Ōsaka Prefecture). Sakai appeared as an estate in thirteenth-century documents. This village then served as a port for transshipment of annual fees supplied by estates situated on the Inland Sea to their proprietors, namely temples and shrines of Nara and Mount Kōya in Wakayama Prefecture. Soon, as in other towns, storage and exchange services evolved. For example, in 1380 a Suō estate (Yamaguchi Prefecture) belonging to Tōdaiji temple in Nara received an order to send its rent, twenty strings of cash, in the form of a letter of exchange that could be converted into specie in Sakai. Another estate, Ōta, situated near modern Hiroshima, sent annual rent to Mount Kōya monastery; in the mid-fifteenth century, this estate had, depending on the year, up to six cargoes of products converted into cash in Sakai.

There certainly were markets in Sakai also, but these were poorly documented. Guilds also existed, albeit to a lesser extent; one guild of lamp oil merchants and two guilds of straw hat traders are known. But the principal activity in Sakai, clearly, was storage and exchange, which entailed important financial transactions: the fees collected could amount to sums of several hundreds of strings per estate. Given that the only coins in circulation were Chinese, it seems natural that the Sakai businesses would turn to trade with China. They were in a privileged situation in this regard because since 1399 the Ashikaga had directly operated the Sakai region military governorship. Thus, in the mid-fifteenth century certain Sakai traders were investors in and owners of Ashikaga-sponsored boats departing for China. One might suppose that the profits from foreign trade equaled, if not at times surpassed, the profits obtained through the other activities and contributed greatly to Sakai's prosperity. Sakai, which in the early sixteenth century had a population of thirty thousand inhabitants, thus became one of three main commercial centers of Japan, the others being Kyōto and Nara. The rapid expansion of the latter two, however, rested on credit, artisanal production, and guild activity.[249]

As a general rule, from the fourteenth century onward trade surpassed the scope of an estate economy. Interregional trade increased and gradually overshadowed the former fiscal economy, which had been characterized by a one-way transfer of goods from the periphery to the tax collection centers, thus exhibiting features of both a market and a monetary economy. Nevertheless, Japan had not yet experienced the rapid urban growth that had characterized Chinese society since the Song Period.

THE ASHIKAGA YOSHIMITSU ERA, 1358–1408

The first official contact between Japan and Ming China took place in 1369. That year a Chinese envoy arrived in Kyūshū carrying a letter from the Hongwu emperor (r. 1368–1399) in which the Chinese sovereign denounced Japanese piracy, which had ravaged the Chinese coast since the 1350s. The Chinese sovereign threatened to impose sanctions. This message was the second addressed to Japan and was part of a series of communiqués sent by China to several countries.

The previous year, in 1368, following his assumption of power, Hongwu had dispatched messengers to Annam, Champa (Zhancheng, South Vietnam), Korea, and Japan to announce his enthronement and the founding of the Ming Dynasty. These steps were intended to legitimate his accession to the throne through the receipt of tribute from barbarian countries, because since ancient times Chinese sovereigns had been considered as ruling" all under heaven." The first delegations bearing tribute landed the following year; others appeared subsequently. The most loyal tributaries were Annam, Champa, Siam (Xianle, Thailand), the Khmer kingdom (Zhenla, Cambodia), Java (Zhuawa), Xiyang (a Southeast Asian region), and soon Korea, Japan, and the Ryūkyū kingdom (Okinawa).

Hongwu's reign was marked by efforts to control trade with foreign countries by channeling it into the bringing of tribute and attempts to reduce the number of embassies in order to alleviate the budgetary strain caused by the reception of foreigners and provision of reciprocal gifts. In 1371 an edict forbidding Chinese to leave the country was promulgated. Hongwu feared that Mongol rebels were linked with pirates of the coastal regions, and through this measure he attempted to sever contact between the continent and the sea. Moreover, the emperor fortified the coast.

In 1374 the Offices of Maritime Trade, just reestablished four years earlier in Ningbo, Canton, and Quanzhou, were abolished. Thus private foreign trade became illegal. This measure was later reinforced by a prohibition on transactions involving imported products in Chinese markets. Hongwu thereby put an end to free trade with foreign countries, which had flourished for centuries. The prohibition on private trade remained in place for nearly two centuries until 1567. Furthermore, in 1374 the Chinese emperor limited the number of Korean delegations bearing tribute to one arrival every three years, and subsequently did likewise with respect to Annam, Siam, Cambodia, and Java. The Ryūkyū kingdom was to bring tribute only once every two years, but later it was authorized to come every year, and Korea was allowed to present tribute several times a year. For these countries, the contribution of tribute conferred the advantage of being able to conduct commercial transactions on an official basis.

As for Japan, the Hongwu emperor was concerned with encouraging the bringing of tribute and eliminating the peril of Japanese pirates. The first Chinese messenger who departed for Japan in 1368 disappeared en route. The next, who carried a letter admonishing piracy, did not reach Kyōto. He was arrested in Kyūshū by Prince Kaneyoshi (1329–1383). Son of Godaigo Tennō, who had founded the southern court at Yoshino, Kaneyoshi had been appointed "great general in charge of supervising the western part of the country" and had occupied the headquarters of the former Kyūshū Headquarters, in the vicinity of Hakata. The prince did not have experience with foreign relations. He had the Chinese envoy seized and imprisoned for three months, and executed five members of his delegation. Then he sent the envoy back to China. The same delegate returned in 1370 accompanied by fifteen Japanese pirates who had been seized in China. This time, Kaneyoshi responded favorably with presents consisting of horses and native products, and he dispatched a Japanese monk to accompany the Chinese, who again set sail for their country. The monk returned the following year, accompanied in turn by monks delegated by the Chinese court and entrusted with gifts of silks and a Chinese calendar. The latter differed from the Japanese calendar with respect to the era names and sometimes slight discrepancies in days. With the use of the Chinese calendar, foreign sovereigns acknowledged their allegiance to the Middle Kingdom, which was precisely Hongwu's goal when he sent this "present" to Japan.

Subsequently other delegations came and went. There were about fifteen of them up to the end of the fourteenth century, the majority sent by Japan. Their respective letters had a tone that was sometimes harsh, sometimes conciliatory. Given that the first contact had been monopolized by Kaneyoshi, who represented the court at Yoshino, it was essential that the Kyōto shogun, Ashikaga Yoshimitsu, make himself known and recognized by the Chinese as the competent authority in foreign relations and as ruler of Japan. He succeeded in doing so from the 1390s onward. At the same time, his ally Imagawa Sadayo (alias Ryōshun), deputy in Kyūshū, succeeded in distancing Prince Kaneyoshi's influence in trade with China. From this time onward through to the sixteenth century, the Ashikaga shoguns placed powerful *daimyōs* loyal to them as their official Kyūshū deputies (*tandai*) in south Japan.[250]

Imagawa Sadayo (1326–?) was the provincial military governor of Tōtōmi (Shizuoka Prefecture) in the Kantō when he was dispatched by Yoshimitsu to Kyūshū in 1371. In this region, several families sometimes shared and sometimes quarreled over rights of dominion. The most powerful were the Shimazu in the southwest, the Kikuchi in the central region, the Ōtomo in the northwest, the Shōni in the northeast, and the Ōuchi in the north. These families became very active in trade with Korea subsequently, but it was Imagawa Sadayo who initiated it.

In 1377 the deputy received a Korean delegation that arrived in Kyūshū. He responded to the demand of the king of Korea, the last Koryô Dynasty sovereign, to combat piracy by sending a Japanese delegation accompanied by a group of Koreans who had been taken prisoner by Japanese pirates and were to be repatriated. Later on, and until 1402, approximately fifteen other Korean and Japanese delegations, primarily bearing messages concerning piracy, crossed the sea. When Imagawa Sadayo was recalled to the capital in 1395, Ōuchi Yoshihiro (1356–1399) acted as main representative for the shogun in external relations. Yoshihiro, a warrior faithful to Ashikaga Yoshimitsu, held the military governorships of six provinces located in the Sakai region, southern Honshū, and northern Kyūshū. In 1397 Yoshimitsu, who had become a monk, continued to lead the Bakufu as retired shogun and conveyed to Korea via Ōuchi Yoshihiro's envoy his good intentions with regard to combating piracy. This message was Yoshimitsu's first contact with the Korean court after he had responded negatively to a letter from the first king of the Yi Dynasty in 1392. Following a response from Korea, the ex-shogun Yoshimitsu dispatched his first official envoy to Korea in 1399. That envoy was followed three years later by several others.[251] Ashikaga Yoshimitsu thereby took relations with foreign sovereigns in hand. From this moment up to his death in 1408, official messengers came and went every year between Japan and both Korea and China.

Trade conditions were determined by Chinese politics. When the Ming emperor received a letter from Yoshimitsu in 1401, he immediately dispatched two Chinese monks to escort the Japanese envoys home. He also entrusted them with a letter, a calendar, and twenty bolts of silks as gifts for the head of the Bakufu. Yoshimitsu sent messengers to the port of Hyōgo to meet the Chinese guests and later received them at his residence in Kitayama, the present-day Kinkakuji in Kyōto. Then he had them accompanied back to China in 1403 by three Japanese monks, among whom was Kenchū Keimitsu (dates unknown), chief abbot of the Tenryūji monastery in Kyōto.

In his letter to the Chinese sovereign, Ashikaga Yoshimitsu referred to himself by the epithet "Your subject Minamoto, king of Japan." The name Minamoto was adopted because the Ashikaga were descended from the Seiwa Genji line of the Minamoto house. The designation "king of Japan" was sharply criticized by Yoshimitsu's contemporaries and by historians of later generations because the term "king" referred to the sovereign of a country owing tribute to China and implied submission to the "universal" supremacy of the Middle Kingdom. No Japanese government leader had adopted so submissive a stance since the founding of the Japanese *tennō*'s realm in the late seventh century. Yoshimitsu thereby inaugurated a policy, which was followed by most of the Ashikaga shoguns, of accepting pro forma the status of vassal because China dealt with only tributary countries. Yoshimitsu and several of his successors thus relinquished their independent diplomatic position so they could conduct commercial transactions in China.[252]

Attached to the 1403 letter was a list of "native products" sent to China. The presentation of tribute, however, was not the only goal of this delegation. Indeed, documents of the Yoshida house, a family affiliated with the shrine of the same name in Kyōto, reveal that "weapons of all sorts, etc., were taken to China; once more [the delegation] departs with a commercial objective (*shōbai*), pursuant to the order of several great lords (*daimyō*)."[253] In fact, the monk Kenchū Keimitsu was accompanied by three hundred persons who, one suspects, were not all official delegates. Thus out of consideration for material profits, and perhaps also under pressure from certain provincial military governors, Yoshimitsu took on a diplomatic compromise.

We know that the Japanese brought to China a certain number of swords and spears intended for sale, apart from those that were presented as tribute, because importation of these weapons provoked active discussion within the Chinese government. The Minister of Rites remarked that "it was forbidden for envoys of barbarian countries to carry weapons for their personal profit when they enter China, and to sell them to the population"; and he suggested therefore that they be confiscated. But the emperor decreed:

> In admiration of the Middle Kingdom, barbarians come to
> bring us tribute. They cross the perilous sea and forge a path
> over thousands of miles. The route is distant and the
> expenses of their voyage are considerable. The payments they
> receive help them to cover the costs, and this is
> understandable. Such a prohibition would paralyze their
> actions. . . . Since the weapons cannot be sold in the public
> market, the government will buy them at the usual price in

China. Do not tie the hands of the barbarians by imposing prohibitions on them. To do so would be contrary to the generous intentions of the imperial court and would discourage the desire of distant peoples to pledge their allegiance.[254]

These remarks precisely reflect the policy of the Yongle emperor (Chengzu, r. 1403–1425), which consisted of encouraging the bringing of tribute. In 1403—the year of a Japanese visit to China—Yongle installed officers responsible for the arrival of tributary missions in some of the ports where the Offices of Maritime Trade had formerly been situated, that is, in Ningbo, Quanzhou, and Canton. He also dispatched delegations to Malaya, Java, Sumatra, and even Cochin on the western coast of southern India. These delegations were followed, between 1406 and 1422, by six large expeditions of armed fleets that advanced as far as the Persian Gulf, the Gulf of Aden, and Mogadishu on the African coast. These expeditions, according to some interpretations, were supposed to demonstrate the power of the Ming empire and prompt payment of tribute. The regions in question were not occupied by military forces, except Annam.

The efforts of the Ming emperor were not in vain, because we can see a definite increase in the number of missions bringing tribute during this period. Therefore thanks to a policy of stimulating tribute, the Japanese benefited from the leniency of the Chinese government concerning their export of weapons to China. Yongle organized a banquet in honor of the guests from Japan and distributed gifts of silk, coins, and paper money to them.

The following year (1404) upon their departure, the Japanese visitors were entrusted with a hooded court robe, fine fabrics, and a golden seal for "the king of Japan"; they were also accompanied by a Chinese delegation of eighty persons. The head of this delegation informed the Bakufu leader of new conditions governing relations between the two countries. This was attested to in the "Standard History of the Ming Dynasty" (*Ming shi*): "At the beginning of the Yongle era, Japan was authorized to send one mission bearing tribute every ten years, counting a maximum of two hundred members per delegation on board two ships at most. It was forbidden to bring weapons, and all groups apart from these missions thereafter would be considered pirates."[255]

Moreover, the Chinese ambassador delivered to Ashikaga Yoshimitsu's administration one hundred or so numbered tallies (*kangō*) bearing the inscription "Japan" and cut into halves. One half was retained by the Chinese authorities. Each boat thenceforth had to possess a tally whose authenticity could be verified with the aid of two registers deposited with the respective administrations of the two countries. This form of supervision had been inaugurated in 1383 for delegations from Siam, Champa, and from the Khmer kingdom; in 1404 twelve countries in all were furnished with these tallies. In part these countries enjoyed somewhat better terms than Japan: that is, a waiting period of one to three years between missions, but with the number of members in their embassies being more limited. This kind of control permitted the Chinese authorities to distinguish official missions from unauthorized commercial delegations and pirates. For the Bakufu, this system had one great advantage, that of obtaining a monopoly on trade with China for itself, especially since the missions were authorized to bring export merchandise.

After having received the tallies from the Chinese delegate, Ashikaga Yoshimitsu immediately sent a delegation to China led by a monk bearing gifts of horses and native products. In return, the Japanese received silks and paper money as reciprocal gifts. Because this was the first mission since the establishment of the new regulations, in theory, the next mission would have to wait ten more years, until 1414. Nevertheless, following a visit from another Chinese envoy, the ex-shogun dispatched his next delegation in 1405, and subsequent ones in 1406, 1407, and 1408. These missions clearly violated the waiting period, but they were all well received in China and were escorted back to Japan. The Japanese sometimes were accompanied by Chinese prisoners who had been liberated from pirate captors and then repatriated, which was considered a gesture of courtesy. Nevertheless, the "Standard History of the Ming Dynasty" stated that the Japanese did not come at all "in accord with the regulation."[256]

The sources do not provide any information about commercial transactions conducted by Yoshimitsu's envoys in China, but they do give some details on the exchange of gifts. The tribute products sent by Japan in 1403 consisted of the following items: 20 horses, 10,000 pounds of sulfur, 32 agates (a total weight of 200 pounds), 3 folding screens with gold backgrounds, [10] spears, 100 long swords, a suit of armor with a case, a *suzuri* ink box in a case, and

100 fans. This list may be considered representative of the missions in general, because the same products were cited on seven occasions up to the sixteenth century, with only slight variations in the number of swords and spears.[257] One notices that gold disappeared from the lists, even though Yoshimitsu had sent some in 1401, at the time of his overtures to the emperor of China. The value of the gifts in 1403 can be estimated at between 600 and 700 strings of cash (at the Japanese rate in 1432).

China responded in 1406 with 378 bolts of brocade, twill damask, *ra* gauze, and *sha* gauze; 500 strings of cash, and 5,000 monetary notes, which at the time, were generally worth 150 to 200 coins per note. A Chinese embassy arrived in Japan the same year, bringing 1,000 ounces of silver, 200 bolts of brocade and colored silk taffeta, 60 embroidered twill monks' robes, 3 silver jars for the preparation of tea, 4 silver cups, embroidered twill fabrics, gauze curtains, mattresses, cushions, lacquer tableware, and 2 boats.

A very complete list of Chinese gifts has survived from the year 1407. In all it comprised, for "the king of Japan and his wife," 1,250 ounces of silver, 20,000 strings of cash, 494 fabric bolts (brocade, satin damask, two kinds of gauze, and silk taffeta), 12 monks' robes, a jade talisman in the shape of a hand, 8 precious stone and pearl rosaries, a felt cushion, 4 other cushions, 2 mattresses and a pillow made of satin damask and brocade, 2 silk curtains, 6 braids, 4 bronze pitchers, 20 trays plus 30 incense boxes made of carved lacquer, and 4 fruit baskets. For 1408, we know only the rewards bestowed upon the Japanese envoy Kenchū Keimitsu, who had come to China for the fourth time. He personally received 100 monetary notes, 10,000 coins, 5 pieces of colored silk taffeta, and a robe.[258]

Just as with China, there was trade with Korea annually. It is remarkable that from 1404 onward the ex-shogun Yoshimitsu even adopted the appellation "king of Japan" in his letters addressed to the king of Korea. This implied, some researches opine, that he put himself on an equal footing with the Korean sovereign, even though the tradition was to treat Korea as a country obliged to present tribute to Japan. The gifts exchanged by the two rulers are not known, but in 1397 Yoshimitsu had requested a bronze temple bell and a copy of the Tripitaka Buddhist canon (Japanese, *Daizōkyō*) from the Koreans.

This latter treasure compiled in more than five thousand volumes the principal texts of Buddhism—the printing of a woodcut edition had been completed for the first time in Korea in 1087. Following the loss of the wood blocks during the wars with the Mongols, a second edition was published on the peninsula in the mid-thirteenth century—the 86,000 wood blocks carved on this occasion are still preserved as a national treasure at Haeinsa temple in Korea. This Buddhist collection, which was printed in Japan only in the seventeenth century, was among the most highly desired Korean items in Japan. The Japanese made approximately sixty requests for this work up to the sixteenth century. Unfortunately it is not known whether the king of Korea responded to the request Yoshimitsu made in 1397. Meanwhile "native products" were presented by the Japanese envoys to Korea, although their content is not mentioned in the sources.

In addition to the exchange of official gifts with Korea, commercial transactions were conducted by the respective missions. In 1399 the head of the Bakufu furnished his delegation with twill fabrics or satin damask (*aya*) as well as two kinds of gauze fabric made for export. On the other hand, two lists of goods imported to Japan have survived from the years 1402 and 1406, including sake barrels, sake pitchers and vessels, kettles, and pots—all in silver—silver sake cups with gilding, leather shoes, straw hats, tiger and leopard furs, various kinds of mats, paper, ginseng, and pine nuts.[259] Silverware had become valuable in Japan because silver had grown scarce following the depletion of the Tsushima Island mines in the fourteenth century.

This list of imported items from China and Korea suggest that in addition to the acquisition of currency, Ashikaga Yoshimitsu also purchased for himself implements for banquets and gatherings. Indeed, the ex-shogun had a pavilion constructed in 1401—a meeting place within the enclosure of his Kitayama residence—where he hosted tea, perfume, and seasonal flower gatherings, poetic composition sessions, banquets, and theatrical presentations of *sarugaku* and *dengaku*. At these gatherings interior decor played an important role, and no doubt on these occasions the Chinese or Korean objects were used or displayed. One notes, however, that the lists of imported items did not contain objects specifically for the tea ceremony.

About this time Nōami, a master of the arts, compiled a list of paintings in Yoshimitsu's collections. This work, entitled "Catalog of Honorable Objects and Paintings [in the Shōgun's Possession]" (*Gyomotsu on'e mokuroku*), presented a classification according to artistic value and was based on the first Chinese works of art criticism. The catalog listed 280 works by more than 31 artists, who took Buddhist deities, portraits, landscapes, or birds and flowers for their subject matter. The most numerous were those by Muqi (103 paintings), followed by Liang Kai (27 paintings), Ma Yuan (17), Xia Gui (17), and Emperor Huizong (r. 1101–1125, 10 paintings), all famous artists of the Song Period. We note the strong preference for Muqi, even though this painter was not so popular in China at this time. Paintings such as these also decorated Yoshimitsu's pavilion.[260]

During this period trade with foreign countries was not limited to society of the capital. Provincial military governors and notable families from southern Japan also conducted trade. The official Korean chronicles of the Yi Dynasty contain accounts of numerous Japanese delegations that had arrived after the establishment of the dynasty in 1392. Until 1408, there were 120 to 130 delegations from northern, southern, and western Kyūshū, and from Tsushima Island.

Imagawa Sadayo, the Kyūshū deputy, and Ōuchi Yoshihiro, the powerful provincial governor in Kyūshū, took the lead as initiators of trade. They were followed by the Ōuchi's successor, a member of the Shōni family, and by a local leader from the Minamoto family who resided in northern Kyūshū. In the south, the Shimazu and Ijūin as well as representatives from Satsuma, Ōsumi (present-day Kagoshima Prefecture), and Hyūga (Miyazaki Prefecture) played roles in trade with Korea. Shimazu Ujihisa (1328–1387) even attempted in 1374 to send a mission to China laden with gifts of horses, tea, fabrics, swords, and fans for the emperor. But the delegation was refused for lack of an official letter from the Japanese authorities. Probably because private trade was forbidden in China, the rich families of Kyūshū turned to Korea in this period.

The system in Korea apparently relied on the acknowledgment of private foreign trade under the auspices of a state monopoly. That is, the court authorized private overseas groups to land in Korea, but trading was conducted exclusively by Korean authorities. The Korean government thus attempted to discourage piracy and hinder contacts between the native population and foreigners. Furthermore, numerous delegations from Kyūshū returned Korean prisoners captured by pirates. Thus missions from southern Japan had both an official and a commercial character.

The greatest number of delegations during this period, about fifty, arrived in Korea from western Kyūshū. The name of Minamoto Yoshihisa (or Yoshiharu, dates unknown), a leader from Iki Island, crops up in particular, as does that of the Shisa, a family originating from the Matsura region. At times they controlled Iki Island. The sources also reveal details about items traded. In 1405, for example, a member of the Shisa family sent two horses, short swords, medicines, and stoneware to Korea. The following year he received from Korean authorities a silver pitcher and basin, 5 bolts of hemp cloth, 5 bolts of ramie cloth, a tiger fur, a leopard fur, 100 pounds of pine nuts, 100 *koku* of rice, and 100 *koku* of beans. That same year delegations of the governors of Hi and Tan each brought sapan-wood, pepper, precious stones, spears, swords, and buffalo horn to Korea. In 1408 another individual received from Korea 105 *koku* of rice and 50 *koku* of beans from Korea.[261]

Relations between Tsushima Island and Korea resumed in 1397. There had been trade between the two regions since the thirteenth century, but no information about trade items survives. We know only that Korea considered Tsushima a pirate base. And piracy was the primary impetus for renewing contact. In 1397 brigands took refuge on Tsushima with a local Korean leader as prisoner, whereupon, an official Korean delegation came bringing a letter addressed to a Tsushima leader. Then, in 1398, eight Korean prisoners were repatriated and nine Japanese were sent to Korea as hostages.

The following year, one Sō Sadashige (?–1418) took matters into his own hands. He sent tribute to Korea and, in a letter addressed to the Korean king, claimed to be the leader of the island's residents. The presents he received from the Korean government on this occasion included 3 bolts of hemp cloth, 3 bolts of ramie cloth, and a tiger fur. Thereafter, Sadashige and other members of the Sō family took part in one or two missions to Korea annually, during which they went laden with gifts, in exchange for which they demanded gifts in return.

In 1402, for example, Sō Sadashige received 20 pounds of ginseng, 6 bolts of hemp and ramie cloth, 40 *koku* of rice, and 20 *koku* of beans. In 1404 he received in exchange 6 bolts of two kinds of cloth, 10 pitchers filled with strong alcohol, 10 *to* of garlic (1 *to* is 8.5 liters), 2 furs, 10 sheaves of dried persimmons, and 10 *to* of chestnuts. Three years later (1407) he brought home 100 pounds of pine nuts, 60 sheaves of dried persimmons, 100 pitchers of strong alcohol, and 30 pitchers of sake. On top of this, Sadashige received annually, from 1406 onward, approximately 200 to 300 *koku* of rice and beans, meaning that relations with Korea were lucrative for the Tsushima leader.[262] At the same time the Korean government benefited from friendly relations because Tsushima was a strategic point from which piracy could be controlled. Trade therefore flourished between southern Japan and Korea.

We have an interesting document on this subject. A manual of protocol for warriors written circa 1400 named special products from all the provinces in Japan, including those of Kyūshū, which were "grains as well as Chinese goods and rare items from Korea, [which are concentrated there] like clouds and mist. Profits from their exchange far surpass those of the Fourth and Fifth Avenue markets in the capital, and there is a constant coming and going of rich and poor, as in Kyōto and Kamakura."[263] According to tradition, Ōuchi Hiroyo (?–1380), founder of the Ōuchi family of Suō Province, spent "thousands of strings of cash" and distributed at will "newly imported Chinese products" to his followers as well as to dancers and theater actors in Kyōto. Hiroyo clearly had acquired his wealth through trade in Kyūshū.[264]

In this period too Japan had its first direct contact with the countries of Southeast Asia. A messenger from the king of Siam carrying tribute to Korea in 1391, claimed to have spent a year in Japan. Another delegation from Siam left Korea for Japan in 1393 accompanied by a Korean delegate, but they fell into the hands of pirates and the entire cargo along with part of the crew was lost. In 1406 a ship from Java landed in Korea. It had suffered losses as well: Japanese pirates had seized the cargo consisting of sapanwood, pepper, camphor, aloe wood, parrots, and peacocks; 60 crew members were taken prisoner, 21 died during the fighting, and only 40 people succeeded in fleeing and taking refuge in Korea. Notably, the leader of Tsushima, Sō Sadashige, sent tribute to Korea that same year—sapanwood, pepper, and peacocks—declaring that they were stolen goods. And many of the same products were offered to Korea by two local leaders from Matsura (sapanwood and pepper), and by Ijūin Yorihisa, who resided in southern Kyūshū (100 pounds of sapanwood). Still later, another delegation from Java landed in Hakata Bay in 1411.[265] Beginning in this period, however, trade with the regions of Southeast Asia came through the Ryūkyū kingdom.

FROM YOSHIMOCHI TO YOSHIMASA, 1408–1449

Ashikaga Yoshimitsu died in the fifth lunar month of 1408; at the same time, the Bakufu's flourishing trade with foreign countries entered a period of stagnation. Yoshimitsu's son and successor, the shogun Ashikaga Yoshimochi (1386–1428), renounced the policies of his father. After the exchange of some courtesy visits with China to declare a state of mourning and accept condolences, the new head of the Bakufu refused to welcome Chinese envoys. The "Account of Good Neighborly Relations" (*Zenrin kokuhōki*) reproduces his response to demands from the Chinese court for the submission of tribute. Yoshimochi wrote: "[Before his death, my father] received from a soothsayer the following prognostication: 'Since antiquity your country has never declared itself a vassal of a foreign country, but you contravened the way of the enlightened sovereigns. You accepted the [Chinese] calendar and the seal [with the title "King of Japan"] and did not refuse them. This is why your illness now occurs.'"[266] Yoshimochi, on the other hand, used the Japanese calendar and Japanese names of eras in his correspondence with foreign sovereigns. He even expressed his indignation when he received a letter from Korea that did not display the Japanese names of eras as well. Exchanges with Korea were reduced to eleven or twelve missions between the two countries until Yoshimochi's death.

Nevertheless, missions that were exchanged were no less lucrative. In 1422 the shogun exported raw silk, copper ore, literary works, aloe, white sandalwood, sapanwood, pepper, liquorice root, and a substance extracted from wood betony; and in 1425, there were fans with silver-plated blades, swords, and raw silk. We note that the plant substances came from Southeast Asia—indeed, after Japan's first contacts with Siam and Java, goods began arriving from Sumatra. One mission sent by the head of Palembang landed in 1408 at the port of Obama on the Sea of Japan coast. He brought an elephant, a mule, and two peacocks as gifts for "the king of Japan." Another delegation from Palembang landed in 1412, when orders from the shogunal residence were placed with him. Two other groups from Sumatra landed later in Kyūshū. Korean sources report the 1411 arrival of an elephant, a gift from Yoshimochi. One can imagine that this animal followed the same route as other products from Southeast Asia that were imported to Japan and then re-exported to Korea. As for the items imported from Korea by the shogun Yoshimochi, the Buddhist canon was foremost among them. Printed editions of this collection reached Kyōto at least five times during this period, while other items included those previously imported by the prominent families of Kyūshū: that is, ramie and hemp cloth, mats, animal furs, and ginseng. One finds here no mention of silverware, however.[267]

Ashikaga Yoshimochi died in 1428. His successors were more favorably disposed toward trade with foreign countries. In China, however, the Ming Xuande emperor (r. 1426–1436) took matters into his own hands: after having acceded to the throne, he revised the regulations concerning relations with Japan. Delegations from Kyōto thereafter were authorized to come in three ships instead of two, carrying three hundred persons (instead of two hundred); but the ten-year waiting period between missions was maintained. This proposal from the Chinese government was transmitted to Japan by an intermediary from the kingdom of Ryūkyū. Ashikaga Yoshinori (1394–1441), the sixth shogun and head of the Bakufu, hastened to reply—in 1432 he dispatched an official delegation led by a monk. At the outset, the mission undoubtedly was to be made up of three ships sponsored respectively by the military government, the Shōkokuji monastery of Kyōto, and the powerful Yamana family. It seems, however, that two more vessels were added, managed by a group of thirteen provincial military governors and religious establishments, and by the Sanjūsangendō, a temple associated with the court. Each ship was furnished with a tally, a hundred or so of which had previously been presented to the Bakufu by the Chinese government, so that it would be recognized as part of the official mission. The following year, 230 delegates arrived in Beijing, while presumably the other members remained in Ningbo. We are particularly well informed about the exchange of gifts and commercial transactions conducted by the group from the shogun's vessel on this occasion.[268]

In the category of "native products" presented by Yoshinori to the Chinese sovereign were 20 horses, 2 swords with ornate guards and gold lacquer sheaths, 10,000 pounds of sulfur, 20 agates, 3 screens with gold backgrounds, 100 spears, 100 short swords with plain guards and black lacquer sheaths, 100 long swords, a suit of armor, a writing case, and 100 fans (see appendix 8). These gifts had been purchased by the Bakufu prior to departure for a sum of 695 strings of cash.

In exchange, the emperor of China sent to the "king of Japan and his wife" the following gifts: 300 ounces of silver, 6 bolts of brocade, 30 bolts of satin damask, 28 bolts of *ra* gauze, 28 bolts of *sha* gauze, 30 bolts of colored silk taffeta, and, as supplementary gifts, 330 bolts of other fine fabrics, a sedan chair, a folding chair, and 2 folding beds—all in carved lacquer inlaid with gold and appointed with cushions made of fine fabric—together with 2 umbrellas, 20 pieces of silverware, 10 mirror cases, 2 carved-lacquer shelves with gold inlay, 2 vases, 2 censers, 2 boxes and 100 incense containers in gilded bronze, 40 carved-lacquer bowls with gold inlay, 4 lanterns, 20 ink sticks, 500 sheets of paper, 300 writing brushes, and one 100 sheets of decorated stationery. There were also 260 snake, monkey, tiger, bear, and leopard skins, 10 boxes containing dichrocephala, and 20 parrots.[269]

Along with the exchange of gifts, commercial transactions were conducted by the parties concerned. The Japanese delegation had been entrusted by the shogun with many supplementary products to be sold to the Chinese court, in particular sapanwood, sulfur, copper ore, swords, and all kinds of refined handicrafts. These products, perhaps, were provided in part by the sponsors of other ships, because a list of items prepared by the Bakufu revealed a smaller number than those sold in China in the shogun's name. Prior to the delegation's departure, the Bakufu had purchased 850 swords, 2,200 fans, 100 bronze pitchers, 100 ounces of gold leaf, and 2,000 pounds of sapanwood, copper ore, and grinding stones, for a total sum of 1,457 strings of cash.

As far as the profits attained in China are concerned, the calculation of payments received for the five items for which quantities are known yields a figure of 69,810 strings of cash. It seems, according to the official Ming chronicles, that the aggregate value of the products sold on behalf of the Bakufu amounted to 217,732 strings of cash, that is, to more than two million coins. This sum corresponds to the total profit realized through trade in the mid-thirteenth century.[270]

Furthermore, not only the Bakufu but also the sponsors of other ships conducted transactions in China for their own benefit. We have information on this subject courtesy of the accounts of a Sakai merchant named Kusuba Sainin (1395–1486), son of a Southeast Asian immigrant, who traveled aboard a ship financed by thirteen sponsors as a representative of the Daijōin, a temple attached to Kōfukuji monastery in Nara. According to Sainin, the hiring of the ship, salaries of the crew, and provisions cost approximately 1,500 strings of cash. The thirteen investors accepted ten individual private traders as passengers aboard their ship in exchange for one-tenth of the value of their imports upon return. In the case of an individual total figure of 10,000 strings of cash, for example, the sponsors collected 1,000 strings (according to an example noted by Sainin himself). The ten merchants therefore could return a sum of 10,000 strings to the thirteen investors, thereby making the investment profitable.

Sainin gave his successors the following advice: nothing was more profitable than trade in silk thread. A pound of thread was worth only 250 *momme* (of silver?) in China, but it was worth 5,000 coins in Japan. In both countries, copper from the Bizen and Bitchū regions cost 10,000 coins per 150 pounds (according to the price in 1453). Instead of selling copper in China, one could trade it for silk thread from Mingzhou and Yunzhou (modern Datong?), yielding a profit of from 40,000 to 50,000 coins upon to return to Japan. Similarly, the price of gold in Japan was 30 strings of cash for 10 ounces; but traded in China for silk thread, this quantity of gold was worth from 120 to 150 strings of cash. Sapanwood could be purchased in Japan for from 50 to 100 coins per pound and resold in China for 1,500 coins. Kusuba Sainin's advice suggests how lucrative the deals conducted in China were, not only for the Bakufu but also for individual investors.

The Japanese delegation's five ships returned in 1434 accompanied by an official mission from China. The Chinese guests presented to the shogun Ashikaga Yoshinori in Kyōto, on behalf of their sovereign, 50 chests filled with gifts, 10 cages of exotic birds, and 300,000 strings of cash. This sum probably included recompense for products exported by the Bakufu. The head of the Chinese delegation also presented the military government with a hundred or so tallies to replace old ones, and asked that the shogun combat piracy and have Chinese prisoners repatriated. The Chinese guests were then escorted back to their country.

A year later a new Japanese mission departed for China. This time it included six boats sponsored by the same investors as before, joined by the Daijōin temple of Nara. The delegation landed in China in 1435, a few months after the Xuande emperor's death, and thus could use the pretext of wanting to convey the Bakufu's condolences to the court—because rules concerning the waiting period and the number and size of missions had again been ignored. It seems that the delegation was well accommodated: it was entrusted by the Chinese court with gifts in exchange for native products presented by the shogun, mainly consisting of the same items as two years before. One can speculate that this delegation also made good profits from trade, although the sources do not give any precise information on this subject. This Japanese mission was the last in the era of Ashikaga Yoshinori. [271]

Yoshinori also entered into relations with Korea. A Japanese delegation departed for Korea in 1432, the same year as the mission that realized such considerable profits in China. On this occasion, Yoshinori exported to Korea Buddhist statues, copper ore, swords, spears, screens, lacquerware, tortoiseshell and lacquer saucers, fish skins, raw silk, crystal, liquorice root, and pepper. In exchange for these "gifts," which can be considered official merchandise, the shogun obtained from the Korean king hemp and ramie cloth, a Chinese edition of the Buddhist canon, cotton cloth, mats of various kinds, animal furs, and a quantity of pine nuts and ginseng. Five or six other Japanese and Korean delegations crossed the sea in this period, and traded products similar to those of the year 1432. [272]

THE ASHIKAGA YOSHIMASA ERA, 1449–1490

After 1432 came a respite in exchanges that lasted about fifteen or so years, interrupted only by two or three arrivals from Korea, one of which received a response from Japan. Ashikaga Yoshinori was assassinated in 1441 by a political adversary. Influential advisers appointed his eldest son head of the Bakufu even though the boy was only eight years old; he died two years later. The advisers then chose another of Yoshinori's sons. Their choice, Yoshimasa (1436–1490), became shogun in 1449 at the age of thirteen, and he remained at the head of the Bakufu for forty years. This period was marked by the blossoming of arts and culture, but also by civil wars. The Ōnin War (1467–1477) in particular broke out during the struggle over succession to the post of shogun waged by families of powerful provincial military governors.

In Yoshimasa's day four missions left for China and about 22 delegations were exchanged with Korea. In 1453 nine Japanese ships, having 1,200 persons on board, arrived in China. The vessels were sponsored by the Tenryūji Zen monastery of Kyōto, the Ise family (which filled important posts in the military government), the deputy of Kyūshū, the Ōtomo family, the Ōuchi family, and

Mount Tōnomine temple, south of Nara (present day Danzan Jinja). Curiously, not one of the ships was sponsored by the Bakufu. Tenryūji assumed responsibility for three boats, and the Ise family provided for two of them. It appears therefore that this mission was organized by Yoshimasa's entourage, since the shogun himself was still too young.[273] Kusuba Sainin, the Sakai trader, took part in the venture, this time as an agent of Mount Tōnomine. He later reported that expenses for the hiring of ships, provisions, and salaries of the crew amounted to 1,820 strings of cash. We also learn that he journeyed to Ningbo, Nanjing, and Hangzhou and that a 10 percent tax was collected by Rokuon'in, a temple that was part of Shōkokuji monastery in Kyōto, which had close relations with the Bakufu.[274]

As far as trade conducted in China in the name of the shogun is concerned, presents and reciprocal gifts included virtually the same items as those received by previous delegations. The volume of trade goods, however, was approximately fifteen times that of the year 1433, at least with respect to the five products whose quantities are known. Given that the Chinese court did not acknowledge the principle of private foreign trade, it was obliged to purchase products brought by representatives of the Bakufu; otherwise it risked losing tribute from Japan or stimulating unauthorized traffic. But in practice, at a certain point the Chinese administration authorized the sale of items too numerous to be absorbed by the authorities.

The main products brought in 1453 would have been worth 615,000 strings of cash—that is, nine times the amount in the year 1433—had the Chinese government applied the same prices of twenty years earlier. The authorities, however, were not ready to make this sacrifice. The prices thus were reduced and calculated partly in silver at a rate of one ounce per string. The total value of the Japanese merchandise was thus fixed at 34,790 ounces of silver, plus 59,400 strings of cash for the swords, and an unknown sum for the rest. Still the court paid only 50,118 strings of cash, and the remainder was paid for in fabric amounting to 688 bolts of silk and hemp cloth. The total sum proposed by the Chinese, therefore, was less than what they had offered previously, even though the volume of imports was much greater. In response to the complaints of the Bakufu's envoy, the Chinese came up with an additional 10,000 strings of cash and, finally, as the Japanese envoy was still not satisfied, the court granted him another 504 bolts of silk taffeta and 1,000 bolts of hemp cloth.

EXPORTS FROM JAPAN TO CHINA IN 1432

Products**	Quantity in 1432-1433	Price per Unit in China*	Price per Unit in Japan*
Sapanwood (pounds)	16,000	1,000	50 to 100
Sulfur (pounds)	22,000	1,000	*
Copper Ore (pounds)	4,300	300	67
Long Swords	2	10,000	1,000?
Short Swords	3,050	10,000	1,000
Spears	*	3,000	*
Fans	(2,200)	300	200
Gilt Bronze Pitchers	(100)	6,000	100
Gold-lacquered ware	*	800	*
Equipped Writing Cases	*	2,000	*
Ink Stones	*	500	*
Daggers	*	500	*
Colored Animal Skins	*	500	*
Fire Tongs	*	300	*
Gold Leaf (ounces)	(100)	*	3,000
Total Amount Paid by the Chinese Court	217,732,100 coins		

* Figure unknown
* In coins
** See the Chinese List of Products in appendix 8

Sources: *Ming shi lu*, p. 170; *Daijōin nikki mokuroku*, p. 157; *Daijōin jisha zōjiki*, p. 249; all excerpted in Yutani Minoru, *Nichi-Min kangō bōeki shiryō* (Tōkyō: Kokusho kankōkai, 1983)

EXPORTS FROM JAPAN TO CHINA IN 1453 AND 1468

Products	Quantity in 1453	Price per Unit in China, 1453*	Quantity in 1468
Sapanwood (pounds)	106,000	70	*
Sulfur (pounds)	364,400	50	30,000
Copper Ore (pounds)	152,000	60	5,250
			(35 *da*)
Long Swords	417	6,000	*
Short Swords	9,483	6,000	500
Spears	51	2,000	40
Fans	250	*	380
Gilt Bronze Pitchers	*	4,000	*
Gold Lacquerware	634	600	*
Equipped Writing Cases	*	1,500	*
Ink Stones	*	*	180
Daggers	*	*	*
Colored Animal Skins	*	*	*
Fire Tongs	*	*	*
Gold Leaf (ounces)	*	*	305 *momme*
Total Amount Paid by the Chinese Court	34,790 ounces silver** 50,118,000 coins 688 bolts of fabric *		38,000 ounces silver

*   Figure unknown
*   In coins
**   Rate: 1 ounce = 1,000 coins in China

The following sources are excerpted in Yutani Minoru, *Nichi-Min kangō bōeki shiryō: Ming shi lu*, pp. 170-171, 220; *Daijōin nikki mokuroku*, p. 157; *Boshi nyūminki*, pp. 200, 213; *Daijōin jisha zōjiki*, p. 249.

Despite a great reduction in prices, they were still higher in China than in Japan, with the exception of the prices of sapanwood and copper. The Japanese, therefore, profited once again. The *Zenrin kokuhōki* records that the Japanese delegation upon departure, was entrusted with a letter from the emperor of China containing the following instructions: "Henceforth, if it is a tribute article, your sulfur should not be classified with the 'supplementary items' and thus be exported unidentified. Sulfur as tribute shall not exceed thirty thousand pounds. Moreover, regarding embassy personnel, you should select only those who are upright and versed in basic principles of behavior respectful of protocol and laws."[275] This last passage alluded to an incident incited by Japanese envoys en route from Ningbo to Beijing—they had looted a shop in a market and wounded local public officials.

The Bakufu responded to these remarks and other Chinese government reprimands with a letter of apology transmitted to the Ming court by the Korean intermediary. Then in 1468 it dispatched a new mission to China. This mission was the first to be in complete accord with the regulations. It arrived more than ten years after the previous mission and traveled in only three ships. It was sponsored by the Bakufu, the Ōuchi family, and the Hosokawa family. The exchange of gifts took place as before. The sources give interesting information about the sums invested this time. Hiring, salaries, and provisions for the crew of the Bakufu's ship cost 2,065 strings of cash; the purchase of export goods and tribute items amounted to a sum of approximately 2,152 strings (Yoshinori's expenses in 1433)—that is, 4,217 strings of cash in total.

The Bakufu nevertheless profited by authorizing as passengers aboard its ship traders who prepaid import duties levied on the anticipated volume of their merchandise. There were fifteen passengers in the 1,000-string category, for example, and eighteen travelers in the 500-string category, yielding amounts that represented one-tenth of the estimated value of the imports upon their return. The Bakufu thus collected from these merchants a total of 24,000 strings, nearly six times the sum invested.

As for the export items supplied by the Bakufu, they were less plentiful than those of previous missions. The Chinese government awarded the Japanese 38,000 ounces of silver in payment for their products, explaining that this would have to suffice. The Bakufu's envoy demanded more, but he was admonished not to bargain. After the departure of two boats, the Ōuchi family envoy addressed a request to the Chinese court for a supplementary payment on the pretext of having lost the Chinese gifts intended for the Bakufu on a previous return attempt. The envoy asked for 5,000 strings of cash, and after some discussion, he finally obtained 500. Furthermore, the Ōuchi succeeded in seizing a part of the cargo of the shogun's ship upon its return as well as the tallies received from the Chinese court.[276]

Thus the shogun was deprived of the official insignia necessary for sending new missions. His response was to have the situation explained to the Chinese court by the Korean intermediaries, and in 1477 a delegation of 300 persons departed for China aboard three ships provided with old tallies. The ships were sponsored by the Bakufu and Shōkokuji temple. The two governments exchanged gifts as in past. In his letter addressed to the emperor of China, Yoshimasa added a postscript requesting currency and books, and he obtained a sum of fifty strings of cash.

It seems that the shogun's ship had been financed by a Sakai trader. The port of Sakai had been governed by the Hosokawa family since the Ōnin War, and thereafter it had become the point of departure for official overseas missions. The sources do not give further details about the volume of sales in 1477, but we know that the Chinese government presented the Japanese with a sum of 16,056 strings of cash, including gifts for the Bakufu and the delegates as well as recompense for imported products.[277]

In 1483 Ashikaga Yoshimasa dispatched his last mission to China, consisting of three ships. The two vessels sponsored by the Bakufu were outfitted by a business from Sakai that paid the Bakufu 4,000 strings of cash per ship for the privilege. Perhaps it was really a tax of 10 percent of the total estimated profit. The third ship, for which the court assumed responsibility, was financed by the Kanroji family, a member of which was then a high dignitary. Investors therefore assumed expenses of approximately 6,000 strings of cash per vessel, including equipment expenses. In return, they made space available to private merchants. In addition to the anticipated 10 percent tax, those travelers also paid transport fees of 20 strings of cash per person and 12 strings per 150 pounds of merchandise.

As usual, the Bakufu sent presents to China and this time requested a supplementary gift of 100,000 strings of cash. It explained that "state warehouses" were empty and praised the generosity of the Chinese court. We do not know, however, if the Chinese acceded to the Bakufu's request. Furthermore, items intended for sale seem to have been numerous. Chinese officials informed the Japanese that sulfur and horses were easy to obtain in China and that sulfur, in particular, reached China in great quantities from the Ryūkyū kingdom. They requested that in the future the Japanese reduce the volume of these items and that preferably they should bring metal handicrafts, such as pitchers, pots, and censers made of gilt bronze.

The military government also sent 3,600 swords as tribute, together with 35,000 swords intended for trade. Once again, the Chinese government was obliged to reduce the price of these swords, which in the meantime had commanded 1,800 coins. Pointing out that the quantities of tribute goods had increased tenfold since 1433, the Chinese court responded that it was prepared to pay only 600 coins per unit. A letter from the emperor of China addressed to the Bakufu and later archived in the "Account of Good Neighborly Relations, Continued" (*Zoku zenrin kokuhōki*) contained the following exhortation:

> Regarding tributary and "supplementary" articles, the
> Ministry of Rites memorialized us and suggested that
> henceforth such items should not be excessive and should
> conform to the precedent of the Xuande era. Swords of all
> kinds shall not exceed a total of three thousand, hereby
> freeing both sides from undue expenses. We have accepted
> this suggestion and hereby inform you of it. It is said of old,
> "Let one give much and receive little." It is also said, "The
> goods may be trifling, but the sentiment is sincere." The
> sincerity of a subordinate in serving a superior is really not
> dependent on goods.[278]

The mission that brought back this letter was the last of Yoshimasa's era, because plans for another delegation were carried out only after his death.

On several occasions the head of the Bakufu also dispatched envoys to Korea and received guests from there in Kyōto. There were approximately seventeen Japanese missions to the peninsula and, perhaps, four or five Korean delegations to Japan. The official Korean chronicles did not always clearly distinguish between the

Bakufu on the one hand and military provincial governors and other local leaders on the other. A source notes that five of the Japanese delegations demanded, on Yoshimasa's behalf, grants for construction or repair work on temples, in particular Tenryūji and Kenninji in Kyōto, Saikōin on Mount Kōya, and Onjōji in Ōtsu. In response to one of these demands, the king of Korea heaped upon his Japanese guests hemp and cotton cloth. In return, Yoshimasa exported to Korea handicrafts (weapons, fans, screens, bronze vessels), copper, raw silk, and aromatic products previously imported from Southeast Asia. Meanwhile, Korea sent plain-woven raw silk, foodstuffs, furs, mats, and printed editions of the Buddhist canon to the archipelago.[279]

Ashikaga Yoshimasa died in 1490. Thus ended a century-long epoch during which the military government of Kyōto had kept a firm grip on relations with China by means of the supervised tally trade, which in theory interdicted private exchange. As far as relations with Korea are concerned, however, the Bakufu was only one of many Japanese participants. Indeed, Yi Dynasty chronicles cite dozens of names of Japanese individuals with whom the Koreans conducted commercial exchanges in an official capacity. Most of those individuals were local leaders from southern Japan. These exchanges assumed such proportions that on several occasions the Korean court was obliged to impose restrictions and implement control measures. Given the important role of these relations, we should recount their principal features.

SOUTHERN JAPAN AND KOREA IN THE FIFTEENTH CENTURY

In the early fifteenth century, many groups arrived in Korea, mostly envoys from western Kyūshū, that is, from the Matsura region and Iki Island as well as northern and southern Kyūshū and Tsushima Island. These delegations, all of which had commercial objectives, averaged thirteen groups per year. To avoid clandestine trade, which could take the form of piracy, the Korean court accommodated all these foreigners and supervised transactions by local authorities in coastal regions.

These exchanges weighed heavily on the kingdom's budget, and in 1407 the Korean monarch introduced a system of accreditation, in accordance with which only groups possessing an access permit (*bun'in*) from their locality in Japan thenceforth would be welcomed. Seven years later, the number of Japanese partners authorized to send commercial delegations was reduced to ten, comprising "the king of Japan," the leader of Tsushima Island, the Ōuchi family, the Shōni family, and the Kyūshū deputy (*tandai*). The Korean court directed the leader of Tsushima, Sō Sadashige, to notify the parties concerned of these conditions. Sō Sadashige thus enjoyed the trust of the Korean king, thanks in part to his efforts to suppress piracy. His death in 1418 was a tragedy for Korea—it was followed by two separate attacks of fifty- and thirty-eight-ship pirate fleets.

King T'aejong (r. 1400–1418), who considered the families of Tsushima to be at the root of the calamity, decided to launch an offensive. His army's attack on Tsushima Island, however, was a failure, and Sō Sadamori (?–1452), Sadashige's son, commenced peace negotiations. Sadamori officially became a vassal of Korea, receiving a title and seal; he was recognized as the sole lord of the island and the legitimate authority for delivering access permits to commercial delegations from Tsushima. Furthermore, the new leader's entitlement to an annual income of two hundred *koku* (seventeen thousand liters) of rice and beans (such as soy beans) from Korea was confirmed. Given that rice was not cultivated on Tsushima and that one hundred *koku* of rice fed thirty persons per year, this income was a significant asset.

During this period, groups from Japan never stopped landing on Korean shores. Yi Dynasty documents reveal no fewer than sixty-two names of Japanese sponsors, families, local leaders, or other individuals who sponsored regular delegations to Korea. In 1419 the Korean court now under King Sejong (r. 1418–1450) decided not to admit commercial delegations any longer, just "diplomatic" missions bearing access permits and official gifts from the Japanese authorities. At this point, Korea recognized only the Kyūshū deputy and the leader of Tsushima as competent authorities, awarding them a seal to be affixed to the access permit. Later these seals of accreditation were granted to other persons. Groups thus accredited were authorized to carry out commercial transactions. In this sense, the system was analogous to the official trade system in China, though without using two-part tallies. Naeip'o (modern Chimhae) and Pusanp'o (Pusan) were designated as the only ports of entry for the Japanese, and inns for foreign guests were established there. Another port, Yomp'o (near modern Ulsan), was added three years later.[280]

Subsequently, Sō Sadamori attempted several times to extend his authority to deliver access permits in order to consolidate his power on Tsushima, chiefly to the detriment of the Sōda family, and to make sure he had new revenue. Indeed, he collected a commission and an import tariff from his clients. In 1438, on his own initiative, Sō Sadamori signed a contract with a messenger from the Korean court, securing for himself the right to accredit not only agents sent to Korea by sponsors from Tsushima but also those delegated by the Shisa of Matsura, the Shisa of Iki Island, the Taira of Kyūshū, and even representatives from the regions of Satsuma, Iwami, as well as those of the Ōuchi family (for a brief period). Sō Sadamori thus became the first authority to control trade with Korea. From 1441 onward, this system was applied also to the fishing rights of Tsushima fisherman in Korean waters.

Around this time, ninety sponsors from southern Japan entered into relations with Korea, most of which were channeled through the leader of Tsushima.[281] Information concerning trade goods is abundant, so we will limit ourselves to a few examples. In the course of the year 1427, for instance, about fifteen Japanese groups landed in Korea. The sponsors and trade products were as follows:

• *Eight Expeditions from Tsushima*

Sō Sadamori exported 2 swords with guards, 300 pounds of sapanwood, 500 pounds of sulfur, and 30 arrowheads; he imported 70 bolts of hemp cloth, 100 *koku* of rice, 100 *koku* of beans, 2 tiger and leopard furs, 20 bolts of ramie cloth, 30 mats of various kinds, 30 of rice liquor, and 5 *koku* of pine nuts (see appendix 8). At least two other delegations were sent to Korea that same year by Sadamori.

Sō Sadazumi exported swords with guards, arrowheads, long swords, and skin-covered trays (?); and he imported 40 bolts of hemp cloth, 50 *koku* of rice, 50 *koku* of beans, 10 bolts of cotton, 10 bolts of ramie cloth, 10 bolts of plain-woven raw silk (*tsumugi*), and 20 pitchers of rice liquor.

Sōda Saemontarō exported 1,000 pounds of sulfur, 500 pounds of sapanwood, 8 pounds of rhinoceros horn, 500 pounds of aromatic wood ("bird plum"), 10 pounds of liquorice root, 2 pounds of birthwort roots (?), 2 pounds of white sandalwood, 30 pounds of mandarin orange rind, 10 pounds of vermilion dye, 2 pounds of aloe, and 100 terracotta bowls; he imported 300 bolts of hemp cloth. Two months later, Saemontarō exported 60 pounds of white wax, 50 pounds of lead, 29 basins, 180 bowls and 290 other stoneware items, as well as 1,000 pounds of sulfur; he imported 59 bolts of hemp cloth, 20 pitchers of rice liquor, and 2 *koku* of pine nuts.

● *Two Expeditions from Iki and Matsura*

Shisa Minamoto Shigeru of Iki exported 2,000 pounds of sulfur, 100 pounds of sandalwood, 5 ounces of camphor, 5 pounds of skullcap, 10 pounds of mandarin orange rind, 3 pounds of areca nut, 50 pounds of copper ore, and 5 short swords. He imported 83 bolts of hemp cloth, an official seal, and a complete collection of the "Great Wisdom Sutra" (Daihannyakyō). Remarkably, Ankokuji temple, on Iki Island, has preserved a Korean edition of this sutra, part of which was printed with the first set of wood blocks from the 1020s. Minamoto Atsuaki of Matsura also sent a delegation, but the goods traded are not known.

● *Two Expeditions from Southern Kyūshū*

Shimazu Takahisa exported 300 pounds of sulfur, 500 pounds of sapanwood, 35 pounds of lacquer, and 5 short swords; he imported 268 bolts of hemp cloth.

   Ijūin Yorihisa exported 1,000 pounds of sulfur, 200 pounds of sapanwood, 3 short swords, 2 spears, 30 pounds of copper ore ("bird's gold"?), and a rhinoceros horn; he imported 30 bolts of cotton cloth and 90 bolts of hemp cloth.

● *Three Expeditions from Northern Kyūshū*

Taira Mitsuchika, "administrator of Ishiki village," dispatched two delegations, and Taira Tsuneyoshi, "*junbushi* of Kyūshū and the former governor of Mimasaka," also sent a mission to Korea. The products traded by the last two individuals are not documented. There were no delegations sent that year by the Ōuchi, the Shōni, or the Ōtomo.

   We also have some information concerning exchange rates. In the 1420s, Sōda Saemontarō received a bolt of hemp cloth in exchange for 4.5 pounds of sapanwood, 9 pounds of sulfur, or 2.5 ceramic basins; he exchanged 5 fans for a tiger fur, and on another occasion, he bartered 22 grinding stones for a *koku* of hulled rice. But the rates seem to have changed depending on the circumstances and the persons involved: for 300 pounds of sapanwood and 1,000 pounds of sulfur, Miura Shirō received 300 bolts of hemp cloth; Saemontarō however obtained only 178 bolts for the same quantities of these items.[282]

In Korea in this period, hemp cloth was the main standard of value used in the fiscal system and as a medium of exchange. But from about the 1460s onward, it was supplemented and then surpassed, by cotton cloth. The cultivation of cotton had been introduced to Korea by the Mongols and expanded quickly. Cotton appeared among the payments made to Japanese traders from the early fifteenth century onward, and it soon became a favorite import item. Between the years 1418 and 1425, Korean sources document annual quantities of up to 5,000 bolts of cotton paid to the Japanese. At the same time, quantities of hemp cloth, ramie cloth, and plain-woven raw silk traded reached seven thousand bolts.

In exchange for these goods, the Japanese exported raw materials, handicrafts, and products from Southeast Asia, including sapanwood, other aromatic woods, and rhinoceros horn. As we have seen, Japan had begun to trade with Southeast Asia in the late fourteenth century. It is known in particular that a group from Sumatra disembarked in Satsuma in 1419 and then proceeded around Kyūshū to land in Hakata. The Kyūshū deputy then had these guest-merchants escorted back as far as Ryūkyū. After this episode, however, there are no further reports of direct trade with the southern regions. It seems that from then on trade in Southeast Asian products essentially was carried out through the Ryūkyū kingdom intermediary. Beginning in the 1370s, one of the local leaders of that archipelago's main island sent missions bearing tribute to China each year, and in the early fifteenth century, he consolidated his power over the entire island. Ryūkyū thus played an important role as an intermediary in trade among China, the countries of Southeast Asia, Japan, and Korea.[283]

Japanese exports to Korea increased despite the restrictive measures taken by the Korean government in 1414 and 1419. For a period of twenty years thereafter, Japanese boats averaged thirty arrivals per year—the example cited above of fifteen arrivals for the year 1427 was unusual. That is why the Korean court drafted new regulations. In 1443 it signed a new contract with Sō Sadamori, the Tsushima Island leader, limiting the number of boats he could send to Korea to fifty per year, a number that could be exceeded only in the event that an urgent communiqué needed delivery. The Korean king upheld Tsushima's right to an annual income of 200 *koku* of rice and beans and Sō's authority to accredit delegations sent to Korea. This contract was the first of many accords intended to limit the number of authorized ships. At the time, 27 Japanese partners had authorization to send one vessel yearly: four partners were authorized to send three, four, five, and seven boats respectively; only the leader of Tsushima was entitled to fifty ships. This sizable number of vessels was permitted Tsushima because this island, situated only a few hours away from Korea by boat (50 kilometers), was even closer to Korea than Kyūshū. Therefore, a total of 72 commercial partners were officially recognized by Korea, and it admitted a maximum of 176 ships per year. In addition to this number, approximately eighty Japanese seem to have received temporary authorizations.

A geographic treatise, "Notes on Countries in the Eastern Ocean" (*Haedong chegukki*) written by a high dignitary of the Korean court, provides invaluable information on the organization of trade, accommodation of foreigners, and trade procedures up to 1471, when it was composed. According to this source, it seems that the Korean government distinguished among four categories of Japanese partners: "the king of Japan," that is, the shogun; "local leaders," consisting of provincial military governors, members of the Shiba, Hatakeyama, Ōuchi, Shōni, Hosokawa, Kyōgoku, and Yamana families; the leader of Tsushima Island; and finally, others granted access permits as well as individuals who previously had received official Korean titles and were therefore authorized to come to Korea themselves. This last group were mainly former pirate leaders whom the Korean court had converted into merchants. Accords limiting the number of ships had only been reached with partners of the last two categories. The Bakufu and a few *daimyō* were free to send as many missions and boats as they wished.[284]

Neither the accords nor strict control, however, could stop the growth of Japanese exports. In 1455, for example, Korean port authorities counted a total of 6,116 "Japanese delegates" who arrived in the course of that year. And later in 1470, King Sŏngjong (r. 1469–1494) made the following remarks in a letter addressed to Sō Sadakuni, leader of Tsushima from 1467 to 1492: "In recent years, ships of envoys from the provinces of your country have been particularly numerous. Not a day passes that the official inns do not see new guests arrive. Given that each vessel transports dozens or hundreds of persons, these visits weigh heavily on our budget and the expenses are enormous. The villages of our coastal garrisons can hardly support this burden."[285]

This letter, archived in the "Chronicles of King Sŏngjong" (*Sŏngjong sillok*), was written at the time of the Ōnin War (1467–1477) in Japan, a period that was marked by a rush of people going to Korea. A large number of persons who did not appear in the registers of the Korean authorities landed there, claiming to be envoys of one or another warrior leader. Furthermore, the privilege of accreditation sometimes was swapped among local Japanese leaders, with the result that Korean seals changed hands, especially after the original owners who had been authorized to use the seals had died. Thus many individuals succeeded in acquiring access permits, and the Korean officials were under obligation to welcome them. Several missives sent by Japanese sponsors to the king of Korea were addressed to "the Yi emperor (*kōtei*)"

Another development made control over Japanese groups in Korea increasingly difficult: the growing numbers of Japanese residents in the three foreign trade ports. The leader of Tsushima earlier had obtained trade-port residency privileges for a certain number of Japanese in order to enjoy their services as commercial agents; Korea had consented because it saw such an agreement as a way to limit contact between the Korean population and foreign guests. Thus 644 Japanese lived in the three ports in 1436, but this number increased to 2,009 individuals in 1475. And since the foreigners sometimes mingled with the native inhabitants in order to prolong their stay, the Japanese presence at times was much greater than the number of registered individuals.

The many arrivals from Japan entailed considerable cost for the Korean government, involving the expense of not only recompense for imported products and reciprocal gifts but also the lodging and sustenance for the Japanese as official guests. Although the Korean court on several occasions had taken measures to reduce prices and limit the duration of visits, the volume of reciprocal gifts, and the number of persons admitted per ship, the sums expended only increased. In 1475 the court awarded a total of 27,208 bolts of cotton cloth to Japanese delegations, for example, and the following year, the amount increased to 37,421 bolts. This sum was as much as ten times the annual payments made in the 1420s. As a proportion of the Korean state budget, expenses in 1475 and 1476 represented between 5 and 15 percent of the national revenue in cotton. These percentages are based solely on known quantities of cotton collected by the state: 200,000 bolts in 1467 and 724,000 bolts in 1485.

The sums spent for unwanted imports from Japan exceeded 100,000 bolts of cotton cloth in the 1480s. Indeed, cotton became the most sought-after Korean item in Japan. In 1464, when an Ōuchi family envoy received in exchange for his cargo of copper and lead 542 bolts of cotton and 1,080 bolts of hemp cloth, he accepted only the cotton and refused the hemp, saying that there was no use for the hemp in Japan. Furthermore, Sō Sadakuni's messenger explained in 1490 that Japan had an abundance of hemp and plain-woven raw silk, but that cotton was scarce. The cultivation of cotton had been introduced to Japan in the mid-fifteenth century, but became widespread only around the eighteenth century.

Sō Sadakuni personally procured considerable quantities of cotton. Between the years 1487 and 1492, the amount imported increased annually to nearly 15,000 bolts. The leaders of Tsushima—Sadakuni and his predecessor—had used every means to increase their exports to Korea. Their requests to have more than fifty ships per year admitted were rejected by the Korean authorities. For people in their entourage who did not yet appear as partners registered in Korea, however, they did secure seals and the right to accredit delegations, as well as authorization for a limited number of ships. Moreover, Sō Sadakuni made extensive use of his license to send supplementary vessels in the event of urgent news. In the 1470s, these special delegations landed in Korea every year.

The latter half of the fifteenth century, therefore, was the high point of Japanese-Korean trade. The number of arrivals of groups from Japan increased incalculably, even though it had already reached a total of approximately 1,300 ships annually in the early fifteenth century. [286]

TRADE AFTER THE ERA OF ASHIKAGA YOSHIMASA

Before his death in 1490, Ashikaga Yoshimasa, then a monk, devised a new plan for a mission to China. The plan was not realized, however, until 1493, after endless discussions had been held about who would have the privilege of sponsoring the ships. The Hosokawa family emerged victorious from these quarrels. It dispatched two vessels for its own benefit and a third on behalf of the Bakufu, led then by shogun Ashikaga Yoshitane (1466–1523). Another subject for debate was financing. The records state that the traders of Sakai, in a quest for profits, had on previous occasions exported mediocre-quality swords, which caused prices to fall. This time it was proposed that the management of ships be entrusted to merchants from Hakata or Nagato. Nevertheless, the men of Sakai ultimately secured the privilege of sponsorship once again by paying 3,000 strings of cash per vessel. When the sponsors discussed gifts to be offered as tribute, they noticed that the number of reciprocal gifts received from China had diminished in recent years. According to information from a Japanese monk, this was the consequence of the inferior quality of Japanese gifts.

Taking all these considerations into account, the delegation took to the seas in 1493. The representatives of the Bakufu were welcomed in Beijing as before. But on the return route from Beijing to Ningbo, the Japanese caused disturbances and some Chinese were killed during a scuffle. Following this incident, the Chinese court decided that henceforth only fifty members of future missions would be authorized to go to the capital. Still, the Japanese were satisfied with their mission. They had sold 7,000 swords on behalf of the Bakufu and had obtained a price of 1,800 coins per unit, even though the importation of swords, in theory, had been limited by the Chinese court in 1483 to 3,000 units per mission. For their part, Sakai traders reaped profits of three or four times the sums invested. It was said that "the three ships brought back tens of thousands of strings of cash."[287] Moreover, representatives of the Bakufu were entrusted with new tallies for their next mission.[288]

No time was lost in planning that mission, but it took thirteen years to happen. The delay, once again, was caused by quarrels between the Hosokawa and Ōuchi families, whose clan leaders at that time found themselves together in Kyōto. For a long period the Hosokawa had had their principal residence in Kyōto and had assumed the functions of the prime minister (*kanrei*) in the Bakufu court. They controlled the provinces near the capital and those in Shikoku as well. In 1508 Hosokawa Takakuni (1484–1531) appointed a new shogun and made himself *kanrei*. The Ōuchi had their main headquarters in Yamaguchi (modern Yamaguchi city), where they had created a "little Kyōto," a flourishing town that subsisted on foreign trade. Ōuchi Yoshioki (1477–1528) was military governor of six provinces in southern Honshū and northern Kyūshū. He allied himself with Hosokawa Takakuni and in 1508 settled in Kyōto, where he performed the duties of vice prime minister for six months. These two individuals initiated a new mission to China.

Three ships set sail in 1510, two sponsored by the Ōuchi, and the third by the Hosokawa. A fourth ship sent by the Hosokawa, however, had secretly departed in advance. It was supervised by Song Suqing (Sō Sokei), a Chinese merchant who had immigrated to Japan. Song was welcomed in China by the authorities; the delegates of the three other ships, who arrived after him, had great difficulty receiving recognition as official envoys. The mission once again carried to China 7,000 swords, but this time the Chinese court accepted just 3,000 of them and paid only 300 coins per unit. The Ōuchi family representative spent the ensuing weeks bargaining, but it seems that the Chinese authorities remained steadfast and refused to respond to his complaints.[289]

The Ōuchi and Hosokawa families dispatched another mission to China in 1520. The two ships sponsored by the Ōuchi were provided with the new tallies obtained by the previous envoy. The Hosokawa boat, again managed by Song Suqing, was furnished with an old tally obtained in 1498. After the arrival of the two groups in Ningbo, there were quarrels about the legality of the respective delegations and the validity of the different tallies. The dispute ended with the assassination of Song's assistant by an Ōuchi representative during an official dinner. Song fled to Shaoxing where he was then seized and imprisoned by the authorities. He died a few weeks later. The Ōuchi envoys had pursued Song along part of the route, then they embarked for Japan. The forbearance of the Chinese government in regard to the behavior of members of the Japanese missions had been put to a rough test. A letter of reprimand was addressed to the "king of Japan" by the Ryūkyū kingdom intermediary. The content of this letter is not known, but the response of the shogun, in which he presented his apologies and claimed that the group sent by the Ōuchi was illegitimate, is recorded.[290]

After an eleven-year disruption, three ships sponsored by the Ōuchi landed in Ningbo in 1539; but this time they had an altogether different reception. They were placed under strict guard by the Chinese provincial army, and the fifty members of the delegation authorized to go to Beijing were forbidden to visit other cities en route. Nevertheless, it seems that this mission was able to complete its commercial transactions successfully.

Upon embarkation, the three ships had been loaded with 24,862 swords and 298,500 pounds of copper ore.[291] The delegation included 464 individuals, among whom were 26 "official delegates," 133 crew members, and approximately 300 traders. Given that the Chinese sources do not report excessive quantities of merchandise, one can assume that the goods were sold mainly in the markets of Ningbo.

Upon its departure, the Japanese delegation received notification that in the future the Chinese court would not permit the disembarkation of more than one hundred persons per mission, and that the waiting period of ten years as well as the three-ship limit would be upheld. Furthermore, the Chinese government granted the Japanese only three tallies bearing the new Chinese era name, even though the Chinese government theretofore had always allocated them a book of one hundred new tallies at the time of era changes. Then the delegates were escorted out to the high seas by an armed fleet.[292]

Ōuchi Yoshitaka (1507–1551), son of Yoshioki and head of the clan after 1528, did not wait ten years before sending his representative to China. In 1547, eight years later, 600 persons embarked on four ships. In one sense this mission might be considered a Chinese diplomatic failure because all the regulations imposed by China were once again violated. Noting this, the Chinese initially refused the Japanese the right to land. After talks within the Chinese government, however, the delegation was authorized to enter the port of Ningbo four months after its arrival. Then the Minister of Rites suggested distributing the usual rewards to only 100 persons and letting the other 500 unauthorized members of the delegation return empty-handed. The emperor's response to this proposal is not known, however. In Beijing the reception of fifty delegates and the exchange of gifts took place as previously. When the Japanese set off on their return journey, they were provided by the authorities with a single new tally. The next mission, therefore, would have to travel in a single boat.[293]

No further Japanese missions departed for China, however. Ōuchi Yoshitaka, a *daimyō* who had strengthened his military power in the provinces under his control while contributing to the rapid cultural growth of Yamaguchi, was betrayed by one of his allies; he committed suicide when Yamaguchi fell into the hands of enemies in 1551. After his death there was no longer anyone capable of organizing delegations and representing the Bakufu in China. Thus the missions to China ended with the fall of the military leader.

In China this was not a disappointment. As we have seen, the Japanese had caused trouble during recent missions. Many times they had violated regulations concerning the frequency of missions and the restrictions on the number of boats and delegation members; they had also brought greater quantities of merchandise than were authorized or desired by the Chinese government. The Japanese probably were, in the eyes of the Chinese, vexing partners with whom they were forced to deal in order to prevent unauthorized traffic from overshadowing official trade. The same was true of the Mongols.

Meanwhile Jurchen tribes in the north and the Oirats in northwestern China also sent excessive numbers of delegations annually, forcing the Chinese court to accept very large quantities of horses that were sometimes of mediocre quality. They caused trouble on the frontiers and along the route to Beijing, compelling the Chinese to deal with them because of the danger of war in these regions. Throughout this era, then, the partner esteemed by the Chinese as "the most faithful of all the countries" was Korea.[294]

As far as Japan was concerned, a Chinese military official submitted the following report in the 1550s:

Memorial Explaining Coastal Defense Strategy—
Strategy for Gaining Control over the Japanese (Pirates)

Since the time of the first sovereign of our dynasty, we have granted to the (government of) Japan the golden seal and tallies, authorizing them to dispatch one mission every ten years, aboard a maximum of three ships, and not numbering more than one hundred persons. Thus we aroused among the distant barbarians a sentiment of esteem and duty toward us, and they could profit through trade for our goods. Thus controlling the outlying barbarians, China continued to discipline them so that they have not practiced piracy for more than one hundred years. In 1523 Shūsetsu [Kendō, an envoy of the Ōuchi] and Song Suqing, in their struggle to present tribute, killed one another, and disaster ensued. Because of this struggle, the submission of tribute was interrupted. In 1539 a group led by the principal envoy [Koshin] Sekitei came to present tribute, carrying a letter expressing their wish to submit to our judgment and noting that they benefited from the benevolence of the emperor, who extends his influence throughout the universe. We again gave them authorization to bring tribute, although the waiting period [of ten years] had not yet expired. In 1547 a delegation led by the principal envoy [Sakugen] Shūryō arrived in four boats to renew tributary relations. We consulted one another. Barely nine years had elapsed since the last visit; that is to say, precedent once again had been disregarded. Subsequently, we deliberately prevented them from coming again, and since that time, the tribute connections have been broken. The Japanese barbarians are of a petty and deceiving character, they exploit our resources, and they do not conform to precedents concerning tribute. Resumption (of relations) with them is not desirable.[295]

Meanwhile, a still more serious problem concerned the Chinese government during this time: the renewal of unauthorized traffic and piracy by adventurers, Chinese merchants operating in part from Japan. For the Japanese, clandestine traffic was a new channel for trading goods with China, one that was beyond the control of the authorities of both countries.

Private foreign trade had been forbidden by China since about 1374, and every individual who went abroad was severely punished. Nevertheless, clandestine traffic had blossomed since the 1520s, especially on Liuheng Island, located in the Zhoushan archipelago across from the Ningbo peninsula, and in the south in Zhangzhou in Fujian Province. The port of Zhangzhou had flourished to such an extent that the Chinese compared this city to Suzhou and Hangzhou; it also was to become the first official port when the ban on private trade was repealed in 1567.

Clandestine traffic was the subject of several works commissioned by the military superintendents responsible for subduing piracy. One of them, the maritime strategy manual "Atlas of the Sea Strategy" (*Chouhai tubian*) and written in 1562, contained a geographic treatise on Japan and a detailed map of Kyūshū as well as a history of Sino-Japanese trade. It presented the activities of traffickers and pirates in each of China's maritime provinces and, in particular, those of fourteen principal leaders. As is common in sources from this period, the distinction between traffickers and pirates is often vague—most unsanctioned trade, whether it entailed violence or not, was classified as piracy. Moreover, the nationality of the participants can be difficult to decipher because many lived beyond the purview of state authority.

Wang Zhi (?–1557) was one such leader. He had enlisted with a major trafficker established on Liuheng Island after having failed in the salt trade. In 1545 he left Japan and escorted three traders from Hakata to Liuheng, which was then a kind of clandestine international market. The three Japanese were the first in a series who came and went between Japan and the Zhoushan archipelago under Wang Zhi's command. When the port of Liuheng was destroyed by the Zhejiang provincial army, Wang Zhi transferred his headquarters to another island, and for a brief time even purchased the protection of the authorities in exchange for helping them fight other traffickers settled in the archipelago. Wang Zhi then controlled all traffic passing by the archipelago. When his new headquarters were destroyed by the provincial army, he fled to Hirado. He then had approximately two thousand Chinese and Japanese under his command then and dispatched large armed ships to trade in China. In 1556 he received envoys delegated by the military commissioner of Zhejiang, who offered him the privilege of conducting business in exchange for his collaboration in subduing piracy. Wang Zhi responded to this request and embarked for the Zhoushan archipelago accompanied by one thousand persons, a significant number of whom were commercial delegates of Ōtomo Sōrin (1530–1587), a *daimyō* who then controlled six northern Kyūshū provinces. Upon his arrival, however, Wang Zhi was seized by the Chinese authorities and executed.

Another more bellicose trafficker, Xu Hai, arrived in Japan in 1551; he was left by his uncle as a hostage of the *daimyō* of Ōsumi (Kagoshima Prefecture) pending settlement of a debt of ten thousand ounces of silver. Beginning the following year, Xu Hai led groups of Japanese, organized traffic between Ōsumi and the Chinese coast, and raided the coasts of Jiangsu and Zhejiang. He then allied himself with Shingorō of Ōsumi, recruited men in southern Kyūshū and Tanegashima Island and, with a squadron of twenty thousand pirates, pillaged the coast of Zhejiang. Xu Hai finally was seized by Chinese officials and put to death. Afterward, piracy continued in the south, the region near Zhangzhou, and Guangdong.

These two leaders exemplify the manner in which the Japanese became involved in piracy and the connections maintained by the traffickers with the lords of the Kyūshū provinces. Since the 1540s ships had landed in Bungo (Ōita Prefecture), where the headquarters of Ōtomo Sōrin were located, as well as in Hakata and in Bōnotsu in Satsuma Province (Kagoshima Prefecture), two ports that for some time had traded with the Ryūkyū kingdom. Moreover, Chinese traffickers established on Hirado Island and the Gotō archipelago traded with other Kyūshū provinces. In a document from Bungo province, Hirado was even called "the western capital" because trade flourished there just as in Kyōto and Sakai. Thus the end of trade via official missions to China went hand in hand with an increase in trade through unofficial channels, continuing up to the 1580s.

Chouhai tubian contains a complete list of goods trafficked, along with commentary thereupon (abridged and in parentheses):

Products loved by the Japanese: silk thread (100 pounds is worth 5 to 10 ounces of silver, but is priced at ten times that in Japan); cotton thread (as much as 200 ounces of silver per 100 pounds); . . . plain-woven raw silk (the Japanese dye it themselves); embroidered brocade (for the use of their theater actors); red thread (for string); mercury (for gilding; worth 300 ounces of silver per 100 pounds in China and ten times more in Japan); sewing needles; an amalgam of iron (*tielian*); iron pots (the Japanese do not have such large ones; they are worth one ounce of silver apiece); ceramics (they prefer pieces with floral motifs, in particular, censers with bamboo motifs, and bowls and cups with chrysanthemums and mallows); old coins (the Japanese do not mint coins and exclusively use vintage Chinese currency; the coins are worth 4 ounces of silver per string of 1,000 coins, but are worth little more than one ounce in the case of counterfeit coins from Fujian; they do not use coins from the Kaiyuan (?) and Yongle eras); old paintings (they especially love the small ones, probably to decorate their libraries, and they take only signed paintings); calligraphy (for their libraries); old books (especially the Five Classics including the *Book of Rites*, the *Analects* of Confucius, etc.; they do not like Mengzi; they appreciate Buddhist works, but not Daoist ones; and without fail they buy all works on medicine); medicines and incense (for example, liquorice root); felt rugs (which they use underneath saddles); lead powder (for makeup); stacked boxes for food (in lacquered bamboo; they prefer old ones); and lacquer objects (especially book stands, writing cases, and round covered boxes with chrysanthemum motifs). In return, the Japanese items that particularly attract attention in China are fans and (lacquer) boxes decorated with gold designs.[296]

Thus it is clear that unauthorized traffic brought about a final wave of intensive trade between the two countries.

As for trade between Japan and Korea, it steadily became more uncontrollable, and Japanese groups disembarked in Korea at will. Moreover, the numbers of Japanese residing in the three Korean ports open to foreign trade grew to more than three thousand in 1494, and they trafficked with the local population. The mismanagement of state affairs by King Yŏnsan (r. 1494–1506) only exacerbated the situation. Finally, Chungjong (r. 1506–1544) took the reform of the country's economy into his own hands and introduced measures to regain control over trade with Japan. Some of his officials, in particular two chief commisioners of the ports of Pusan and Naeip'o, abused their authority: they manhandled the Japanese residents; repeatedly refused envoys passage to the capital; failed to pay subsidies to the leader of Tsushima Island, Sō Yoshimori; and deprived Japanese fishermen of protection.

Afterward, in 1510, the leader of Tsushima sent a fleet of a few thousand soldiers to attack several Korean coastal towns and seize some local leaders, and had the chief commissioner of Pusan killed. After his first victory Sō Yoshimori demanded restoration of trade terms that had been set down in the late fifteenth century. But the Tsushima forces were pushed back to the sea and forced to retreat. Relations with the island were broken off.

Later, a few delegations came on behalf of the Bakufu and the Ōuchi family in order to negotiate a new contract; they were successful in their endeavors. In 1512 a contract was signed with the following terms: all Japanese residents were to be repatriated; the number of Japanese partners trading with Korea was reduced to slightly less than half of those then active; two Korean ports were closed to foreign trade; for Tsushima, the annual income was reduced by 50 percent, and the leader of the island became the sole authorized trade partner; and finally, the number of boats authorized annually was reduced to twenty-five. The ensuing years were marked by Tsushima's attempts to improve trade conditions, but in vain. The island had lost its key position in relations between Japan and Korea.

Sources for this period reveal few details about the content of trade. We know that some delegations, on behalf of the Bakufu, requested contributions for construction of temples and that others came to purchase silver. Relations, once again broken off in 1544 following an attack by Japanese troops, were renewed in 1547. Other contracts negotiated in the course of the following decades granted slight advantages to the Japanese, but trade no longer had the same rapid growth as in the previous century. The end of an epoch was marked by two invasions of Korea led by Toyotomi Hideyoshi in 1592 and 1597.[297]

EXPORT AND IMPORT PRODUCTS

As we conclude this chapter, it seems useful to make a few observations about the products that crossed the sea from the end of the fourteenth century up to the end of the sixteenth century. As for imports to Japan, they were of a very different nature depending on where they came from. The majority of products imported from Korea consisted of foodstuffs—rice, beans (*mame*), sake, a rice liquor (*shōshu*) resembling Japanese *shōchū*, ginseng (*ninjin*)—and ordinary fabrics, such as hemp (*mafu*) and ramie cloth (*chofu*), plain-woven raw silk (*tsumugi*), and cotton (*menpu*, from the mid-fourteenth century onward). Japan also imported mats (*mushiro*) made of plant fibers, which were used as carpets or cushions, animal furs, and quantities of pine nuts. Printed copies of the Buddhist canon and silverware, comprising vases, pitchers, barrels, kettles, pots, and sake cups, were sent only to the Bakufu and certain military leaders in the provinces. Silverware was a strong point for Korean handicrafts. The silversmiths of Korea had a good reputation from the Koryô Period (918–1392) onward, and they were sought as masters of this art by the Khitans and Jurchen. Beginning in the Yi Period (1392–1910), the Koreans acquired the habit of eating out of metal tableware—a tradition that continues—even though the Chinese and Japanese had always used ceramics and lacquerware.

Imports from China comprised currency, silver, textiles, silk thread, ceramics, and curios (including paintings and stationery). The item most in demand, at least until the mid-fifteenth century, was currency. Like the Kamakura regents before them, the military government of Kyôto did not mint Japanese currency, and the country thus depended on Chinese currency. Coins reached the Bakufu through the two channels of official gifts and trade. Principal representatives of the Bakufu also received from the Chinese authorities rewards that, in theory, amounted to ten strings of cash (*kan*), that is, 10,000 coins.

In 1405 the military government in Kyōto received for instance 500 strings of cash among the reciprocal gifts from the Chinese court. Two years later, the sum amounted to 15,000 for "the king of Japan" and 5,000 strings "for his spouse." In 1411, the shogun Yoshimochi is thought to have again received 5,000 strings. Thereafter, currency was missing from such gifts. In a letter addressed to the Chinese court in 1464, the head of the Bakufu asked that the Chinese emperor continue to send coins in accord with precedents of the Yongle era (1403–1424) and called for a sum of 5,000 strings of cash. Nonetheless the Chinese government granted him just 500 strings. Ashikaga Yoshimasa renewed the request in 1476:

> [In my country] currency has been scattered by wars and state warehouses are empty. The land is poor and the people are poverty-stricken. How then can I restore them to prosperity? During the Yongle era, gifts of currency frequently came from your court; this has been recorded in our documents. Furthermore, books were burned in the course of fighting, as in the Qin Dynasty (221–206 B.C.E..). These are the two things for which we have the most urgent need in our country, which is in a sad state. We note this respectfully and present to you this request.[298]

The request for books probably was made merely for appearance sake; undoubtedly it was intended to elevate the tone of the letter, because Chinese books were not exported to Japan much in this period. In response to the missive, the Chinese authorities sent 50,000 coins (fifty strings). Seven years later, Yoshimasa repeated his request for cash. This time he asked for no fewer than 100,000 strings, but the response is unknown.[299]

The main reason why the Ming court ceased offering monetary gifts was probably the shortage of cash in China. The first Ming emperor, Hongwu (r. 1368–1399), had issued convertible paper bills and made every effort to stimulate their circulation. The value of these bills (Ch. *chao*, J. *satsu*) was fixed at one string of cash, or one ounce of silver; but by about 1400 they had already depreciated and were not worth more than about one-sixth of their original value. Fifty years later, a bill was worth not even one coin, which is perhaps an exaggeration on the part of the Chinese chroniclers. Gifts of bills to the Japanese were noted only in 1404 and 1405.

Moreover, the Bakufu obtained currency also through commercial exchanges. In this sense 1432 was an uncommonly good year: receipts for exported products amounted to more than 200,000 strings of cash, which corresponds to the best figures attained in the thirteenth century. Twenty years later the volume of exported items had increased nearly tenfold. After the steep reduction in prices imposed by the Chinese court, however, the sums were more modest and only a portion of the payments came in cash. The Japanese then received 50,000 strings of cash, approximately 35,000 ounces of silver, and 688 bolts of fabric, before complaints by the military government's envoy yielded an additional 10,000 strings of cash. Thereafter, the sales figures achieved by the Bakufu amounted to 38,000 ounces of silver in 1468, and 16,000 strings in 1478.[300]

Considering that in Japan the average rents remitted by estates amounted to a few dozen strings per year for small estates and a few hundred strings for large ones, one could suppose that the payments received by the Ashikaga military government from China were considerable. Indeed, in the fifteenth century foreign trade constituted a significant part of the Bakufu's revenues. The same was true for the other military leaders and religious establishments that sponsored trade ships.

Chinese currency in circulation in Japan consisted of coins of varying issue, which seemed to have disparate value: coins from the Song Dynasty were worth more than those of the later periods. A member of a Japanese delegation explained what transpired in 1483 in these terms:

> The Chinese are thieves. Among the Japanese who departed for China, those who went to the capital sold native products to the Chinese authorities. The Chinese government set the prices and paid in currency, that is, in new coins. Then, the Japanese insistently demanded the older currency, because this is the good currency and the new coins are bad coins.[301]

It is difficult to say whether the journal writer was referring to a recent issue or to counterfeit coins, because the latter had reached

Japan as well. From the mid-fifteenth century onward, the Bakufu on several occasions forbade the circulation of counterfeit currency, and in 1505 it decreed that the Song, Yuan, and Ming currencies were of identical value.

Archaeological excavations have provided evidence of the circulation of different currencies. In Kusado-Sengen village, located on the Inland Sea (near Fukuyama, Hiroshima Prefecture), approximately 7,400 loose coins were unearthed amid everyday items scattered throughout the site; there were also 30,000 strings consisting of one hundred coins each. In 1971 seven large terracotta jars filled with approximately 200,000 coins were discovered in Takarazuka, not far from the old port of Hyōgo. These jars dated from the early sixteenth century, but the contents came from all periods, from the Later Han (25–220 C.E.) to the Yongle (1403–1425). They even contained a small number of Japanese coins from the eighth century as well as coins from Korea and the kingdom of Annam. Other jars containing 500,000 coins in total were uncovered in Hakodate, Hokkaidō; and numerous coins were excavated in Ichijōdani (Fukui), headquarters of the Asakura *daimyō* family from the mid-fifteenth century onward. At all these sites Song Dynasty currency was by far the most plentiful, even though the sites date from a period contemporaneous with the Ming Dynasty. Also the circulation of currency spread even to regions far removed from the foreign trade circuits and the headquarters of the great families.[302] In fact, in fifteenth-century Japan currency had achieved broad distribution and a fairly high degree of convertibility. Consequently, Japan depended more than ever on trade with China, and to a greater extent than other countries that had their own specie or were less reliant on cash. For example, in Korea, the principal means of payment was hemp and cotton cloth.

Sometimes silver was imported into Japan as a substitute for currency, as was the case in 1453 and 1468. At the time, the official rate was one ounce of silver per string of copper cash. Gifts of silver from China initially amounted to one thousand ounces, and from 1433 onward, to three hundred ounces.[303] Thereafter, the Chinese court paid for imported products partly in silver instead of currency because silver was then the primary means of payment in domestic trade. In Japan, silver had been scarce since the depletion of ore on Tsushima Island. Japan again became an exporter of silver in the mid-sixteenth century, when new mines were exploited in the regions of Tamba (Hyōgo Prefecture) and Iwami (Shimane Prefecture), thanks to extraction techniques adopted from Korea. Textiles constituted another large category of imported products in Japan. Chinese gifts primarily consisted of four kinds of fabric: brocade, satin damask, *ra* gauze, and *sha* gauze, in each instance amounting to a total of one hundred or so bolts of fabric (except in 1405 and 1407, when the figure was four hundred bolts). *Kinran*-quality brocade, called *zhijin* (*shokukin*, "woven gold") and *jin* (*nishiki*) in the Chinese texts, was decorated with gold thread or sometimes had motifs filled entirely with gold weft fibers. Satin damask, designated in the documents as *zhusi*, corresponds to modern *donsu*. It was heavier than traditional Song-dynasty twill damask (*wenqi*). Satin and twill, regardless of whether they were damask or not, were designated by a single Japanese term, *aya*.

Chinese fabrics were highly valued merchandise on the Japanese market. For this reason, traders who accompanied missions to China, unlike the Bakufu, were not content with acquiring merely currency. They also traded their merchandise for fabrics and other items. The merchant Kusuba Sainin, for example, recommended the following items for importation: "Silk thread, silk taffeta from northern China (*hokuken*, from Shandong and Henan), satin damask (*donsu*), gold gauze (*kinra*), musk, and old monks' and nuns' robes." He commented on the latter item in these terms: "they involve fabrics with gold leaf appliqué (*inkin*, "golden seal"); they are not prized highly in China . . . but among these old, damaged, and folded garments, one sometimes finds magnificent pieces of three or five thumbs (11 or 18 centimeters)."[304]

Monks' garments appeared also among the Chinese gifts in 1406, 1407, and 1408. Well before the beginning of the fifteenth century, monks sent to China by the Kamakura Bakufu often were presented with robes from the Chinese court. Fine fabrics from China were used for ceremonial garments of the high aristocracy and the military, as Nō theater costumes, and as covers for sacred texts. But the rarest bolts of fabric, such as those acquired by Sainin, were carefully guarded as objects of curiosity. They were called "specialty fabrics" (*meibutsu-gire*), and played an important role in the tea ceremony, as wrappings for powdered tea boxes.[305]

The item that yielded the best profits for Kusuba Sainin, however, was silk thread. His strategy was to take copper, gold, and sapanwood to China, and rather than procuring currency he sought out silk thread to resell in the Japanese markets. As a result, he earned sums several times the amount invested for the purchase of raw materials. According to his indications, the price of silk thread was 250 *momme* (of silver?) per pound in China, and 5,000 coins in Japan. Silk thread was also much desired by pirates in the mid-sixteenth century, because at that time it sold for ten times more in Japan than China.[306] One wonders whether the Japanese demand for silk thread resulted from the discrepancy in price between the two countries or from a disparity in quality. The quantity of silk thread manufactured was probably lower in Japan than in China, and sericulture techniques less advanced. In fact, the cultivation of mulberry trees, breeding of silkworms, and spinning of silk did not progress significantly in Japan until the beginning of the eighteenth century.

Chinese ceramics, until the mid-fourteenth century, were one of the most sought-after items in Japan. It is surprising, however, that from the mid-fourteenth until the mid-fifteenth century they disappeared from lists of imported objects, even though China produced a porcelain of very high quality that later enjoyed worldwide renown. This was the famous blue-and-white porcelain, which was developed from the 1330s to 1350 in the Jingdezhen kilns of Jiangxi (perhaps under the influence of Persian models), following an increase in cobalt imports from the Near East under the Mongol Yuan Dynasty. Designs were painted directly on bisque using blue cobalt ore applied with a brush, then covered with a transparent glaze and fired once at a high temperature (more than 1,000 degrees) in a reducing atmosphere—the brightness and purity of the blue mainly depended on the degree of reduction. Until that time, monochrome ceramics (celadons), had always undergone two firings: one at a high temperature and, after the bisque was glazed, a second at a lower heat (approximately 800 degrees). These glazes did not permit the creation of refined designs. Shortly after developing blue-and-white, the Chinese introduced another high-heat-fired color: copper oxide red. So were born the polychrome ceramics that in subsequent centuries were exported to the countries of Asia, the Middle East, and Europe.

Archaeological excavations have unearthed a large number of Ming-dynasty ceramics in Indonesia, the Philippines, and other Asian countries; celebrated collections have been preserved in Istanbul in the fifteenth-century Topkapi Palace Museum and in the Ardebil mosque in Iran. The former contains 3,900 pieces; and the latter holds 1,400 Yuan- and Ming-dynasty ceramics. In Istanbul, however, only 70 pieces could be identified as polychrome artifacts from the Yongle era (1403–1425); no more than 200 are held in the Iranian collection. Neither collection apparently contains pieces from the Xuande era (1426–1436). And all this Yongle-era porcelain came from the imperial kilns of China, even though its exportation was strictly forbidden. Thus porcelain came into these countries through official channels, as gifts, perhaps in exchange for tribute. Relations with the Middle East had been established at the time of the great Chinese expeditions launched by the Yongle emperor: four of them had reached Hormuz on the Persian Gulf and Aden, while another had navigated the Red Sea as far as Mecca.

The rarity of blue-and-white porcelains from the first century of the Ming Dynasty is not particular to the two collections discussed above. On the contrary, it is generally true for the Middle East and Asia and can, perhaps, be attributed to China's restriction of foreign trade to official delegations—a regulation that, in theory, remained in force until the mid-sixteenth century. In Japan, only a few Chinese pieces from the Yongle and Xuande eras have been discovered. One was found in the Asakura's Ichijōdani. We do not know why Chinese ceramics did not appear on the lists of the official presents from China in the fifteenth century, or why traders accompanying the Japanese missions did not show interest in them. Notably, Kusuba Sainin did not cite porcelain among the Chinese products he recommended for purchase.[307]

In 1452, however, Sainin received an order for 100 celadon tea bowls and 30 blue-and-white porcelain tea bowls (*sometsuke*).[308] Furthermore, another merchant, upon returning from China, offered the following imported objects to a friend in Sakai: paper, ink, writing brushes, and silk taffeta as well as 20 porcelain tea bowls and plates.[309] Then in 1510 Ryōan Keigo (1425–1514), a Rinzai sect monk and associate of the court, was the principal envoy on a mission to China, and he seems to have had a particular interest in ceramics. On his way to the Chinese capital he bought "ceramic bowls and white porcelains" in Ningbo and Hangzhou, and he also entrusted to a Chinese trader 500 ounces of silver for an order of white porcelain and medicines. But he was deceived: upon the monk's return to the city, the family of the Chinese trader claimed that he had not yet returned from a business deal in Nanjing, and they returned only 100 ounces of silver to the monk.[310]

Later, the same blue-and-white Ming porcelain also appeared in the notes of Sakugen Shūryō (1501–1579), a Tenryūji temple monk and renowned writer. Shūryō accompanied the last two delegations to China in 1539 and 1547, and he noted in detail his purchases in the markets of Ningbo and Suzhou: a censer and 15 or so dishes made of Cizhou porcelain; 7 white Ding pieces; some celadons; 100 or so dishes with polychrome decoration; 20 white dishes with chrysanthemum motifs; 330 "dishes for vinegar and salt" (*sushiosara*); 20 sets of stacked boxes for foodstuffs (generally made of lacquered wood); metal vases; 110 sheets of paper; cymbals; 5 metal paperweights; 16 ink sticks; some writing cases; 73 pounds of angelica (a medicinal plant); 40 pounds of sugar; thousands of sewing needles; a copy of the 1317 compendium *Wenxian tongkao* (General Observations on Texts and Documents) by Ma Duanlin; a painting; 5 celadon tea bowls; 4 ceramic covered containers for powdered tea; 7 square dishes; 3 lacquered-wood stands for tea bowls; 5 water scoops; and a fine pair of fire tongs.[311]

The items enumerated above, following the entry for *Wenxian tongkao*, were all used for the tea ceremony (*chanoyū*), which was the stylistic outgrowth of tea gatherings that had been in vogue since the beginning of the fourteenth century. The tea-ceremony ritual was laid out for the first time by Murata Jukō (1422–1502). Although earlier tea gatherings primarily had featured objects from China, this master introduced an austere style and plead for the use of both Chinese and Japanese objects. He wished to realize a perfect marriage between the taste for Chinese things and the abstemious aesthetic of Japan.

For military leaders, the tea ceremony was also a way to demonstrate their authority. They engaged experts (called *dōbōshu*) responsible for the preservation and assessment of paintings and Chinese objects as well as the decoration of reception pavilions. Nōami, Geiami, and Sōami succeeded one another as "masters of protocol" in the residences of the shoguns and ex-shoguns Ashikaga Yoshimitsu, Yoshinori, and Yoshimasa.

These were also the authors of the "Catalog of Objects and Paintings Belonging to the Residence" (*Kundaikan so'u chōki*), two versions of which were completed in 1476 and 1511. The first part contained a catalog of about 300 paintings and 160 Chinese authors, listed in categories according to their artistic value. The most-cited painters were Wang Wei of the Tang Dynasty, Muqi, Emperor Huizong, Li Guanglin, Li Anzhong, Liang Kai, Xia Gui, Ma Lin, and others from the Song period. One finds several names from the *Kundaikan so'u chōki* in the collection of Yoshimitsu. Surprisingly the

Japanese did not rank either of the great painters Guo Xi or Ma Yuan, or any painters from the Yuan Period, in the top category. A second part of the work stipulated the arrangement of Chinese objects in a reception pavilion (i.e., a building built in *shoin-zukuri* style) and on staggered shelves (*chigai dana*). A third part contained a list of objects and implements used in the tea ceremony, at gatherings, for writing, and for entertainment including lacquerware (with enumeration of a dozen sculptured-lacquer techniques), tea bowls, ceramic jars for the preparation of tea, other types of ceramics, and writing implements. For the warrior aristocracy, therefore, the tea ceremony was the principal reason behind the demand for special objects imported from China.[312]

Japanese exports consisted of gifts and other merchandise sent abroad by the military government and numerous other sponsors. They can be divided into three categories: handicrafts, consisting mainly of weapons (swords, spears, breastplates), bronze housewares, lacquer, and gold lacquerware (writing cases are not mentioned for Korea), screens, and fans; raw materials, that is, copper, sulfur, gold (more rarely mentioned), and agates (as presents for China); and products from Southeast Asia imported via the Ryūkyū kingdom and then reexported, consisting of sapanwood, sulfur, pepper, rhinoceros horn, and other items.

The sword was the preeminent Japanese manufactured item. In the fifteenth century, a blade of older style—of average length (*uchigatana*), between forty centimeters and one meter—reappeared. The blade was narrower than that of previous centuries and it curved toward the point, which permitted it to be unsheathed more easily. Demand for this weapon was high in Japan in a period of incessant warfare, and thus developed true mass production. The most-renowned centers of production were the three provinces of Bizen, Bitchū, and Bingo (Okayama and Hiroshima prefectures), where iron and copper mines were located. The sword of this period, although of inferior quality as a mass-produced article, was known for the power of its cutting edge. Perhaps it was because of this quality that the Japanese sword attracted the attention of several Chinese authors in the Ming Period, who saw therein the symbol of the striking force of Japanese warriors—in the present cases, pirates.[313]

This weapon therefore was exported to China by the thousands. Two types of *uchigatana* were distinguished: long swords of more than two *shaku* (sixty centimeters), called *katana*, and those of less than two *shaku*, called *wakizashi*. They were designated in the Chinese and Korean sources by the terms "long sword" (*chōtō*) and "short sword" (*tachi*, broad sword). The former was carried at the waist, suspended by two rings, with its cutting edge turned downward, while the second was tucked under the waist, with the cutting edge turned upward.

We have some information about the quantities the Bakufu exported: the gifts sent to the Chinese sovereign generally consisted of 100 long swords, 100 short swords, and 2 dress swords with ornate guards. The weapons sold to the Chinese government and the prices paid were as follows: 3,052 swords in 1432, at 10,000 coins per unit, which was ten times the price in Japan; 9,900 swords in 1452, at 6,000 coins each; 7,000 swords in 1478, at 3,000 coins each. The price then fell to 1,800 coins per unit. In 1483, 35,000 swords netted only 600 coins.

That year the Chinese government limited the number of imported swords to 3,000 per Japanese mission. Ten years later, the envoys, who were supposed to represent the Bakufu, brought 7,000 swords, and the same number was brought in 1511. This time, the Chinese court accepted only 3,000 swords and paid a mere 300 coins per unit. Finally, a Japanese delegation sold 24,862 swords in the Chinese markets in 1539, but these sales probably were made privately on behalf of traders, not the Bakufu. The figures for Korea are not known. Given that the importation of weapons had been strictly forbidden in China since the beginning of the fifteenth century, the attitude of the Chinese authorities was astonishingly tolerant. The reason put forward by the Chinese court in this period was that it did not wish to discourage the Japanese from bringing tribute.[314]

"Bronze pitchers, pots, and censers," also were appreciated in China, according to a declaration by Chinese officials in 1483. Metalwork experienced a revival in Japan as internal demand grew for cast-iron kettles used in the tea ceremony. The objects exported to China and Korea, however, were of gilt bronze and resembled ritual utensils. Around the fifteenth century, Japanese artisans loved to imitate Chinese tiger and dragon motifs, particularly on censers. In China, these objects cost 6,000 coins in 1432, and 4,000 coins in 1453; from this standpoint, they ranked second behind swords.[315]

Screens and painted fans were the most exotic Japanese export products. The former appeared only among gifts from the Bakufu intended for Chinese and Korean sovereigns. They had gold backgrounds, made of paper stretched over a wood frame and covered entirely with gold leaf affixed in the same manner as their joints—visible to the eye, but imperceptible to the touch. This background was given a polychrome decoration painted in gouache. The panels were framed with lacquered-wood listels. We find the first mention of them in written sources in a list of presents sent by Ashikaga Yoshimitsu to the emperor of China in 1402. Thenceforth, three screens always appeared among the official gifts for China, and an indeterminate number were sent to Korea as presents. Even in Japan, these were rare objects, worth 35,000 coins, and they were the most valuable of the gifts sent to foreign sovereigns—the second most expensive being swords with ornate guards, which cost 27,000 coins. The screens offered to the king of Korea in 1443 and 1487 were decorated with flowers, pines, and cranes. In 1539 Ōuchi Yoshitaka, for his mission to China, commissioned three screens from Kanō Motonobu (1476–1559), one of the greatest painters in Japan.[316]

Folding fans, another Japanese creation, enjoyed particular success abroad. One hundred or so were normally included among official gifts sent to China. At least 2,200 fans were sold to the Chinese government in 1433, 250 in 1453, and in 1468 the number was 380. In 1539 Ōuchi Yoshitaka exported 100 fans painted by Kanō Motonobu. This item was often exported to Korea as well. Japanese production was concentrated in Kyōto, where guilds soon took form. We know that Kanō Motonobu, together with another individual, even asked the Bakufu to grant him commercial monopoly rights. Fans were decorated either with ancient Japanese-style paintings (*Yamato-e*, which experienced a rebirth in the fourteenth century thanks to the Tosa school) or with Chinese-style images that had been introduced by Zen monks.

From the thirteenth century onward, Japan imported monochrome ink paintings from China. Only toward the fifteenth century did a Japanese style of monochrome painting emerge, unveiled by the painters Josetsu (dates unknown), Shūbun (dates unknown), and Sesshū Tōyō (1420–1506). The latter two made visits to Korea and China, respectively. A Japanese school of Chinese-style painting that also took into account the new decorative painting of the Ming Dynasty (often having flowers and birds as themes) was founded in the sixteenth century and experienced its zenith in Japan under Kanō Motonobu. The Chinese, therefore, could sometimes recognize a Japanese version of their own style of painting on imported screens and fans.

Since antiquity, the Chinese had used round, fixed fans. Folding fans were familiar because they had appeared a few times among the presents received from Japan since the tenth century and had also reached China through Korea (see the "Exports" section in chapter 3). Nevertheless, the use of the folding fan was not widespread in China prior to the fifteenth century. According to information from certain authors, in China the folding fan up to that time was considered an object used exclusively by uncivilized men, and at the thirteenth-century Chinese court official envoys from Southeast Asia who made use of folding fans were ridiculed. The situation changed altogether when the Yongle emperor received one hundred folding fans as gifts from Ashikaga Yoshimitsu in 1401, and again in 1402. The Chinese sovereign in turn made a gift of these Japanese objects to his brother, the Prince of Zhou; thenceforth the folding fan was in favor among the aristocracy and Chinese elites. The Japanese thus, in a sense, had created a new market.

The Koreans soon began to manufacture folding fans in imitation of Japanese products. They first offered them as presents to the Yongle emperor, then exported them via commercial channels. According to a Chinese source, however, Korean fans were worth only one-tenth as much as those from Japan. In 1432 the price of folding fans in China was three hundred coins. At the end of the sixteenth century, fans made in Korea even reached Japan, in Hakata. After that time, China also made folding fans decorated with paintings; later, fans would undergo true large-scale mass production in Ningbo. These objects subsequently aroused the admiration of European missionaries in China, and they brought them back to Europe.[317]

Finally, lacquerware was another category of manufactured items exported to China and Korea. The Korean chronicles record that among the products received from the Ashikaga military government were bowls, square trays, and hot water pitchers, most often produced in red lacquer and lacking gold decoration; gold lacquer bowls were commissioned from craftsmen and sent to Korea by the head of the Ōuchi clan.

Invariably, among the gifts sent to the Chinese court as tribute by the Bakufu were a writing case and a box containing fans, both of which were ornamented with refined gold lacquer designs (*makie*) on backgrounds of *nashiji*-type translucent gold dusting. These boxes ranked third in value among the gifts: in Japan, the writing case cost 24,450 coins, and the fan box was worth 23,850.

Lacquer objects also appeared among the merchandise exported to China. In 1453 they numbered 634; the number of writing cases was not known. Lacquerware was described in the Ming-dynasty chronicles in the following fashion: round and square boxes in the form of flowers or other shapes; large and small censers and other black-lacquered wares painted with gold, dusted with gold, and inlaid with mother-of-pearl; and gold-lacquered writing cases appliquéd and sprinkled with gold, containing ink stones and small bronze water flasks (see appendix 8).

The lacquerware exported from Japan through commercial channels, however, was far less valuable than what was presented as gifts to the Chinese court. The prices of commercial lacquerware in China amounted to only 800, then 600 coins for the various boxes, and 2,000, then 1,500 coins for the writing cases. One can suppose, therefore, that these were mass-produced goods, especially since unauthorized traffic in the sixteenth century brought gold-decorated lacquerware to China.

As with fans, the Chinese also began to manufacture imitations of Japanese lacquerware, according to an article on "Japanese Things" in the nineteenth-century "Encyclopedia of Qixiu" (*Qixiu leigao*):

> We [the Chinese] manufacture lacquerware inlaid with gold, but not those pieces painted with gold; we decorate with gold appliqué, but not with sprinkled gold dust and painted gold outline; we have fixed screens [or panels], but not folding screens; we manufacture carved lacquerware, but not those decorated with extremely delicate motifs. All these techniques come from Japan. The Japanese transmitted the techniques of gold outlining and gold dusting to Ningbo, but the Chinese have not succeeded to the same degree as the Japanese. For a long time, the Ningbo artisans have also manufactured imitation Japanese fans; the Japanese decorate them with lacquer blades painted in gold and fine colored designs. They transmitted this manufacturing method to us during the Xuande era (1426–1436), and brought the folding screens to us as tribute in the Hongzhi Period (1488–1506).[318]

Therefore, for these few products, the Japanese became exporters of techniques, having previously imported the crafts of gold inlay and lacquer sculpting themselves. The Japanese also developed the technique of lacquering carved wood (*kamakura-bori*).[319]

The three raw materials that predominated on the lists of exports to China and Korea were sulfur, copper, and sapanwood. This last traditionally appeared on the list of imports to Japan; it came from Southeast Asia, and in the fifteenth century was imported in sufficient quantity to be reexported. This undoubtedly was a particularly lucrative trade because China engaged only in limited trade with the countries of Southeast Asia in this period. The price of a pound of sapanwood in 1432 was 100 coins in Japan, and 1,000 coins in China. But by 1453 in China, it was reduced to 70 coins. This was because between 1432 and 1453 the volume imported from Japan had increased from 16,000 to 106,000 pounds. In the same period, the merchant Kusuba Sainin of Sakai recommended the sapanwood trade as yielding good profits.

Exports of copper ore to China progressed as follows: 4,300 pounds (i.e., 2.6 tons if a pound weighed 600 grams) in 1432, 152,000 pounds in 1453 in the name of the Bakufu; and 295,500 pounds in 1539, carried by Japanese traders.

Sulfur was the only raw material that appeared among not only merchandise but also official presents, amounting to 10,000 pounds per visit to China. The quantities exported to China by the Bakufu as merchandise in 1432 amounted to 22,000, and in 1453 to 364,000 pounds. The Chinese court was particularly bothered by these imports because sulfur was brought in similar quantities from the Ryūkyū kingdom. Also, in 1453 the Japanese were aware that China no longer was inclined to accept quantities greater than 30,000 pounds, and even then, as a rule, only as tribute. In 1468 the Bakufu's representatives did not bring more than the stipulated quantity to China, but in 1495 the Chinese court refused a cargo of sulfur whose volume in all likelihood exceeded the established threshold.[320]

Sapanwood and sulfur probably were undesirable imports to China and Korea. Korea, in particular, imported sapanwood from Southeast Asia and sulfur from the Ryūkyū kingdom in such great quantities that it reexported them to China. Korea also exported copper. China and Korea, presumably, resigned themselves to bearing the burden of imports from Japan in order to maintain their systems of state-controlled foreign trade. Kusuba Sainin provided a list of Japanese products recommended for export that sold better in the Chinese markets, including sea otter furs, pepper, short swords, long swords, spears, pitchers, pots, copper, gold, sapanwood, and folding fans.[321]

It is interesting to compare the proportion of raw materials and manufactured products among the Japanese exports. In 1433 earnings from sales of sapanwood, sulfur, and copper in China amounted to 39,290 strings of cash in all, while those from sales of swords amounted to 30,520 strings. Twenty years later total sales of the three raw materials yielded 34,760 strings of cash, whereas swords were sold for a price of 59,400 strings. Furthermore, if we take into account an indefinite number of other manufactured items, we can estimate that the two categories of exported products (raw materials and manufactured goods) in 1433 were nearly equal in value. But in 1453 the value of manufactured items amounted to roughly double that of raw materials. In other words, after a steep reduction in the price of raw materials, sales of manufactured products enabled the Japanese to maintain their profit margin. The figures for other years are not known, but we can assume that the export of finished goods assumed growing importance in Japan's foreign trade.

In this sense Japan differed from other countries that exported to China. Ming-dynasty Chinese sources acknowledged about sixty tributary countries, but we can estimate that only twenty or so regularly presented tribute to China, either accompanied by merchandise or consisting itself of commercial products. These tributary countries were Korea, Ryūkyū, some Southeast Asian countries, and a few Mongol tribes of Central Asia. The products exported to China as merchandise were recorded in the "Regulations of Great Ming" (*Da ming huidian*, book 113), and in a "Continued Treatise of Siming [Ningbo] of the Zhizheng era" (*Zhizheng Siming xuzhi*, book 6). One finds therein:

- raw mineral materials (precious metals, other metals, sulfur, precious stones, jade), plants (wood, other rare plants and aromatics, fragrant substances extracted therefrom, and some foodstuffs), animal materials (ivory, tortoiseshell, horn, coral, pearls)

- animals (horses, camels, birds)

- products of simple manufacture (animal skins, straw mats, felt, hemp cloth, cotton, wool)

- highly finished goods necessitating advanced manufacturing techniques (swords, knives, bows, arrows, saddles, decorative items—carved of jade, ivory, or tortoiseshell—paper, metal dishes and utensils, ceramics, lacquered wood).

These Chinese import items comprised nearly three hundred varieties, among which aromatic materials accounted for an especially sizable share. On the other hand, the volume of highly finished goods can be estimated at 10 percent at the very most. The suppliers of finished goods were Korea, a few Central Asian tribes, and Japan. The countries of Central Asia manufactured only a few weapons and carved objects. Korea delivered to China bronze and silver dishes, celadons, paper, and lacquerware; the quantities of these items were minute, however, compared to raw materials from Korea and Southeast Asia, and to simple products exported by Korea. Therefore, we can assume that Japan, in terms of both the value and volume of products, was the largest supplier of highly finished goods manufactured with advanced techniques.

From the Japanese perspective, foreign trade from the fifteenth century onward was a source of revenue for the military government of Kyōto and a few great *daimyō*, as well as for a certain number of commercial enterprises (such as those in Sakai) and many small entrepreneurs from the Kyūshū region. Foreign goods reached a larger proportion of the population and achieved broader geographic distribution than ever before because nearly all the imported products were marketed domestically. For the first time foreign trade had direct repercussions on the domestic economy.

The link between foreign trade and the domestic market stimulated exports. In one sense, we can speak of a balance of payments favorable to Japan because Japan succeeded in exporting a higher volume of products to China and Korea than those countries demanded, and that in spite of the restrictions that were imposed upon Japanese trade. On the other hand, China and Korea saw themselves as obliged to permit the outflow to Japan of considerable quantities of items, even those which they themselves lacked, such as coins and cotton. In this sense Japan had the upper hand, whereas its partners were at a disadvantage. This situation resulted partly from the commercial dynamism of the Japanese and partly from the differences in the trade systems of the three countries. Due to their state monopolies, in conjunction with bans on people leaving their respective countries, China and Korea tied the hands of their traders and thus hindered the export of their surplus goods.[322] The balance of trade with Japan would not have been the same if each year many Chinese and Koreans had come to Japan to unload cargoes of ceramics, hemp fabrics, and plain-woven raw silk. The third reason for the trade imbalance lay in the nature of the items exported by the Japanese: exports of products manufactured with advanced techniques accounted for a high percentage of sales figures.

As for trade between Japan and China, even though profits were registered on the Japanese side, the volume of trade expressed in absolute terms was considerably lower than in preceding periods. Only twenty or so Japanese delegations went to China between 1400 and 1548, in contrast to the annual arrivals from China in the Song and Yuan periods (during the tenth to the fourteenth centuries). Furthermore, trade with China in the fifteenth and early sixteenth centuries was only a minute part of Japan's foreign trade, the greatest part then being trade with Korea. The number of Japanese groups that departed for Korea, as recorded in the Korean chronicles of the Yi Dynasty, increased to nearly three thousand up to the end of the fifteenth century. Therefore Korea was by far Japan's primary commercial partner.

In the sixteenth century, while trade with China and Korea took on the semblance of unauthorized traffic, two new partners appeared: Portugal and Spain. They first introduced Christianity to Japan. Ōuchi Yoshitaka, who had been part of the last two delegations to China, was the first *daimyō* in Japan to authorize a Christian mission in his territory. He received as presents from the missionary Francis Xavier a clock, binoculars, a glass mirror, an arquebus, crystal glasses, a bottle of wine, brocade fabrics, and a manichordion. All these objects until then were unknown in Japan. Thereafter, Portuguese and Spanish trade ships landed in Hirado and Nagasaki. Ōtomo Sōrin, who had participated in unauthorized traffic with China, was one of the first to be baptized. Moreover, he dispatched the first Japanese delegation to Europe. The Japanese horizon then opened toward the West, and Japan entered a new era in foreign trade.

CONCLUSION

From the beginning of its history Japan found itself on the periphery of the Asian continent, where China played a dominant role. Chinese cultural imperialism determined an international order with China at its axis. Thus goods converged upon China; and it was China that, according to particular eras, imposed upon confederates its own concept of trade. Until the tenth century the system was based on the tributary model; then Song-dynasty China instituted a free-trade policy that was perpetuated and institutionalized under the Yuan Dynasty. In the Ming Period, China reverted to the tributary system, which afforded the best means of control. On the basis of these policies a considerable volume of products circulated between the Middle East and China, either via land routes or by maritime routes passing through Southeast Asia, and ultimately were traded between China and the countries of Eastern Asia.

Japan thus found itself at the eastern periphery of this international network. Throughout a period of nearly a millennium, Japan accommodated itself to the trade structures imposed by China. Sometimes Japan abided by the rules, sometimes it imposed further restrictions, and sometimes it went well beyond the limits. Japan did not develop its own trade policy adapted to its domestic situation as, for example, did Korea, where the Yi Dynasty instituted a system of accredited delegations. Rather than create a trade structure that was suitable to it and impose this system upon its partners, Japan preferred to use the structures defined by others to its own advantage. The Japanese lack of interest in formulating their own commercial strategy went hand in hand with a pragmatism so developed that they sometimes even sacrificed their national pride and desire to place themselves on a diplomatic footing equal to that of China and above that of Korea. Thus the Japanese leader Taira no Kiyomori in the latter half of the twelfth century, and the Ashikaga shoguns from the fifteenth century onward, adopted the attitude of a tributary country intent on increasing foreign trade. The commercial pragmatism of the Japanese can be summed up for each period as follows. Up to the eighth century: *assimilation* of foreign knowledge and techniques; up to the twelfth century: *importation* of luxury items, but solely for the Japanese court; from the twelfth century onward: importation, at all costs, of Chinese currency; and, finally, from the fourteenth century onward: ever-increasing *exports*.

To realize these objectives, the Japanese did not hesitate to bend the rules that were imposed by themselves or foreign authorities. The Heian court, for example, limited the arrival of foreign traders in theory, but nonetheless proved tolerant at times when it needed Chinese products. When Ming-dynasty emperors and the Yi-dynasty court limited imports from Japan, the Japanese habitually exceeded the authorized number of delegations and increased the volume of exports. Such dexterity at handling regulations no doubt was the result of a Japanese ideological indifference: regulations were not so strictly observed in Japan, because they did not issue from a comprehensive policy, but rather from ad hoc measures adopted in response to immediate needs. In Japan, rules were adapted to practical situations; whereas in China, rules were adapted to policy. At the time of an unlawful arrival of Japanese swords at the beginning of the fifteenth century, for example, instead of refusing them the Chinese monarch declared: "Do not tie the hands of the barbarians by imposing prohibitions on them. To do so would be contrary to the generous intentions of our imperial court, and would discourage the desire of distant peoples to pledge their allegiance." The Chinese thus were prepared to pay for their imperialist ideology. The Japanese, on the contrary, had a tendency to compromise their imperialist ideology to achieve their commercial objectives.

Thanks to this pragmatism, Japan profited greatly from trade with foreigners, especially once imported products were no longer hoarded by aristocrats, and became available for marketing. Foreign trade then had repercussions on the domestic economy: from the thirteenth century onward, the importation of Chinese currency became the predominant concern. Given that Japan did not mint its own currency, and that Chinese currency had attained a relatively broad distribution and high degree of convertibility, the domestic economy to a great extent depended on the importation of Chinese money.

This peculiarity gave impetus to exports and initially resulted in the outflow of a quantity of gold to China. But, gradually, the Japanese turned to exportation of finished goods as a complement to that of raw materials. They soon succeeded in mass production of high-quality items necessitating sophisticated techniques that had developed in Japan over several centuries, since the period when the country had imported handicrafts from the continent. The Japanese created their own techniques, and their products achieved a quality that was appreciated by the Chinese and Koreans; they even exported some manufacturing techniques. The increasing volume of high-quality products represented a significant share of foreign sales in the fifteenth and sixteenth centuries. Japan, formerly an importer of handicrafts, had become an exporter of finished goods.

NOTES

All lunar calendar dates are rendered in the year/month/day format and are accompanied by the equivalent Gregorian calendar year in parentheses. Intercalary months are designated by an asterisk. Publishing data for sources appear in the bibliography. All translations of source texts are the author's own unless otherwise indicated.

1. See *Nihon shoki* Suiko 31 (623) 7/. For an English translation of the *Nihon shoki*, see W. G. Aston, *Nihongi* (Rutland, Vt.: Charles E. Tuttle, 1972).

2. *Hou Han shu*, book 115. For an English translation see Homer Dubs, *Pan Ku's History of the Former Han Dynasty*, 3 vols. (Baltimore: Waverly Press, 1938-1955).

3. *Nihon shoki* Suiko 16 (608) 9/11; *Sui shu*, book 81.

4. *Nihon shoki* Suiko 7 (599) 9/.

5. *Nihon shoki* Suiko 10 (602) 10/.

6. *Nihon shoki* Suiko 13 (605) 4/.

7. *Nihon shoki* Suiko 15 (607) 2/15; Suiko 16 (608) 4/, and 6/15; and Suiko 18 (610) 3/.

8. *Nihon shoki* Suiko 26 (618) 8/; and Suiko 31 (623) 7/.

9. *Nihon shoki* Suiko 33 (625) 1/7.

10. *Nihon shoki* Kōgyoku 1 (642) 2/21.

11. *Nihon shoki* Kōtoku 3 (647) 12/.

12. *Nihon shoki* Hakuchi 4 (653) 5/12; and Hakuchi 5 (654) 7/24; *Cefu yuangu*, book 971; *Song shi*, book 491.

13. *Nihon shoki* Saimei 2 (656) 9/; and Saimei 3 (657) 9/.

14. *Nihon shoki* Saimei 5 (659) 7/.

15. *Nihon shoki* Tenji 4 (665) 2/; and (Winter 666) 5/.

16. *Nihon shoki* Saimei 6 (660) 10/.

17. *Nihon shoki* Tenji 10 (671) 1/; and Tenmu 14 (686) 2/.

18. The official register referred to herein is titled *Shinsen shōjiroku*, a register of noble families of the Kinai region compiled in 815.

19. *Nihon shoki* Tenji 6 (667) 7/11.

20. *Nihon shoki* Tenji 6 (667) 11*/11; and Tenji 7 (668) 11/1.

21. *Nihon shoki* Tenji 10 (671) 6/15.

22. *Nihon shoki* Tenji 10 (671) 11/29.

23. *Nihon shoki* Tenmu 1 (673) 5/23.

24. *Nihon shoki* Tenmu 8 (680) 10/17; Tenmu 10 (682) 10/20; Tenmu 14 (686) 5/26; Shuchō 1 (686) 2/19; Jitō 2 (688) 2/2; and Jitō 3 (689) 4/20.

25. See *Taihō ritsuryō*; Toyoda Takeshi et al., eds., *Ryūtsūshi* (Tōkyō: Yamakawa shuppansha, 1969-1975), pp. 15-39; and Ishino Tōru, ed., *Nara, zusetsu nihon bunka no rekishi* (Tōkyō: Shōgakkan, 1979), 3:81-93.

26. Embassies exchanged between Japan and foreign countries during the seventh, eighth, and ninth centuries:

Missions	7th century	8th century	9th century
to China	10	7	2
from China	4	2	50
to Korea	20 (?)	16	2 (?)
from Korea	105 (?)	21	30
to Parhae	0	12	1
from Parhae	0	14	18

27. *Shoku nihongi* Yōrō 3 (719) 7*//7.

28. *Shoku nihongi* Tenpyō 4 (732) 5/19.

29. *Shoku nihongi* Monmu 4 (700) 10/19.

30. *Shoku nihongi* Taihō 3 (703) 10/25.

31. *Shoku nihongi* Wadō 2 (709) 5/27.

32. *Shoku nihongi* Hōki 1 (770) 3/4.

33. *Samguk sagi*, book 10, Aejang 5 (804) 5/, in *Chūgoku-chōsen no shiseki ni okeru nihon shiryō shūsei*, Sangoku kōrai no bu, p. 23.

34. *Shoku nihongi* Tenpyō-Shōhō 4 (752) 3*/22, 4/6/14, and 4/7/24. See also Erling von Mende, *China und die Staaten auf der koreanischen Halbinsel bis zum 12. Jahrhundert: Eine Untersuchung zur Entwicklung der Formen zwischenstaatlicher Beziehungen in Ostasien* (Wiesbaden: Steiner, 1982), pp. 180-181.

35. See the table by Sekine Shinryū in Mori Katsumi and Tanaka Takeo, eds., *Kaigai kōshōshi no shiten*, 1:160. See also the Shōsōin archives (*Shōsōin komonjo*) in *Dai nihon komonjo*, 25:49. The identification of the plants is thanks to the assistance of Georges Métaillié of the Centre National de la Recherche Scientifique.

36. *Shoku nihongi* Reiki 1 (715) 3/23.

37. *Shoku nihongi* Jingo-Keiun 2 (768) 10/24.

38. *Shoku nihongi* 3 (769) 11/12.

39. *Samguk sagi* Sondok 30 (731) 4/, in *Chūgoku-chōsen no shiseki ni okeru nihon shiryō shūsei*, Sangoku kōrai no bu, p. 22; *Shoku nihongi* Tenpyō-Hōji 3 (759) 6/18 to 3/9/19.

40. *Song shi*, book 491, regarding the Japanese monk's mission to China in 983.

41. *Jiu Tang shu*, book 17b, with respect to Japanese silks in 734; and *Cefu yuangu*, book 972, concerning silks and pearls in 734 and 838.

42. *Engi shiki*, book 30, p. 738.

43. *Shoku nihongi*, Tenpyō-Hōji 5 (761) 10/10.

44. *Xin tang shu*, p. 220. Regarding paper, see *Zhiyiji*, book 11, quoted in Mori Katsumi, "Nitchū bunka no kōryū," *Gekkan bunkazai* 62 (November 1968):10-16.

45. See Jugaku Bunshō, *Nihon no kami* (Tōkyō: Yoshikawa kōbunkan, 1967).

46. *Nihon kōki* Enryaku 24 (805) 7/24; *Nihon kiryaku* Daidō 2 (807) 1/27.

47. *Shoku nihongi* Yōrō 3 (719) 1/10.

48. *Shoku nihongi* Tenpyō-Hōji 5 (761) 8/12; and Tenpyō-Hōji 6 (762) 1/28.

49. *Cefu yuangui*, book 999 (734); *Shoku nihongi* Tenpyō 7 (735) 4/26.

50. *Engi shiki*, book 30, p. 737.

51. *Shoku nihongi* Hōki 7 (776) /4/15; *Nihon kiryaku* Enryaku 22 (803) 3/29. See also *Shoku nihon kōki* Jōwa 3 (836) 4/23 in reference to gold allowances.

52. Edwin O. Reischauer, *Ennin's Travels in T'ang China* (New York: Ronald Press, 1955).

53. Hayashi Ryōichi, *The Silkroad and the Shōsōin, The Heibonsha Series of Japanese Art*, vol. 6 (New York: Weatherhill, 1975).

54. *Shoku nihongi* Tenpyō-Hōji 1 (757) 11/9.

55. For specifics see *Nihonkoku genzaisho mokuroku kaisetsu kō*.

56. *Jiu Tang shu*, p. 199. See also Ikeda On, "Gudai Riben shequ Zhongguo dianji wenti," in International Conference on Sinology, ed., *Zhongyang yanjiuyuan guoji Hanxue huiyi lunwenji*, part 1 (lishi kaogu) (Taibei: Academia Sinica, 1981), pp. 345-367.

57. *Shoku nihongi* Jingi 5 (728) 1/17.

58. *Shoku nihongi* Tenpyō 11 (739) 12/10; and *Nihon sandai jitsuroku* Jōgan 14 (872) 5/18.

59. *Engi shiki*, book 30, p. 738.

60. *Shoku nihongi* Jingi 5 (728) 4/16.

61. *Shoku nihongi* Hōki 8 (777) 5/23.

62. *Nihon kiryaku* Enryaku 17 (798) 5/19.

63. *Ruiju sandai kyaku*, book 18, Tenchō 1 (824) 6/20; *Ruiju kokushi*, book 194, Tenchō 1 (824) 5/15 and Tenchō 3 (826) 3/1.

64. *Nihon sandai jitsuroku* Gangyō 1 (877) 6/25.

65. *Engi shiki*, book 30, p. 735.

66. *Nihon sandai jitsuroku* Jōgan 14 (872) 5/20, 14/5/21, and 14/5/22; Gangyō 6 (882) 11/28; and Gangyō 7 (883) 5/7, and 7/5/8.

67. *Nihon sandai jitsuroku* Ninna 1 (885) 10/20.

68. See Jacques Gernet, *Le monde chinois* (Paris: A. Colin, 1972); and Étienne Balazs, "Beiträge zur Wirtschaftsgeschichte der T'ang-Zeit (618-906)," *Mitteilungen des Seminars für Orientalische Sprachen* 34 (1931):1-92; 35 (1932):1-73; and 36 (1933):1-62. See also Kawahara Yoshirō, *Sōdai shakai keizaishi kenkyū* (Tōkyō: Keisō shobō, 1980) with regard to the Chinese economy, and the economic treatise in *Song shi*, books 177-186.

69. *Song shi*, book 186.

70. See Umehara Kaoru, ed., *Sō ōchō to shinbunka, zusetsu chūgoku no rekishi*, 5 (Tōkyō: Kōdansha, 1981):150.

71. See Shiba Yoshinobu, *Sōdai shōgyōshi kenkyū* (Tōkyō: Kazama shobō, 1968), pp. 56-71, with respect to Song boats.

72. Netolitsky, Almut, trans., *Das Ling-wai tai-ta von Chou Chü-fei: Eine Landeskunde Südchinas aus dem 12. Jahrhundert*, p. 54.

73. *Song shi*, book 186.

74. Quoted in *Yuehaiguan zhi*, book 3 (for 1137), by Liang Tingnan. A Qing-dynasty edition of the nineteenth century is preserved in the Tōyō Bunko, Tōkyō.

75. On Song foreign trade, see Friedrich Hirth and W. W. Rockhill, trans., *Chau Ju-kua: His Work on the Chinese and Arab Trade in the Twelfth and Thirteenth Centuries, Entitled Chu-fan-chi*; Kuwabara Jitsuzō, "On P'u Shou-keng," *Memoirs of the Research Department of the Tōyō Bunko* 2 (1928):1-79; Kawahara, *Sōdai shakai keizaishi kenkyū*; and Morris Rossabi, ed., *China among Equals: The Middle Kingdom and Its Neighbors, 10th–14th Centuries*. Figures for government revenue are derived from *Song shi*, book 186, but the calculations are my own. Note, however, that Shiba Yoshinobu arrived at a figure of 2–3% in Rossabi, *China among Equals*, p. 106.

76. See Francine Hérail, "La circulation des biens au Japon aux Xᵉ et XIᵉ siècles," unpublished seminar paper (1983); Toyoda et al., eds., *Ryūtsūshi*; and Akiyama Ken et al., eds., *Heian, Zusetsu nihon bunka no rekishi*, 4 (Tōkyō: Shōgakkan, 1979):73-93.

77. *Shōyūki* Jian 3 (1023) 6/17; and Akiyama Ken, pp. 90, 91.

78. See, for instance, tales from the Japan (honchō) section of the *Konjaku monogatarishū*, book 29, no. 36; and book 28, no. 40.

79. Regarding fairs see *Heian ibun*, doc. nos. 4701, 3753-3762, and 3788.

80. *Nihon kiryaku* Kōnin 9 (818) 1/13; and Kōnin 11 (820) 5/4, and 11/4/27; and *Ruiju sandai kyaku*, book 18, Tenchō 8 (831) 9/7.

81. *Shoku nihon kōki* Jōwa 9 (842) 1/10; *Nihon Montoku Tennō jitsuroku* Ninju 1 (851) 9/26; and *Shoku nihon kōki* Jōwa 9 (842) 8/15.

82. *Nihon sandai jitsuroku* Jōgan 16 (874) 6/17. See also Verschuer, *Les relations officielles du Japon avec la Chine*, chap. 4.

83. *Nihon sandai jitsuroku* Gangyō 1 (877) 8/22 and Gangyō 3 (879) 10/13.

84. *Ruijū sandai kyaku*, book 19, Engi 3 (903) 8/1. The other decrees can be found in *Shoku nihon kōki* Jōwa 8 (841) 2/27; *Nihon sandai jitsuroku* Ninna 1 (885) 10/20; and *Ruiju sandai kyaku*, book 14, Kanpyō 7 (895) 3/23.

85. On the rights of preemption and setting prices, see the penal code sections in *Taihō ritsuryō*, book 2 (Shikiinryō), article 67; and book 27 (Genshiryō), articles 8 and 20.

86. With respect to missions from Parhae, see *Engi shiki*, book 30; *Nihon sandai jitsuroku* Jōgan 14 (872) 5/20, 14/5/21, and 14/5/22; and Gangyō 6 (882) 11/28.

87. The waiting period (*nenki*) imposed on foreign traders is noted in Fujiwara no Tadahira's *Teishinkō ki* Tengyō 8 (945) 7/29; in *Hyakurenshō* Chōtoku 3 (997) 11/11; in *Shōyūki* Kankō 2 (1005) 8/21, and Chōgen 1 (1028) 11/29; and in *Gonki* Chōhō 5 (1003) 7/20, and Kankō 2 (1047) 8/21.

88. Prohibitions against leaving the country appear in *Hyakurenshō*, in entries dated Eishō 2 (1047) 12/24, and Kahō 1 (1094) 3/6; and in *Honchō monzui*, book 7, Tenryaku 7 (953)/7. Prohibitions against private trade can be found in *Fusō ryakki* Enchō 7 (929) 5/17, and 7/5/21; and in *Chōshūki* Chōshō 2 (1133) 8/13.

89. *Nihon kiryaku*, Engi 3 (903) 10/20, and Engi 9 (909) 2/17; *Fusō ryakki* Engi 9 (909) 8*/9, and 9/11/27; and *Nihon kiryaku* Engi 19 (919) 7/16.

90. *Honchō monzui*, book 12, Engi 22 (922) 6/5; and *Fusō ryakki* Enchō 7 (929) 5/21.

91. *Nihon kiryaku* Enchō 5 (927) 1/23; and *Fusō ryakki* Enchō 4 (926) 5/21.

92. *Nihon kiryaku* Jōhei 5 (935) 9/, and Jōhei 6 (936) 7/13 and 6/8/2; *Honchō seiki* Tengyō 1 (938) 7/21 and 1/8/23; and *Teishinkō ki* Tengyō 1 (938) 8/8.

93. *Nihon kiryaku* Jōhei 7 (937) 8/5, and Tengyō 2 (939) 2/11; *Teishinkō ki* Tengyō 2 (939) 2/15, and Tengyō 3 (940) 6/21 and 3/6/23; *Nihon kiryaku* Tengyō 3 (940) 7/; *Honchō seiki* Tengyō 8 (945) 7/26, 8/8/5, and 8/10/20; *Teishinkō ki*, Tengyō 8/7/29; *Honchō monzui*, book 7, Tenryaku 1 (947) 7*/27, Tenryaku 7 (953) 7/; *Nihon kiryaku*, Tentoku 1 (957) 7/20, and Tentoku 3 (959) 1/12. With respect to the letters written in 947 and 953, see *Honchō monzui*, book 7, Tenryaku 1 (947) 7*/27, and Tenryaku 7 (953) 7/.

94. *Nihon kiryaku* Tenroku 3 (972) 9/23; *Hyakurenshō* Tenroku 3 (972) 10/20; *Nihon kiryaku* Ten'en 2 (974) 10*/30; *Shōyūki* Tengen 5 (982) 3/25, and 5/3/26; *Gonki* Chōtoku 4 (998) 7/13. Regarding Chōnen, see Kimiya Yukihiko, *Nissō sō chōnen no kenkyū: shū to shite sono zuishinhin to shōraihin* (Tōkyō: Kashima shuppankai, 1983) and *Song shi*, book 491. See the list of Chōnen's gifts in the section "Exports" in chapter 3, p. 70; and in appendix 8.

95. Regarding Zhu Rencong, see *Hyakurenshō* and *Nihon kiryaku* Chōtoku 1 (995) 9/6; *Honchō seiki* and *Gonki* Chōtoku 1 (995) 9/24; *Nihon kiryaku* Chōtoku 2 (996) 10/6, and 2/11/8; *Hyakurenshō* Chōtoku 3 (997) 11/11; *Gonki* Chōhō 1 (999) 7/19 and 1/7/20; and Chōhō 2 (1000) 8/17, 2/8/18, 2/8/19, 2/8/20, 2/8/24, and 2/10/17.

96. *Hyakurenshō* Chōtoku 3 (997) 6/13; *Gonki* Chōhō 1 (999) 7/19; and Chōhō 2 (1000) 7/13, and 2/7/14.

97. *Gonki* and *Hyakurenshō* Chōhō 5 (1003) 7/20.

98. *Midō kanpaku ki* Kankō 1 (1004)1/27, 1/8/20, 1/8/21, 1/10/3, and 1/11/3. For a French translation see Francine Hérail, *Notes journalières de Fujiwara no Michinaga, ministre à la cour de Heian (995-1018): Traduction du Midō kanpaku ki*, 1:307, 407, 436, and 448.

99. *Nihon kiryaku* Kankō 2 (1005) 8/14.

100. *Hyakurenshō* Kankō 2/8/21; *Gonki* Kankō 2/8/21; and *Shōyūki* Kankō 2/8/21.

101. *Midō kanpaku ki* Kankō 2 (1005) 12/15, and Kankō 3 (1006) 10/20. In Hérail, see 1:582, and 2:89. Also see *Shōyūki* Kankō 2 (1005) 8/21 and 2/8/24.

102. *Midō kanpaku ki* Chōwa 1 (1012) 9/2, 1/9/21, and 1/9/22; and Chōwa 2 (1013) 2/2, 2/2/3, and 2/2/4. In Hérail, see 2:619, 624-625, and 714-715. Also see *Hyakurenshō*, *Fusō ryakki*, and *Nihon kiryaku*, Chōwa 4/6*/25.

103. Concerning the gifts sent by Michinaga, see *Midō kanpaku ki* Chōwa 4 (1015) 7/15 (Yōmei Bunko manuscript); in Hérail, see 3:124.

104. In regard to gifts from Sanesuke, see *Shōyūki* Chōwa 4 (1015) 6/19.

105. *Chōya gunsai*, vol. 20, Kannin 3 (1019) 4/16; *Nihon kiryaku* Kannin 3 (1019) 4/17, 3/4/18, and 3/5/26; and Kannin 4 (1020) 2/16, and 4/4/11; *Sakeiki* Kannin 3 (1019) 9/22; and *Hyakurenshō* Kannin 4 (1020) 2/16.

106. Regarding Zhou Liangshi, see *Sakeiki* Manju 3 (1026) 7/17; *Ukaikishō* Ninpyō 1 (1151) 9/24; *Shōyūki* Manju 3 (1026) 6/26 copy of Kunaichō, and Chōgen 1 (1028) 10/10 and 1/10/15; *Song shi*, book 491; Mori Katsumi, "Tōgū to sō shō Shu Ryōshi," in Mori Katsumi, *Zoku nissō bōeki no kenkyū*, pp. 269-279, and 253-258. Regarding Fujiwara no Korenori, see *Shōyūki* Chōgen 1 (1028) 10/10; and Chōgen 2 (1029) 7/11; and Mori, *Zoku nissō bōeki no kenkyū*, pp. 256-259.

107. Concerning Zhou Wenyi, see *Shôyûki* Chôgen 1 (1028) 11/23, and 1/11/29; and Chôgen 2 (1029) 3/2; *Sakeiki* Chôgen 1 1028) 11/23, and 1/11/29. With respect to Sanesuke's imports, see *Shôyûki* Chôwa 2 (1013) 7/25, and 2/8/7. See appendix 8 for the list of products from 1028 in Chinese.

108. *Chôgen shichinen shôgatsu tôka tôgū onteseki* quoted in Mori, "Tôgū to sô shô Shu Ryôshi."

109. *Konjaku monogatarishū*, book. 26, no.16.

110. *Hyakurenshô* Eishô 2 (1047) 12/24.

111. *Fusô ryakki* Kôhei 3 (1060) 7/; and *Hyakurenshô* Kôhei 3 (1060) 8/7.

112. Concerning Japanese traders' activities in Korea, see *Koryôsa*, books 9-11, in Nihon shiryô shûsei hensankai, *Chûgoku-chôsen no shiseki ni okeru nihon shiryô shûsei*, kôrai no bu, pp. 63-66; and *Song shi*, book 491.

113. *San tendai godaisan ki*, book 1; and *Song shi*, book 491.

114. Regarding gifts, see *Hyakurenshô* Enkyū 5 (1073) 10/, Jôhô 2 (1075) 1/26, 2/10/26, and 2/11/5; Jôhô 3 (1076) 6/2; Jôryaku 1 (1077) 5/5; and Jôryaku 2 (1078) 10/25; *Suisaki* Jôhô 2 (1075) 10/26, and Jôhô 3 (1076) 6/2. The rendering of Sun Zhong's name differs depending on the sources.

115. Regarding Sun Zhong's second visit, see *Ikoku chôjô no koto* Jôryaku 4 (1080) 9/, in *Dai nihon shiryô*, series VII, vol. 28, pp. 63-70; *Sochiki* Jôryaku 4 (1080) 4/21, 4/5/27, 4/8*/14, 4/8*/26, 4/9/6, 4/9/10, 4/9/19, and 4/9/20; Jôryaku 5 (1081) 3/5; Eiho 1 (1081) 5/2, and 1/10/25; *Suisaki* Jôryaku 4 (1080) 8*/14, 4/8*/26, 4/8*/30, 4/9/10, 4/9/19, 4/9/20, and 4/11/3; Jôryaku 5 (1081) 10/8, 5/10/24, and 5/10/25; *Fusô ryakki* Jôryaku 4 (1080) 8*/30, and 4/9/9; and *Hyakurenshô* Eihô 2 (1082) 11/21, and Jôryaku 4 (1080) 8*/13.

116. *Suisaki* Jôryaku 4 (1080) 8/7, 4/8*/5, 4/8*/11, 4/8*/13, 4/8*/14, 4/8*/23, 4/8*/24, 4/8*/26, 4/9/3, 4/9/4, 4/9/6, 4/9/12, 4/9/17, 4/9/18, 4/9/24, 4/10/10, 4/10/11, and 4/11/3; *Sochiki* Jôryaku 4/8*/5 (1080), 4/8*/14, 4/8*/22, 4/8*/25, 4/9/2, 4/9/3, and 4/9/4; and *Hyakurenshô* Jôryaku 4 (1080) 8*/5.

117. Copies of the letter from Korea and the response from Japan appear in *Chôya gunsai*, book 20; *Honchô zokumonzui*, book 11, Jôryaku 4 (1080); and *Sochiki* Jôryaku 4 (1080) 9/4.

118. *Hyakurenshô* Kanji 6 (1092) 6/27, and 6/9/28; Kahô 1 (1094) 3/6, and 1/5/25; *Chûyûki* Kanji 6 (1092) 6/27; Kanji 8 (1094) 5/3, 8/5/14, 8/5/25; and Eichô 1 (1096) 7/14, and 1/9/22; and *Gonijô Moromichi ki* Kanji 6 (1092) 10/23; and Kanji 7 (1093) 3/12, 7/10/14, and 7/10/15.

119. *Ikoku chôjô no koto* Jôtoku 1 (1097) 9/; *Moromori ki* Jôtoku 1 (1097) 9/, and 1/12/24 as quoted in *Dai nihon shiryô*, series III, vol. 4, p. 873; *Hyakurenshô* Eikyū 4 (1116) 5/16, Gen'ei 1 (1118) 6/8, and Hôan 2 (1121) 3/26; *Chûyûki* Gen'ei 1 (1118) 2/29; and *Zenrin kokuhôki* Gen'ei 1. See Verschuer, "Japan's Foreign Relations 600-1200: A Translation of *Zenrin kokuhôki*," p. 35.

120. *Chôshûki* Chôshô 2 (1133) 8/13.

121. *Chôshûki* Chôshô 3 (1134) 5/2.

122. *Ukaikishô* Ninpyô 3 (1153) 1/15; *Taiki* Kyūan 3 (1147) 11/14; and *Honchô seiki* Kyūan 4 (1148) 6*/5.

123. See entries about Chinese residents in Kyûshû in 1151 and 1152 in *Aogata monjo* Juei 2 (1183) 3/22.

124. *Hyakurenshō* Ninpyō 1 (1151) 9/24; *Hyōhanki* Nin'an 3 (1168) 9/17. See Mori Katsumi, *Nissō bōeki no kenkyū*, pp. 245-263; and Mori, *Zoku nissō bōeki no kenkyū*, pp. 260-262.

125. The translated passage is in *Gyokuyō* and *Hyakurenshō* Ka'ō 2 (1170) 9/20.

126. About the Nakahara criticism, see *Moromoriki* Jōji 6 (1367) 5/9. On Kiyomori, see Gomi Fumihiko, *Taira no Kiyomori*. See also *Gyokuyō* Jōan 2 (1172) 9/22; Jōan 3 (1173) 3/13; *Hyakurenshō*, Jōan 3 (1172) 3/3; *Ikoku chōjō no koto*, Jōan 3/2 (1172); and *Song shi*, book 491.

127. Zhou Mi, *Guixin zazhi xuji, xia*. See Wada Sei and Ishihara Michihiro, eds., *Kyū tōjo wakoku nihon den, Sōshi nihon den, Genshi nihon den*, p. 183.

128. See *San tendai godaisan ki*, book 4, with respect to Jōjin's testimonial.

129. The list of Chinese products is drawn from the *Shinsarugakuki* account of the episode titled, "Hachirō Mahito." See appendix 8 for the list in Chinese.

130. *Gonijō Moromichi ki* Kanji 5 (1091) 10/25. See *Engi shiki*, book 37, concerning the list of Japanese medicines.

131. Regarding incense, see Mori, *Nissō bōeki no kenkyū*, pp. 196-199.

132. With respect to the quotation about perfumes, see *Genji monogatari*, "Mume gae jō," book 16, p. 164. The English translation is taken from Edward G. Seidensticker, *The Tale of Genji* (New York: Alfred A. Knopf, 1987), p. 514.

133. *San tendai godaisan ki*, book 6.

134. *Engi shiki*, books 22-25.

135. *Murasaki Shikibu nikki*, book 19, pp. 507-508. For an English translation see Annie Shepley Omori and Kochi Doi, *Diaries of Court Ladies of Old Japan* (Boston: Houghton Mifflin, 1920), pp. 143-144.

136. *Genji monogatari*, "Wakana jō," book 16, p. 231; Seidensticker, *The Tale of Genji*, p. 546.

137. *Makura no sōshi*, book 19, p. 136. For the English translation see Ivan Morris, *The Pillow Book of Sei Shonagon*, (New York: Columbia University Press, 1967).

138. *Utsubo monogatari*, in *Nihon koten bungaku taikei*, 11:217-218, "Hatsu aki." For the English translation see Ziro Uraki, trans., *Tale of the Cavern (Utsuho Monogatari)*, (Tokyo: Shinozaki shorin, 1984).

139. Regarding *kara aya* fabric in Japan, see *Meigetsuki* Kangi 1 (1229) 12/29; *Minkeiki* Jōei 1 (1232) 5/8-1/5/23; and Nishimura Heibe, "Orimono," *Nihon no bijutsu* 12 (April 1967):54. See also "aya," in *Kokushi daijiten* I, p. 317.

140. Concerning fabric from Shu, see *Unshū shōsoku*, book 3, in *Gunsho ruijū*, vol. 9, Shōsokubu; *Teikin ōrai*, notes on *kara aya* in the 6th and 7th months, in *Tōyō bunko* 242; *Genpei seisuiki* 28; and *Taiheiki*. Thanks to Mrs. Ogasawara, curator of the Tōkyō National Museum, and Jane Cobbi of the Centre National de la Recherche Scientifique for their assistance.

141. On imported and domestic ceramics, see Kamei Meitoku, *Nihon bōeki tōjishi no kenkyū* 1986, with an English abstract, pp. 6-16. Hayashiya Shōzō, "Chawan," *Nihon no bijutsu* 14 (June 1967); Yabe Yoshiaki, "Tōji chūsei hen," *Nihon no bijutsu* 236 (January 1986); Nakazawa Fujio et al., "Sō gen no tōji kōeki," *Kobijutsu* 68 (1983): 52-71; Madeleine Paul-David, "L'évolution de la céramique japonaise de l'époque des grandes sépultures à celle de Heian," in *Mélanges offerts à M. Charles Haguenauer, en l'honneur de son quatre-vingtième anniversaire: Études japonaises*, pp. 527-568.

142. See *Chōya gunsai*, book 20, for gifts in 1080; as well as Mende, *China und die Staaten*, pp. 345-350.

143. Verschuer, *Les relations officielles du Japon avec la Chine*, p. 242.

144. *Nihon Montoku Tennō jitsuroku* Ninju 1 (851) 9/26.

145. *Midō kanpaku ki* Kankō 1 (1004) 10/3, and 1/11/3; and Kankō 3 (1006) 10/20. In Hérail, 1:436, 448, and 2:89.

146. *Midō kanpaku ki* and *Nihon kiryaku*, Kankō 7 (1010) 11/28. In Hérail, see 2:443-445. In fact this date corresponds to January 5, 1011.

147. *Nihon kiryaku* Jōhei 7 (937) 10/13.

148. *Fusō ryakki* Eishō 3 (1048) 11/16. However, *Hyakurenshō*'s entry for Eishō 3/5/2 mentions a Korean calendar from Silla.

149. See also *Hyakurenshō* and *Nihon kiryaku*, Eien 1 (987) 2/11.

150. *Unshū shōsoku*, book 3.

151. Regarding titles cited by Jakushō, see *San tendai godaisan ki*, book 5, Enkyū 4 (1072) 12/29; *Hyakurenshō* Enkyū 5 (1073) 10; and in *Ukaikishō* and *Hyakurenshō*, see Ninpyō 1 (1151) 9/24.

152. *San tendai godaisan ki*, book 5, Enkyū 4 (1072) 12/29, which quotes *Huang Chao leiyuan*, book 43. On "Riben seng," see Wada and Ishihara, *Ku tōjo wakoku nihon den*, pp. 181-182. See *Midō kanpaku ki*, Chōwa 2 (1013) 9/14. In Hérail, see 3:35.

153. *Taiki* Kōji 2 (1143) 11/3, and 2/11/24.

154. *Hyakurenshō* Jishō 3 (1179) 12/16; and *Sankaiki* Jishō 3 (1179) 2/13.

155. See Mori Katsumi, *Nissō bunka kōryū no shomondai*, pp. 163-192; and *Koryōsa*, 10:65-66.

156. *Hyakurenshō* Kanji 2 (1088) 10/17.

157. *Taiki* Kyūan 6 (1150) 5/16.

158. *Shōsōin-ten mokuroku* 1981. One of the legends is cited in the collection of reminiscences known as the *Kojidan*, in section 6.

159. *Hyakurenshō* Jiryaku 2 (1066) 5/1, and Eiho 2 (1082) 8/8; and *Honchō seiki* Kyūan 4 (1148) 6*/5.

160. *Makura no sōshi*, book 41, "Tori wa." For a French translation see André Beaujard, *Notes de chevet*, p. 67. A different version (from a different manuscript) is in *Makura no sōshi*, p. 89. For an English translation, see Ivan Morris, trans., *Pillow Book of Sei Shonagon*, 2 vols., New York: Columbia University Press, 1967.

161. Regarding Cui Duo, see *Nihon sandai jitsuroku* Gangyō 3 (879) 10/13.

162. According to *Midō kanpaku ki* Kankō 1 (1004) 1/27, the purchase was made via the governor of Bitchū.

163. *Gyokuyō* Bunji 3 (1187) 9/29.

164. *Song shi*, book 491; *Zhufan zhi* 1, "Woguo," in Friedrich Hirth and W. W. Rockhill, trans., *Chau Ju-kua: His Work on the Chinese and Arab Trade in the Twelfth and Thirteenth Centuries, Entitled Chu-fan-chi*, pp. 170-175. Regarding metals and pearls in China and Japan, see Edward Schafer, *The Golden Peaches of Samarkand: A Study of T'ang Exotics*; and Kobayashi Yukio, *Kodai no gijutsu*.

165. *San tendai godaisan ki*, books 1 and 2: 3rd to 6th months, 1072.

166. *Xu Zizhi tongjian changbian*, book 343, for the Mingzhou prefect's sulfur order of 1084.

167. Regarding the importation of pearls into China, see *Wei shu*, book 102; *Song shi*, book 186; and *Zhufan zhi*, book 2, "Pearls." With respect to the exportation of pearls from Japan, see *Uji shūi monogatari*, tale no. 180, p. 395; *Konjaku monogatarishū*, book 25, p. 456; and *Unshū shōsoku*, book 3.

168. *Baoqing Siming zhi*, book 6, in Wada and Ishihara, *Ku tōjo wakoku nihon den*, p. 183. See appendix 8 for the list of products in Chinese.

169. With regard to Chinese praise for Japanese paper in 1008, see "Riben seng" in *Huang Chao leiyuan*, book 43, in Wada and Ishihara, pp.181-182. See *San tendai godaisan ki*, book 1, regarding Jōjin's allotment of paper.

170. *Chosôn wangjo sillok*, book 41, Sejong 10 (1428), which is quoted in Ikeda On, "Zenkindai tōa ni okeru kami no kokusai kōryū," in Tōhō gakkai, ed., *Tōhō gakkai sōritsu yonjisshūnen kinen Tōhōgaku ronshū*, p. 4; also see Dard Hunter, *Papermaking: The History and Technique of an Ancient Craft*; and *Washi no bi*.

171. *Zhufan zhi*, in Fujiyoshi Masumi, trans., *Shobanshi (Zhufan zhi)*, p. 243.

172. Regarding wood for construction, see *Zhufan zhi*, book 1, "Woguo," translated in Hirthand Rockhill, *Chau Ju-kua*, p. 171; and Fujiyoshi Masumi, trans., *Shobanshi*, p. 243. See also Kimiya Yasuhiko, *Nikka bunka kōryūshi*, pp. 331-333.

173. For the list of Chōnen's gifts, see *Song shi*, book 491. See appendix 8 for the list in Chinese.

174. *Bozhaibian*, book 3, a commentary on Japanese mother-of-pearl, quoted in Mori, "Nitchū bunka no kōryū," p. 13.

175. See Kawada Sadamu, "Raden," *Nihon no bijutsu* 211 (December 1983); Arakawa Hirokazu, "Makie," *Nihon no bijutsu* 35 (March 1969); Beatrix von Ragué, *Geschichte der japanischen Lackkunst* (Berlin: W. de Gruyter, 1967); and *Asahi shinbun*, October 24, 1986. See also the section "Export and Import Products" in chapter 5 of this volume.

176. See Nagata Seiji, "Ōgi no hensen to kinsei kami ōgi ni tsuite," *Kobijutsu* 75 (July 1985):4-52; and Nakamura Kiyoe, *Nihon no ōgi* (Kyōto: Kawahara shoten, 1942).

177. Mori Katsumi, "Tairiku bunka to nihon ōgi," in *Nissō bunka kōryū no shomondai*, p. 312.

178. *Huang Chao leiyuan*, book 60, in Wada and Ishihara 1986, p. 182.

179. *Tuhui baojian*, quoted in Mori Katsumi, "Tairiku bunka to nihon ōgi," in *Nissō bunka kōryū no shomondai*, pp. 313.

180. Regarding prices and the popularity of fans, see also the section "Export and Import Products" in chapter 5 of this volume.

181. See Schafer, *The Golden Peaches of Samarkand: Weapons and Armor of Ancient Japan*, exhibition catalog; *Samurai*, exhibition catalog; Sato Kanzan, "Tōken," *Nihon no bijutsu* 6 (October 1966); and Joe Earle, trans., *The Japanese Sword*. See also the section "Export and Import Products" in chapter 5 of this volume..

182. In the prehistoric era, the Kun tribe, in the vicinity of Hami, had sent mysterious red swords to the Zhou sovereign.

183. This refers to a Chinese legend according to which Xu Fu, a Taoist magician, was ordered by Emperor Qin Shi Huangdi (r. 246–210 B.C.E.) to depart, accompanied by thousands of children, to research medicinal herbs that could render a person immortal. Xu Fu never returned from his mission, however.

184. Certain authors compared the legendary island of Penglai, to which Xu Fu traveled, with Japan, giving rise to a Xu Fu cult there. Certain Japanese shrines still celebrate the memory of this Chinese magician. See Verschuer, "Tō-sō ni okeru nihon hōrai kan to suigin yunyū ni tsuite."

185. In the third century B.C.E. Emperor Qin Shi Huangdi had many of early China's books burned. In the eleventh century, numerous Buddhist texts lost in the aftermath of persecutions were purchased in Korea and Japan and reintroduced in China.

186. *Ouyang wenzhonggong ji*, book 54 and *Wenguo wenzheng Sima Guang ji*, book 3, as quoted by Wada and Ishihara 1986, p. 182. I am indebted to Ikeda On and Chu Yung-ch'uan for information regarding the poem's authorship. See also note 313.

187. *Kaiqing siming xuzhi*, book 8.

188. See *Song shi*, book 491, in reference to Japanese voyages to China in 1175, 1176, and 1183. Also see *Gyokuyō*, Jishō 3 (1179) 7/27; *Hyakurenshō* Jishō 3 (1179) 6/; and *Sankaiki* Jishō 4 (1180) 10/10.

189. *Azuma kagami* Bunji 1 (1185) 10/20.

190. *Zuoshi jiancao*, quoted and interpreted in Mori and Tanaka, p. 200; and *Shimazu-ke monjo*, book 1, doc. 298.

191. *Genkō shakusho*, book 2, biography of Myōan Yōsai (1191); *Gyokuyō* Shōji 2 (1200) 2/5; *Sennyūji Fukaki hōshi den*, biography of Shunjō (1166-1227); *Gyokuyō* Kenkyū 2 (1191) 2/15, 2/2/19, and 2/6/12; *Song shi*, book 491 (1193, 1200, and 1202). Shōjirō's name is cited in *Sennyūji Fukaki hōshi den*, for which see Charlotte von Verschuer, "Le moine Shunjō: Sa jeunesse et son voyage en Chine," *Bulletin de l'École Française d'Extrême Orient* 88 (2001):171.

192. *Koryōsa*, book 22, pp. 67-68.

193. *Meigetsuki* Karoku 2 (1226) 10/16, and 2/10/17.

194. *Azuma kagami* Antei 1 (1227) 5/14; *Minkeiki* Antei 1 (1227) 5/1, and 1/5/15; and *Hyakurenshō* Antei 1 (1227) 7/21. See also Seno Seiichirō, *Matsura-tō kankei shiryōshū*, esp. vol. 1.

195. *Goseibai shikimoku*, article 3; and *Azuma kagami* Jōei 1 (1232) 9*/17.

196. *Koryōsa*, book 23 (1243 and 1244).

197. *Koryōsa*, book 82 (1251), book 25 (1259 and 1263), and book 26 (1265).

198. See Kimiya, *Nikka bunka kōryūshi*, pp. 334-351; *Shōichi kokushi nenpu* in *Dai nihon bukkyō zensho*, vol. 95, p. 135; Mori Katsumi, "Nihon kyoryū no sō shōnin," in Mori, *Zoku nissō bōeki*, pp. 260-262; *Koipponki* Ninji 3 (1242) 7/4 in Mori and Tanaka, p. 203. With regard to the capacity of ships, see Tanaka Takeo, ed., *Kamakura bakufu to mōkō shūrai*, pp. 42-43.

199. *Gyokuyō* Jishō 3 (1179) 7/27.

200. *Zuoshi jiancao*, quoted and interpreted in Mori and Tanaka, p. 200.

201. *Song shi,* book 37 (1199); Kobata Atsushi, *Nihon no kahei,* pp. 38-74; Kuwabara, "On P'u Shou-keng," pp. 24-27; Mori, *Nissō bōeki no kenkyū,* pp. 474-506; and *Song shi,* book 181.

202. Quoted in Kuwabara, "On P'u Shou-keng," p. 26.

203. *Chūyūki* Kanji 6 (1092) 6/27.

204. Kobata, *Nihon no kahei,* pp. 39-41.

205. *Tōdaiji monjo* and *Tōji hyakugō monjo,* quoted in Mori and Tanaka, p. 200; and Mori, *Nissō bōeki no kenkyū,* p. 476.

206. *Hyakurenshō* Jishō 3 (1179) 6/.

207. Regarding property transactions, see for instance a statistic in Kobata, *Nihon no kahei,* p. 58.

208. *Gyokuyō* Jishō 3 (1179) 7/25.

209. *Gyokuyō* Bunji 3 (1187) 6/13, and Kenkyū 3 (1192) 10/1; and *Hossō shiyōshō,* book 2, entry on "Suiko," Kenkyū 4 (1193) 7/4.

210. *Kachō yōryaku,* book 121, which quotes *Tendai zasuki,* book 2 in regard to the denunciation of private trade by the Mount Hiei monastery. See Mori, *Nissō bōeki no kenkyū,* p. 479.

211. *Shōkyū sannen guchūreki* and *Tōji hyakugō monjo* quoted in Mori, *Nissō bōeki no kenkyū,* pp. 481-482 (Karoku 2, 1226). *Azuma kagami* Karoku 2 (1226) 8/1.

212. See the statistic of payments in Uwayokote Masataka, ed., *Kamakura,* in *Zusetsu nihon bunka no rekishi,* 5:84.

213. *Samuraidokoro satahen,* in *Gunsho ruijū,* vol. 22, Bukebu, Ennō 1 (1239) 4; and *Azuma kagami* Kōchō 3 (1263) 9/10, quoted in Mori, *Nissō bōeki no kenkyū,* p. 486. See also note 297 below.

214. Regarding coin supply, see the table in Uwayokote, p. 84.

215. *Azuma kagami,* Kenchō 6 (1254) 4/29.

216. *Shinpen tsuika,* addenda to *Goseibai shikimoku.* See *Tsuikahō,* book 422, in Satō Shin'ichi and Ikeuchi Yoshisuke, eds., *Chūsei hōsei shiryōshū,* vol. 1, dated Bun'ei 1 (1264) 4/.

217. See Wei Jung-chi [Gi Eikichi], *Gen nichi kankeishi no kenkyū,* pp. 27-223; and Mori, *Nissō bōeki no kenkyū,* pp. 506-517, with regard to *Yuan shi* books 94 and 10; see books 208 (1277) and 10 (1278) as to the measures taken by Khubilai Khan.

218. See the *Kamikaze* citation in von Verschuer 2002, p. 432.

219. *Yuan shi,* book 10 (1279); *Kenji sannen ki,* Keinji 3 (1277) 6/.

220. See *Bukkō kokushi goroku,* on the arrival of Mugaku Sogen in Japan.

221. *Kanchūki* Kōan 10 (1287) 7/13.

222. *Daihiōin monjo* Shōō 3 (1290) 4/25 in Mori, *Nissō bōeki no kenkyū,* p. 523.

223. *Aogata monjo,* six documents from Einin 6 concerning the boat of 1298 under Tōtarō's supervision. See also Tanaka, *Kamakura bakufu to mōkō shūrai,* pp. 126-127.

224. *Yuan dianzhang,* book 22 (1322), in reference to the regulations issued in 1293.

225. *Yuan shi,* books 17 and 21, as to the installation of the special guard at Qingyuan in 1292 and the Dinghai watch post in 1304.

226. *Shingen daishō zenji ryūzan ōshō gyōjō* (for 1305) quoted in Wei, *Gen-nichi kankeishi no kenkyū*, pp. 225-244; Mori and Tanaka, pp. 232-237; and Herbert Franz Schurmann, *Economic Structure of the Yuan Dynasty: Translation of Chapters 93 and 94 of the Yüan shih*, pp. 223-236.

227. *Hossō shiyōshō*, book 2; *Yuan shi*, book 21 (1306). On Shōmyōji see also "Kanesawa Sadaaki shojō," in *Sō-gen bunka to Kanazawa bunkoten*, exhibition catalog, p. 34.

228. *Shingen daishō zenji Ryūzan ōshō gyōjō* (1307), in *Mingzhou xinianlu*, book 4 (1309), and *Yuan shi*, book 99 (1311); quoted in Wei, *Gen-nichi kankeishi no kenkyū*, pp. 241-242.

229. See Kimiya, *Nikka bunka kōryūshi*, pp. 445-464 (table listing monks).

230. *Hishijima monjo* Karyaku 1 (1326) 9/4, in Mori and Tanaka, p. 235.

231. "Hōjō Sadaaki shojō," in *Sō-gen bunka to Kanazawa bunkoten*, p. 34.

232. *Sumiyoshi jinja monjo* (1332, Settsu), quoted in Mori and Tanaka, p. 234.

233. See Kimiya, *Nikka bunka kōryūshi*, pp. 417-420, for the following: *Tenryūji zōeikiroku*; *Daitsū zenji goroku* 6, "Nenpu"; and *Taiheiki*, book 24, "Tenryūji konryū no koto."

234. Tōkyō kokuritsu hakubutsukan, *Shin'an kaitei hikiage bunbutsu: The Sunken Treasures off the Sinan Coast*, exhibition catalog; *Asahi shinbun*, June 8, 1987.

235. *Koryōsa*, books 37, 38, 114, and 134; and *Koryōsa chōryo*, books 26, 28, 30, 31, and 34, pp. 109-113, and 297-352.

236. *Moromori ki* Jōji 6(1367) 4/.

237. Henri Cordier and Sir Henry Yule, trans., *The Travels of Marco Polo: The Complete Yule-Cordier Edition*, pp. 253-255.

238. *Taiheiki*, book 39, "Kōraijin raichō no koto."

239. *Zhizheng Siming xuzhi*, book 5.

240. Regarding the *Taiping yulan*, see *Yōkōki* Hōji 1 (1247) 9/20.

241. *Sō-gen bunka to Kanazawa bunkoten*. Numerous works originally belonging to this archive are now held in other libraries. See also lists of Chinese books in *Isei teikin ōrai*, "7ᵗʰ month," and *Tōfukuji monjo*, vol. 1, doc. 28.

242. See Kimiya, *Nikka bunka kōryūshi*, pp. 510-519, which cites the *Kissa ōrai* and *Isei teikin ōrai*.

243. For a description of tea gatherings at Sasaki Takauji's residence, see *Taiheiki*, books 33 and 39.

244. With regard to Hōjō Sadaaki's manuscripts, see *So-gen bunka to Kanazawa bunkoten*, pp. 34-37.

245. See *Butsu nichian kōmotsu mokuroku*, by Hōsei, 1363, in *Kamakura shishi: Shiryō hen*, part 2, vol. 5.

246. *Tsurezuregusa*, by Yoshida Kenkō, ca. 1330-1335, in *Nihon koten bungaku teikei*, vol. 30, no. 120.

247. *Zenrin kokuhōki* in Yutani Minoru, *Nichi-min kangō bōeki shiryō*, p. 36, as translated in Wang Yi-t'ung, *Official Relations between China and Japan, 1368-1549*, p. 22. However, there were no double-edged swords in medieval Japan; see the section on swords in chapter 3 above. *Zenrin kokuhōki*, "Account of Good Neighborly Relations," is considered the first Japanese collection of diplomatic documents. See

Charlotte von Verschuer, "Japan's Foreign Relations 600 to 1200: A Translation of *Zenrin kokuhōki*," p. 1. The best Japanese edition is Ishii Masatoshi, "*Zenrin kokuhōki*." Yutani's *Nichi-min kangō bōeki shiryō* offers a convenient compendium of original Chinese and Japanese sources concerning relations between the two countries from the fourteenth to the sixteenth centuries. Wang's *Official Relations between China and Japan*, the only western-language monograph of its kind, contains numerous translations of official diplomatic correspondence and an analysis of commercial trade.

248. See *Chosŏn wangjo sillok*, book 5, 1420/10/8; see also *Nosongdong ilbon haengnok*, in Murai Shōsuke, trans. *Rōshōdō nihon kōroku: Chōsen shisetsu no mita chūsei no nihon*.

249. Toyoda et al., eds., *Ryūtsūshi*, pp. 67-92; V. Dixon Morris, "Sakai: From Shōen to Port City," in John Whitney Hall and Toyoda Takeshi, eds., *Japan in the Muromachi Age*, pp. 145-148.

250. See Cheng Liang-sheng, *Min-nichi kankeishi no kenkyū*, pp. 58-71, 194, 195 and table at the end; Tanaka Takeo, ed., *Dai minkoku to wakō*, in *Kaigai shiten nihon no rekishi*, vol. 7, pp. 34-67; Tanaka Takeo, *Chūsei taigai kankeishi*, pp. 52-63; and Wang, pp. 10-33.

251. See Tamura Hiroyuki, *Chūsei nitchō bōeki no kenkyū*, pp. 405-414, which presents a chronology of the relations of each region of Japan with Korea based on *Chosŏn wangjo sillok*; Tanaka, *Chūsei taigai kankeishi*, pp. 95-109; Tanaka Takeo, *Taigai kankei to bunka kōryū*, pp. 25-39.

252. See *Zenrin kokuhōki* in Yutani, p. 38, concerning Yoshimitsu's letter containing the phrase "king of Japan"; for letters from China addressed to the king of Japan in 672, 704, and 736, see *Zenrin kokuhōki*, jō; and *Tang chengxiang Qujiang Zhang xiansheng wenji*, book 7, in Wada and Ishihara, *Ku tōjo wakoku nihon den*, p. 165; with respect to Taira no Kiyomori's use of the term "king," see chapter 2 above, and note 126; and for use of this appellation by Prince Kaneyoshi and the Ashikaga, see Tanaka Takeo, "Ashikaga shōgun to nihonkoku ō no gō," in Tanaka Takeo, ed., *Nihon zenkindai no kokka to taigai kankei*.

253. *Yoshida-ke hinamiki*, in Yutani, p. 47.

254. *Ming shi lu*, in Yutani, p. 83.

255. *Ming shi*, book 322, "Riben zhuan" ("Nihon den"), in Nihon shiryō shūsei hensankai, *Chūgoku-chōsen no shiseki ni okeru nihon shiryō shūsei*, seishi no bu, 1:289; and *Ming shi gao* in Yutani, p. 88. See also note 271 below regarding the submission of tribute by the countries of Southeast Asia subsequent to the Chinese expeditions. Also see the table and appendix in Cheng, *Min-nichi kankeishi no kenkyū*.

256. See the previous note 255 for references. During the tally trade regime, Japan sent official delegations to China in 1405, 1406, 1407, 1408, 1433, 1435, 1453, 1468, 1477, 1484, 1495, 1511, 1523, 1539, and 1548.

257. See the list of gifts sent to China in 1403 and noted in *Zenrin kokuhōki*, in Yutani, p. 38. I have translated "ten" instead of "thousand" spears by reading *sen* as a mistake for *jū*, in accordance with Tanaka Takeo, ed., *Zenrin kokuhōki, Shintei zoku zenrin kokuhōki*, p. 112. The other lists of Japanese gifts are cited in Yutani: *Zenrin kokuhōki*, p. 36 (1401), pp. 107-108 (1433), p. 151 (1452), p. 226 (1475-1477), and p. 258 (1483); *Boshi nyūminki*, pp. 199-202 (1468); *Inryōken nichiroku*, p. 312 (1493); *Myōchiin monjo*, pp. 437-446 (1538) as well as *Da ming huidian* 105.

258. See *Ming shi lu* in Yutani, pp. 84, and 86, concerning the Chinese gifts in 1406 and 1407. See appendix 8 for the 1407 list drawn from the *Ming shi lu*. For a detailed description of fabrics and other gifts in 1403, 1406, and 1407, see *Myōchiin monjo* in Yutani, pp. 446-465. See hereafter the section "Export and Import Products." For other lists of Chinese gifts, consult the following sources excerpted in Yutani: *Ming shi lu*, p. 84 (1405), p. 86 (1408 and 1411), p. 137 (1435), p. 221 (1468), and p. 228 (1478); *Zenrin kokuhōki*, pp. 100-106 (1433), p. 108 (1435), and pp. 151-154 (1451); and *Zoku zenrin kokuhōki*, p. 261 (1485). See also *Da ming huidian*, book 111, and Cheng, p. 208 (1435 and 1485); and *Tokugawa monjo* in Yutani, pp. 77-81 (1407).

259. Tamura, pp. 405-428; and Tanaka, *Chūsei taigai kankeishi*, pp. 95-108. The last item in the list (*shōshi*) seems to be pine nuts, rather than pine wood. In the fourteenth century, this item was also among the high-value medicinal and aromatic substances imported by China, as per *Zhizheng siming xuzhi*, book 5. However, Mende's *China und die Staaten*, p. 346, holds that Korea exported pine wood (*shōshi*) to China in 929, 945, 1072, and 1080.

260. See *Gyomotsu on'e mokuroku*, in *Dai nihon shiryō*, series VII, 10:131-137; Tanaka, *Chūsei taigai kankeishi*, pp. 104-109; and Tamura, pp. 405-424.

261. Tamura, pp. 171-370, and 283-284; and with regard to the delegations from Shisa, Tan, and Hi, see pp. 180-181.

262. Concerning the delegations from Tsushima, see Tanaka, *Chūsei taigai kankeishi*, pp. 108-113.

263. *Teikin ōrai*, "Fourth month."

264. With respect to Ōuchi Hiroyo, see *Taiheiki*, book 39, "Ōuchi no suke rakusan no koto."

265. Wada Hisatoko, "Nanbansen no nihon kaigan raichaku," in Tanaka, ed., *Dai minkoku to wakō*, pp. 114-125; and Tamura, pp. 179, 283, and 336. In English see Richard Pearson, "Port, City and Hinterlands: Archaeological Perspectives on Quanzhou and Its Overseas Trade," in Angela Schottenhammer, ed., *Emporium of the World: Maritime Quanzhou, 1000-1400.*

266. The quotation, from one of Yoshimochi's letters written in 1419, is drawn from the *Zenrin kokuhōki*. See Yutani, p. 96.

267. Tanaka, *Chūsei taigai kankeishi*, pp. 116-118; Nakamura Hidetaka, *Nihon to chōsen*, pp. 93-102; Tamura, pp. 412-425; and Wada, "Nanbansen no nihon kaigan raichaku."

268. As to the regulation of missions see *Ming shi*, book 322 in Nihon shiryō shūsei hensankai, *Chūgoku-chōsen no shiseki ni okeru nihon shiryō shūsei*, seishi no bu, 1: 289. Interpretations differ with respect to the dates of these regulations: see Tanaka, *Chūsei taigai kankeishi*, p. 158; and Cheng, pp. 68-71.

269. See *Zenrin kokuhōki*, in Yutani, pp. 100-110, regarding the lists of gifts and reciprocal gifts.

270. See *Ming shi lu*, in Yutani, pp. 137, 138, and 170, concerning the lists of trade goods; and *Boshi nyūminki*, in Yutani, pp.199-200, regarding prices.

271. *Daijōin jisha zōjiki*, cited in Yutani, p. 429 (Kusuba Sainin's entries); Wang, pp. 60-64; and Tanaka, *Chūsei taigai kankeishi*, pp. 153-156. The following sources are excerpted in Yutani: *Kanmon gyoki*, pp. 126-128; and *Mansai jugō nikki*, pp. 111-125.

272. Tamura, pp. 415-424.

273. Regarding the 1453 mission, see the *Inryōken nichiroku* in Yutani, p. 293.

274. Wang, pp. 64-67; *Daijōin jisha zōjiki*, pp. 251-253, in reference to Kusuba Sainin's notes; *Rokuon nichiroku*, pp. 285-286, regarding taxes; and *Ming shi lu*, pp. 170-171, on trade goods.

275. *Zenrin kokuhōki*, in Yutani, pp. 149-155, regarding the gifts and the letter from China about sulfur. In English, see Wang, p. 67. For other sources, see Yutani, pp. 143-175, and 293.

276. The sources are excerpted in Yutani: *Ming shi lu*, pp. 220-221; *Boshi nyūminki*, pp. 198-219, concerning expenses; *Zenrin kokuhōki*, pp. 184-187, and 226; and *Daijōin jisha zōjiki*, p. 250. For other sources, see Yutani, pp. 175-222; and Wang, pp. 67-71.

277. *Zenrin kokuhōki* in Yutani, pp. 223-226; *Zoku zenrin kokuhōki* in Yutani, pp. 227-232; *Ming shi lu* in Yutani, p. 243; *Taishi Wang Duanyi gongzuoyi*, book 4, quoted in Cheng, p. 215; and in English, Wang, pp. 71-72.

278. *Zoku zenrin kokuhōki*, in Yutani, p. 260, translated into English in Wang, pp. 73-74. On the 1483 mission, see also the following sources, all excerpted in Yutani: *Zoku zenrin kokuhōki*, pp. 259-261, regarding the limitation on the number of swords; *Rokuon nichiroku*, pp. 285-287; *Zenrin kokuhōki*, pp. 258-259; *Inryōken nichiroku*, pp. 291-293; and *Riben yijian*, book 7, "Qionghe huahai" section, p. 615.

279. Nakamura, *Nihon to chōsen*, pp. 93-102; and Tamura, pp. 416-425.

280. On the subject of access permits, see Kenneth R. Robinson, "The Tsushima Governor and Regulation of Japanese Access to Chosōn in the Fifteenth and Sixteenth Centuries," *Korean Studies* 20 (1996):23-50.

281. Mori Katsumi and Numata Jirō, eds., *Taigai kankeishi*, pp. 103-110; Tanaka, *Chūsei taigai kankeishi*, pp. 109-122, 138, and 167; Mori and Tanaka, pp. 273-276, and 281; Tanaka, ed., *Dai minkoku to wakō*, pp. 74-85, and 129-131; and Tamura, pp. 171-370.

282. Regarding the expeditions sent in 1427, see Tamura, pp. 193, 203, 292, 308, 337, 375, and 389 (the readings of names were adopted in an arbitrary manner). Regarding the value of trade, see Tamura, p. 425; and Tanaka, *Chūsei taigai kankeishi*, pp. 172-175. I had the opportunity to view the Daihannyakyō at Ankokuji in 1980.

283. See Tanaka, *Chūsei taigai kankeishi*, p.174, regarding the quantities of fabric in the years 1418 to 1425; Tanaka, ed., *Dai minkoku to wakō*, pp. 121-125, concerning the groups from Sumatra, and pp. 150-161, with respect to Ryūkyū; and Charles Haguenauer, "Relations du royaume des Ryūkyū avec les pays des mers du Sud et la Corée," *Bulletin de la Maison Franco-Japonaise* 3 (1931):1-2 .

284. Mori and Tanaka, pp. 274, and 280-281; Tanaka, ed., *Dai minkoku to wakō*, pp. 87, 127-129; and *Haedong chegukki*, 1471.

285. Tanaka, *Chūsei taigai kankeishi*, pp. 167-195, including the letter from the Korean king, p. 169 (drawn from *Sōngjong sillok*, book 2).

286. Tanaka, ed., *Dai minkoku to wakō*, pp. 129-134; and Mori and Tanaka, pp. 278-283. The figure of 1,300 arrivals of Japanese in Korea is based on Tamura (see note 282 above). For the entire fifteenth century, Japanese arrivals in Korea can be estimated at about 4,000 groups.

287. *Daijōin jisha zōjiki*, in Yutani, p. 331.

288. See the sources excerpted in Yutani: including *Jinshin nyūminki*, pp. 365, 371, and 378; *Rokuon nichiroku*, pp. 285-287; and *Inryōken nichiroku*, pp. 291-321. In English see Wang, pp. 74-75.

289. *Jinshin nyūminki* in Yutani, *Nichi-min kangō bōeki shiryō*, pp. 363-381; and *Ming shi lu* in Yutani, pp. 402-403.

290. See the following sources excerpted in Yutani: *Ming shi lu*, pp. 402-406; *Wu xuebian*, p. 417; and *Gen'un monjū*, pp. 399-400. See also *Chouhai tubian*, book 2.

291. *Ekiteiroku* in Yutani, pp. 473-474, in reference to the figures for swords and copper.

292. *Ming shi lu* in Yutani, p. 596.

293. *Sakugen oshō saitoshū* in Yutani, pp. 566-587; *Ming shi lu* in Yutani, pp. 596-597; *Myōchiin monjo* in Yutani, pp. 433-446; and Kobata Atsushi, *Chūsei nisshi tsūkō bōeki shi no kenkyū*, pp. 191-202, regarding tallies.

294. *Da ming huidian*, book 105.

295. *Huang ming jingshi wenbian* in Yutani, p. 631. This is a document authored by the military official Tang Shunzhi (1507-1560), who from 1555 onward was in charge of combating piracy. See also Henry Serruys, *Sino-Mongol Relations during the Ming: The Tribute System and Diplomatic Missions (1400-1600)*.

296. See *Chouhai tubian*, book 2, for the list of products; also see Tanaka, ed., *Dai minkoku to wakō*, pp. 143-149; and Cheng, pp. 194-205, 222-224.

297. Mori and Tanaka, eds., pp. 278 and 283; Tanaka, *Chūsei taigai kankeishi*, pp. 200-204; and Nakamura, *Nihon to chōsen*, pp. 163-173.

298. *Zenrin kokuhōki* in Yutani, p. 226.

299. See *Zoku zenrin kokuhōki* in Yutani, p. 231, regarding the excerpt of Yoshimasa's missive; *Zenrin kokuhōki* in Yutani, pp. 226, 259; *Ming shi lu* in Yutani, p. 243; *Da ming huidian*, chapter 115, concerning rewards given to envoys. See note 258 above for references to Chinese gifts. For more details about coins, see Kobata, *Nihon no kahei*, pp. 38-55. Specialists postulate three reasons for the absence of minting in Japan: the Bakufu lacked authority and credibility; importation was more convenient than minting; and importation permitted the Bakufu to maintain a tight rein over trade.

Yoshimasa enclosed along with his letter of 1476 a list of twelve titles that, with one exception, were duplicates from a list of fifteen titles that had been sent to China in 1468. These works had been recommended to the head of the Bakufu by the monk Zuikei Shūhō and included an array of Song-dynasty works as well as two or three Tang-dynasty titles, although there were none from the Ming Dynasty. Among these titles was an important Song-dynasty literary collection, *Baichuan xuehai*, that had reached Japan in 1433, but was not yet complete. See *Zenrin kokuhōki* in Yutani, pp. 187 and 227; and *Gaun nikkenroku* in Yutani, pp. 158 and 182. Yoshimasa did not requisition any Confucian titles, even though in that era they were much studied in the great Zen monasteries. It was only from the late sixteenth century onward that Japan imported books by contemporary Chinese authors, in particular those of the Neo-Confucianists.

300. On the value of monetary notes, see *Ming shi*, book 81 and *Ming shi lu*, book 15. Regarding the figures, see *Ming shi lu* in Yutani, pp. 170,171, and 220; and Cheng, p. 215. A portion of the 1432 payment, perhaps, was remitted in fabric and silver.

301. *Rokuon nichiroku,* in Yutani, p. 286.

302. See Kawahara Sumiyuki, "Ichijōdani iseki," *Nihon no bijutsu* 214 (1984); Matsushita Masashi, "Kusado-Sengen machi iseki," *Nihon no bijutsu* 215 (April 1984); and Tanaka, ed., *Dai minkoku to wakō,* p. 91. See above in this chapter regarding imports of coins by traffickers.

303. See note 258 above. In the sources, silver is designated either as *baijin* (*shirogane*), or as *jin* (*gin*).

304. *Daijōin jisha zōjiki* in Yutani, p. 251.

305. See note 258 above for references pertaining to gifts. Therein are cited, inter alia, colored silk taffetas (*cai, ayaginu*), embroidered twills, and brocade with gold-leaf applique (*inkin*). All the fabrics are described in detail in *Zenrin kokuhōki* in Yutani, pp. 101-103. Concerning the gifts of monks' robes, see *Ming shi lu* in Yutani, pp. 84 and 86; as well as *Myōchiin monjo* in Yutani, pp. 450 and 454. See also Ogasawara Sae, ed., *Hakusai no senshoku* (Tōkyō: Chūō kōronsha, 1983); and Nishimura, "Orimono."

306. *Daijōin jisha zōjiki* in Yutani, p. 249; Tanaka, ed., *Dai minkoku to wakō,* p. 92. With respect to imports in the mid-sixteenth century, see *Chouhai tubian,* book 2; and above in this chapter.

307. The lists of Chinese gifts (see note 258 above) mention only lacquerware and bronze vessels, except for ten *tenmoku* bowls from Jian with gilt bronze settings noted in a list dated 1406.

308. Regarding Kusuba Sainin's itemized order see *Keikaku shiyōshō* (or *Shiyōshō*), book 26, dated Hōtoku 4 (1452) 5/6, in Yutani, p. 156.

309. See *Shoken nichiroku* in Yutani, pp. 283-284.

310. *Jinshin nyūminki* in Yutani, pp. 370, 373, and 375 (Ryōan Keigo here notes *jiwan* and *hakufun,* "white powder"). See Yabe Yoshiaki, "Tōyō no sometsuke, minchō zenki no sometsuke jiki to nishi ajia," *Kobijutsu* 68 (October 1983):72-87, discussing the *Rokuon nichiroku.*

311. See *Sakugen oshō shotoshū* and *Saitoshū,* in Cheng, pp. 218-222.

312. See *Kundaikan so'u chōki,* dating from the late fifteenth or early sixteenth century.

313. Ishihara Michihiro, "Nihontō ka nanashu," *Ibaragi daigaku bunrigakubu kiyō* 11 (December 1960):17-26. This article quotes three poems featuring Japanese swords as themes, one of which is "Riben dao ge" by Tang Shunzhi, together with texts contained in *Wubei zhi* ("Riben kao"), *Chouhai tubian* ("Wo dao"), *Riben yijian* ("Qionghe huahai" and "Riben dao"). See also p. 76 above.

314. Sources are excerpted in Yutani: *Ming shi lu,* pp. 170 and 171; *Rokuon nichiroku,* p. 287; *Daijōin nikki mokuroku,* p. 157; *Riben yijian,* p. 615; *Jinshin nyūminki,* pp. 367-373, and 378; *Ekiteiroku,* pp. 473 and 474. The *Ming shi lu* notes *gundao* (*kontō,* royal sword) instead of *chōtō,* and *yaodao* (*koshigatana*) for *tachi.*

315. See the tables in the section "The Ashikaga Yoshimasa Era" above.

316. For the references to gifts sent to China, see note 257 above; *Myōchiin monjo* in Yutani, p. 439, gives a detailed description of Motonobu's folding screens; and *Boshi nyūminki* in Yutani, p. 199, cites prices. See also Bettina Geyger-Klein, "Japanese

Kinbyōbu: The Gold-Leafed Folding Screens of the Muromachi Period (1333-1573),"
Artibus Asiae (1984).

317. For the prices, see note 257 above, and the table in the section "The Ashikaga Yoshimasa Era" above. Also see *Ming shi lu*, books 24 and 28, which notes the Yongle emperor's gift of fans to the Prince of Zhou. Regarding the popularity of fans, see *Liangshan motan*, book 18; *Meibutsu rokujō*, 3rd chō, *kizaisen* 5; *Shimai monjo* in *Fukuoka-ken shi shiryō*, 6:176-181 (quotation from "Chōsen sensu" for the years 1588 and 1589); and Ch'oe Sangsu, "Les éventails," *Revue de Corée* 13:2 (1981):63-70. Also see notes 176 and 177 above.

318. *Qixiu leigao*, book 45.

319. Tamura, pp. 422 and 423; *Minkoku to nihon*, exhibition catalog, pp. 9, and 47-51; *Boshi nyūminki* in Yutani, p. 199; *Myōchiin monjo* in Yutani, p. 440; *Ming shi lu* in Yutani, p. 170; *Daijōin nikki mokuroku* in Yutani, p. 157, notes 634 pieces of gold lacquerware.

320. *Boshi nyūminki* in Yutani, p. 200; *Daijōin jisha zōjiki* in Yutani, p. 249; *Ming shi lu* in Yutani, p. 170; *Ekiteiroku* in Yutani, pp. 473, 474. Also see tables on pp. 128-129 above, and *Jinshin nyūminki* in Yutani, p. 371.

321. *Daijōin jisha zōjiki* in Yutani, p. 251.

322. With regard to the organization of foreign trade in the fifteenth century, see appendix 6.

APPENDICES

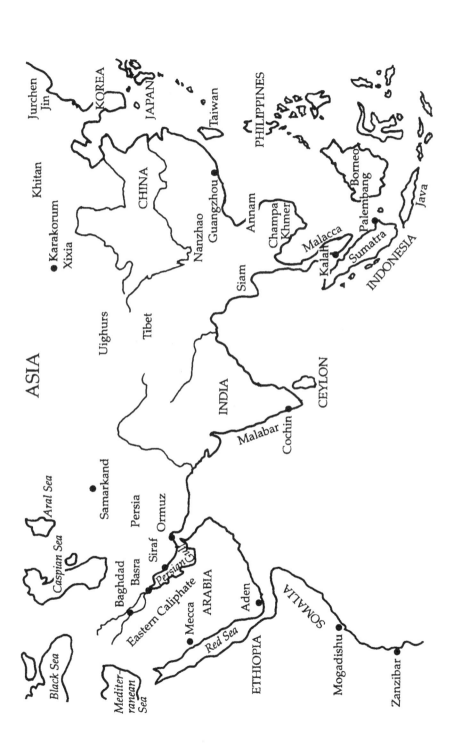

CHINA AND KOREA

JAPAN

N

HONSHŪ

Sea of Japan

OKI ISLANDS

MUTSU

DEWA

SADO ISLAND

ECHIGO

SHIMOTSUKE

KŌZUKE

HITACHI

ETCHŪ

SHINANO

MUSASHI

SHIMOSA

KAGA

HIDA

ECHIZEN

MINO

KAI

SAGAMI

KAZUSA

YAMASHIRO

WAKASA

TANGO

OWARI

TŌTŌMI

SURUGA

IZU

AWA

27

4

OMI

MINO

IGA

OWARI

MIKAWA

TŌTŌMI

2

IZU

TAJIMA

TAMBA

INABA

HARIMA

SETTSU

IZUMO

MIMASAKA

BITCHŪ

BIZEN

13

12

ISE

IWAMI

BINGO

14

AWAJI

IZUMI

7

10

15

KII

AKI

16

SANUKI

AWA

11

TSUSHIMA

NAGATO

SUŌ

Sea

KAWACHI

Iki

IYO

TOSA

19

18

BUZEN

SHIKOKU

CHIKUZEN

Inland

21

HIZEN

BUNGO

20

HIGO

HYŪGA

22

GOTO ISLANDS

CHIKUGO

23

KYŪSHŪ

SATSUMA

24

ŌSUMI

TANEGASHIMA

YAKUSHIMA

Pacific Ocean

1 Kamakura
2 Fuchū
3 Seto
4 Hiei
5 Kyōto/Heian
6 Ōsaka/Naniwa
7 Nara/Heijō
8 Fujiwara-kyō
9 Yoshino
10 Tōnomine
11 Kōya
12 Kōbe/Ōwada/
  Hyōgo/Fukuhara

13 Murotsu
14 Kusado-sengen
15 Onomichi
16 Itsukushima
17 Yamaguchi
18 Hakata
19 Hakozaki
20 Matsura
21 Hirado
22 Aokata
23 Shimazu
24 Bōnotsu
25 Ichijōdani
26 Tsuruga
27 Obama

APPENDIX FOUR
Comparative Number of Japanese and Foreign Groups Exchanged
7th to 16th Centuries

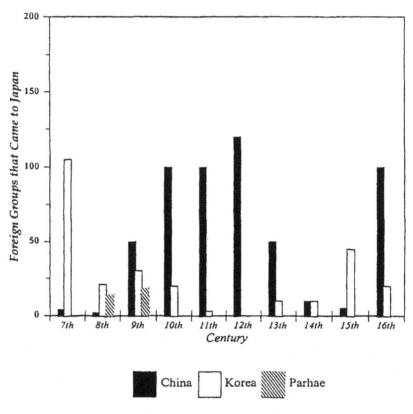

These graphs are based on estimates of the numbers of groups that crossed the ocean in each century. Precise figures are available only for the eighth century and the first half of the fifteenth century. This graph does not take into account the number of boats per group, exchanges with Ryūkyū (14th-15th centuries), Korean piracy (9th century), or the Mongol invasions (13th century). The number of groups dispatched to Korea in the 14th and 15th centuries, and to both Korea and China in the 16th century, include pirates. Furthermore, figures for the 15th and 16th centuries also include Koreans and Chinese who resided in, or acted from, Japan. Similarly, Japanese pirate groups comprised non-Japanese as well. For more precise figures for the 7th-9th centuries, please see note 26. Approximately 4,000 Japanese groups travelled to Korea in the 15th century.

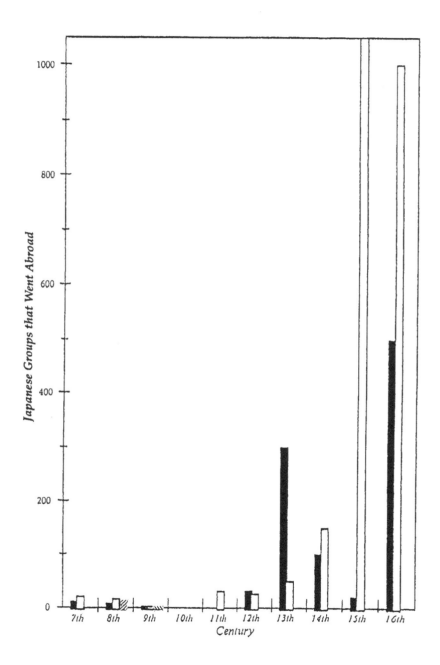

APPENDIX FIVE
Comparison of Official Systems of Foreign Trade
in the 11th Century

CHINA	JAPAN
Free trade	Government monopoly on trade
Trade stimulated by the court	Limitation of arrivals, free trade prohibited
Trade managed by Offices of Maritime Trade	Trade managed by Kyūshū Headquarters
Export of certain items forbidden	Export of weapons forbidden
State monopoly on certain imported items	State preemption of certain imports
Active and passive trade: foreign traders permitted entry, Chinese traders allowed to go overseas	Passive trade: foreign traders arrived in Japan, Japanese subjects forbidden to go overseas
Partners: Korea, Japan, Asia, Orient	Partners: China, Korea
Import taxes	No taxes
Four ports	One main port (Hakata)
Traders were private individuals, they had to finance their travels themselves	Traders enjoyed guest treatment, the costs of their stay were underwritten by the State, the duration of their sojurn in Japan was limited
Export and import	Imports predominate
Price of imports set by the State	Price of imports set by the State
Means of payment: coin	Means of payment: fabric, gold dust

Appendix Six
Comparative Organization of Foreign Trade in the 15th Century

China	Japan	Korea
Government trade monopoly	Free trade (with Korea), trade on behalf of the Bakufu (with China)	Government trade monopoly
Agreements: 2-3 boats, 200-300 persons, arrivals every 10 years	Agreements on the number of Japanese boats departing for Korea	
Trade managed by the State	Trade managed by the Bakufu (for China), by local elites (for Korea)	Trade managed by the State
Prohibition against Chinese leaving the country	Free entry and departure	Prohibition against Koreans leaving the country
Regulation: tallies granted to the Bakufu by the Chinese court	Regulation: access permits from Japanese elites required by the Korean court; traders as government guests	
Traders were members of official missions	Active trade: the Japanese departed for foreign countries	Passive trade: foreign traders came
Traders were guests of the government	Traders were sent by the Bakufu/sponsors	Traders were guests of the government
Imports predominated	Exports predominated	Imports predominated
Partners: tribute-bearing countries	Partners: China, Korea, Ryūkyū	Partners: Japan, Ryūkyū, China, Southeast Asia
No taxes	Taxes on imports (from China), tax on accreditation to depart for Korea	No taxes
Three ports	Several ports	Three ports
Import prices set by the court	Unrestricted prices	Prices set by the court
Means of payment: coins, silver, fabrics		Means of payment: hemp, plain-woven raw silk, cotton, etc.

Several of the respective characteristics of the eleventh-century Chinese and Japanese trade systems had been transposed by the fifteenth century.

Appendix Seven
Table of Principal Trade Goods

	EXPORTED BY JAPAN	IMPORTED INTO JAPAN
7th - 9th Century		
CHINA	silk (plain-woven raw, taffeta, floss, thread), hemp, gold (9th century), pearls	brocade, twill, medicinal and aromatic plants, books, handicrafts (metal, wood, ceramics)
KOREA	silk (plain-woven raw, taffeta, floss, thread)	medicinal and aromatic plants, musk, mineral substances for dyes, handicrafts
PARHAE	silk (plain-woven raw, taffeta, floss, thread)	furs, ginseng, honey
10th - 12th Century		
CHINA	gold, mercury, sulfur, pearls	medicinal and aromatic plants, mineral substances, musk, brocade, twill, ceramics
KOREA	mercury, pearls, sulfur	medicinal and aromatic plants, musk, brocade, twill
13th - 14th Century		
CHINA	gold, mercury, sulfur, pearls, construction wood, swords, gold lacquerware	coins, ceramics, medicinal and aromatic plants, musk, books, objects of curiosity (i.e., paintings, stationery; fabric?)
KOREA	?	?
14th - 16th Century		
CHINA		coins, silver, brocade, satin, other silks, silk thread, metal and lacquer crockery, ceramics, objects of curiosity
KOREA	copper, sulfur, fans, swords, spears, bronze crockery, gold lacquerware, gold, products from Southeast Asia (sapanwood, etc.)	rice, beans, ginseng, textiles (plain-woven raw silk, hemp, ramie, cotton), mats, furs, (silverware and the Buddhist canon for the military leaders)
RYŪKYŪ	?	medicinal and aromatic plants, rhinoceros horn and other products from Southeast Asia

APPENDIX EIGHT
Lists of Products

p. 12　丁香，青木香，薰陸香，甘松香，龍腦香，沈香，麝香，呵藜勒，大黃，人參，甘草，蜜汁，桂心。胡粉，黃丹，同黃，雌黃，朱沙，金青，蘇芳。

p. 27　金銀，綵錢，鉛錫，雜色帛，瓷器，市香藥，犀象，珊瑚，琥珀，珠琲，鑌鐵，氄皮，玳瑁，瑪瑙，車渠，水精，蕃布，烏樠，蘇木等物。

p. 42　翠紋花錦壹疋，小紋綠殊錦壹疋，大紋白綾參疋，麝香貳臍，丁香伍拾兩，沈香伯兩，薰陸香貳拾兩，可梨勒拾兩，石金青參拾兩，光明朱砂伍兩，色色餞紙貳伯幅，絲鞋參足。

p. 51　沈，麝香，衣比，丁子，甘松，薰陸，青木，龍腦，牛頭，雞舌，白檀，赤木，紫檀，蘇芳，陶砂，紅雪，紫雪，金益丹，銀益丹，紫金膏，巴豆，雄黃，可梨勒，檳榔子，銅黃，綠青，燕脂，空青，丹，朱砂，胡粉，豹虎皮，藤茶碗，籠子，犀生角，水牛如意，瑪瑙帶，瑠璃壺，綾，錦，羅，穀，吳竹，甘竹，吹玉等。

p. 68　細色金子，砂金，珠子，藥珠，水銀，鹿耳，茯令。麤色硫黃，螺頭，合罩，松柏，羅板。

p. 70　佛經，納青木函；琥珀，青紅白水晶，紅黑木槵子念珠各一連，並納螺細花形平函；毛籠一，納蝶朴二口；葛籠一，納法蝶二口，染皮二十枚；金銀蒔繪筥一合，納髮鬟二頭，又一合，納參議正四位上藤佐理手書二卷，及進奉物數一卷，表狀一卷；又金銀蒔繪硯一筥一合，納金硯一，鹿毛筆，松烟墨，金銅水瓶，鐵刀；又金銀蒔繪扇筥一合，納繪扇二十枚，蝙蝠扇二枚；螺細梳函一對，其一納赤木梳二百七十，其一納籠骨十蔽；螺細書案一，螺細書几一；金銀蒔繪平筥一合，納白細布吾匹；鹿皮籠一，納狃裝一領；螺鈿鞍轡一副，銅鐵鐙，紅絲鞦，泥障；倭畫屏風一雙；石流黃七百斤。

p. 117　賜王白金一千兩，銅錢一萬吾千緡，錦，紵絲，紗，羅，絹四百一十匹，僧衣十二襲，帷帳，衾裯，器皿若干事；╫賜王妃白金二百五十兩，銅錢五千緡，錦，紵絲，紗羅絹八十四匹。

p. 123　馬貳拾匹　撒金鞘太刀貳把　硫黃壹萬斤　硫腦大小貳拾塊　金屛風參副　鎗壹百柄　黑漆鞘柄太刀壹百把　長刀壹百柄　鎧壹領　硯壹面并匣　扇壹百把

p. 128　蘇木　硫黃　生紅銅　衷刀　腰刀　鎗　扇　抹金銅銚　黑漆泥金麗金嵌螺甸花大小方丹箱盒　╫香壘等器皿　貼金麗金硯匣╫硯銅水滴　花硯小帶刀　印花鹿皮　火筋　延金

p. 135　環刀二，柄丹木三百斤，石硫黃五百斤，箭簇三十個。
正布七十匹，特賜米豆各一百匹，虎皮豹皮各二領，紵布二十匹，雜彩花席三十張，燒酒三十瓶，松子五石

BIBLIOGRAPHY

Primary sources have been arranged by title rather than by author, and notations concerning authorship and publication/compilation dates have been included wherever possible.

A considerable number of the primary sources listed below appear in the following collections:

Dai nihon shiryō. Comp. Tōkyō daigaku shiryō hensanjo. Tōkyō: Tōkyō daigaku, 1901-.
Gunsho ruijū. Comp. Hanawa Hokiichi. 29 vols. Tōkyō: Zoku gunsho ruijū kanseikai, 1959–1960.
Nihon koten bungaku taikei. 100 vols. Tōkyō: Iwanami shoten, 1957–1969.
Nihon shisō taikei. Ishii Susumu et al. 67 vols. Tōkyō: Iwanami shoten, 1970–1982.
Shintei zōho kokushi taikei. Comp. Kuroita Katsumi. 66 vols. Tōkyō: Yoshikawa kōbunkan, 1929–1964.
Zōho shiryō taisei. 50 vols. Kyōto: Rinsen shoten, 1965.

Publication data cited in this bibliography pertain to those editions used in this book and do not necessarily include the most recent editions. Note that primary sources included in only one section of a collection volume cannot be found under their own titles. They will be given as: [Source title]. In [Collection title and volume].

PRIMARY SOURCES

Aogata monjo. 2 vols. Tōkyō: Zoku gunsho ruijū kanseikai, 1975–1976.
Azuma kagami. Early 14th century C.E. In *Shintei zōho kokushi taikei*, vols. 32-33.
Baoqing Siming zhi. Luo Jun. 1225–1227 C.E. In *Song Yuan fangzhi congkan*, vol. 5. Beijing: Zhonghua shuju, 1990.
Bukkō kokushi goroku. Isshin. Late 13th century C.E. In *Taishō shinshū daizōkyō*, vol. 80. Tōkyō: Daizō shuppan, 1924–1935.
Butsu nichian kōmotsu mokuroku. Hōsei. 1363 C.E. In *Kamakura shishi: Shiryō hen*, vol. 5, part 2. Kamakura and Tōkyō: Yoshikawa kōbunkan hatsubai, 1956.
Cefu yuangui. Comp. Wang Qinruo et al. 1013 C.E. 20 vols. Taibei: Qinghua shuju, 1967.

Chōshūki. Minamoto no Morotoki. 1087–1136 C.E. In *Zōho shiryō taisei,* vols. 16–17.

Chosŏn wangjo sillok. 48 vols. Reprint. Seoul: Kuksa p'yŏnch'an wiwŏnhoe, 1955–1958.

Chouhai tubian. Hu Zongxian. 1624 C.E. Original Ming-dynasty edition preserved in the Tōyō Bunko, Tōkyō.

Chōya gunsai. Comp. Miyoshi no Tameyasu. 12th century C.E. In *Shintei zōho kokushi taikei,* vol. 29.

Chūyūki. Fujiwara no Munetada. 1087–1138 C.E. In *Zōho shiryō taisei,* vols. 9–15.

Da ming huidian. Comp. Li Dongyang. 1587 C.E. 5 vols. Taibei: Dongnan shubaoshe, 1963.

Dai nihon komonjo: Hennen monjo. Comp. Tōkyō daigaku shiryō hensanjo. 25 vols. Tōkyō: Tōkyō daigaku shuppankai, 1901–1940.

Engi shiki. Comp. Fujiwara no Tokihira et al. 927 C.E. In *Shintei zōho kokushi taikei,* vol. 26.

Fusō ryakki. Comp. Kōen. 12th century C.E. In *Shintei zōho kokushi taikei,* vol. 12.

Genji monogatari. Murasaki Shikibu. 1001–1010 C.E. In *Nihon koten bungaku taikei,* vols. 14–18.

Genkō shakusho. Kokan Shiren. 1322 C.E. In *Shintei zōho kokushi taikei,* vol. 31.

Genpei seisuiki. Circa 14th century C.E. In *Kōchū nihon bungaku taikei,* vols. 15–16. Tōkyō: Kokumin tosho, 1926.

Gonijō Moromichi ki. Fujiwara no Moromichi. 1083–1099 C.E. 3 vols. In *Dai nihon kokiroku* Tōkyō: Iwanami shoten, 1956–1958.

Gonki. Fujiwara no Yukinari. 991–1011 C.E. In *Zōho shiryō taisei,* vols. 4–5.

Goseibai shikimoku. Hōjō Yasutoki et al. 1232 C.E. In *Nihon shisō taikei,* vol. 21.

Gyokuyō. Kujō Kanezane. 1164–1203 C.E. 3 vols. 1906–1907. Reprint. Tōkyō: Kokusho kankōkai, 1965.

Gyomotsu on'e mokuroku. Nōami. 15th century C.E. In *Dai nihon shiryō* VII: 10:131-137.

Haedong chegukki. Sin Suk-chu. 1471 C.E. Original Korean edition preserved in the Tōyō Bunko, Tōkyō.

Heian ibun. Comp. Takeuchi Rizō. 13 vols. 1963–1974. Reprint. Tōkyō : Tōkyōdō shuppan, 1992.

Honchō monzui. Comp. Fujiwara no Akihira. 1037–1046 C.E. In *Shintei zōho kokushi taikei,* vol. 29.

Honchō seiki. Fujiwara no Michinori. 12th century C.E. In *Shintei zōho kokushi taikei,* vol. 9.

Honchō zokumonzui. Attributed to Fujiwara no Suetsune. 1147–1155(?) C.E. In *Shintei zōho kokushi taikei,* vol. 29.

Hossō shiyō shō. Sakanoue Akikane and Sakanoue Akimoto. Late 12th century C.E. In *Gunsho ruijū,* vol. 6, Ritsuryōbu.

Hou han shu. Comp. Fan Ye. 445 C.E. 18 vols. Beijing: Zhonghua shuju, 1965.

Hyakurenshō. 13th century C.E. In *Shintei zōho kokushi taikei,* vol. 11.

Hyōhanki. Taira no Nobunori. 1132–1171 C.E. In *Zōho shiryō taisei*, vols. 18–22.

Ikoku chōjō no koto. 14th century C.E. In *Dai nihon shiryō* VII: 28, pp. 63–70.

Isei teikin ōrai. 14th century C.E. In *Gunsho ruijū*, vol. 9, Shōsokubu.

Jiu tang shu. Comp. Liu Xu. 945 C.E. 16 vols. Beijing: Zhonghua shuju, 1975.

Kaiqing Siming xuzhi. Mei Yingfa. 1259 C.E. In *Song Yuan fangzhi congkan*, vol. 6. Beijing: Zhonghua shuju, 1990.

Kanchūki. Fujiwara (Kadenokōji) Kanenaka. 1275–1300 C.E. In *Zōho shiryō taisei*, vols. 34–36.

Kenji sannen ki. Late 13th century C.E. Ōta Yasuari. In *Zōho zoku shiryō taisei*, vol. 10.

Kissa ōrai. Late 14th century (?) C.E. In *Gunsho ruijū*, vol. 19, Inshokubu.

Kojidan. Minamoto Akikane. 13th century C.E. In *Shintei zōho kokushi taikei*, vol. 18.

Konjaku monogatarishū. 12th century C.E. In *Nihon koten bungaku taikei*, vols. 22–26.

Koryôsa. Kim Chongsô. 1451 C.E. In *Nihon shiryō shūsei hensankai, Chūgoku-chōsen no shiseki ni okeru nihon shiryō shūsei, sangoku kōrai no bu*. Tōkyō: Kokusho kankōkai, 1978.

Koryôsa chôryo. Kim Chongsô. In *Nihon shiryō shūsei hensankai, Chūgoku-chōsen no shiseki ni okeru nihon shiryō shūsei, sangoku kōrai no bu*. Tōkyō: Kokusho kankōkai, 1978.

Kundaikan so'u chōki. Late 15th or early 16th century C.E. In *Nihon shisō taikei*, vol. 23.

Liangshan motan. Chen Ting. Late 15th century C.E. In *Li Xiling, Xiyinxuan congshu*, vol. 24. Taibei: Yiwen yinshuguan, 1967.

Makura no sōshi. Sei Shōnagon. Ca. 1001 C.E. In *Nihon koten bungaku taikei*, vol. 19.

Meibutsu rokujō. Itō Tōgai. 1714 C.E. 6 vols. Kyōto: Keibunkan nakko, 1721, 1859.

Meigetsuki. Fujiwara no Sadaie. 1180–1235 C.E. 3 vols. Tōkyō: Kokusho kankōkai, 1911–1912.

Midō kanpaku ki. Fujiwara no Michinaga. 998–1021 C.E. 3 vols. In *Dai nihon kokiroku*. Tōkyō: Iwanami shoten, 1952–1954.

Ming shi. Comp. Zhang Tingyu. 1739 C.E. 28 vols. Beijing: Zhonghua shuju, 1974.

Ming shi lu. Comp. Hu Guang et al. 1411–1628 C.E. 69 vols. Nangang: Zhongyang yanjiuyuan lishi yuyan yanjiusuo, 1966.

Minkeiki. Fujiwara Tsunemitsu. 1226–1272 C.E. 7 vols. In *Dai nihon kokiroku*, Tōkyō: Iwanami shoten, 1975- .

Moromori ki. Nakahara Moromori. 1339–1374 C.E. 11 vols. In Fujii Sadafumi and Kobayashi Hanako, eds. *Shiryō sanshū*. Tōkyō: Zoku gunsho ruijū kanseikai, 1968–1982.

Murasaki shikibu nikki. Murasaki Shikibu. Circa 1010 C.E. In *Nihon koten bungaku taikei*, vol. 19.

Nihon kiryaku. 11th–12th century C.E. In *Shintei zōho kokushi taikei*, vols. 10–11.

Nihon kōki. Fujiwara no Fuyutsugu et al. 840 C.E. In *Shintei zōho kokushi taikei,* vol. 3.

Nihon Montoku Tennō jitsuroku. Fujiwara no Mototsune et al. 878 C.E. In *Shintei zōho kokushi taikei,* vol. 3.

Nihon sandai jitsuroku. Fujiwara no Tokihira et al. 901 C.E. In *Shintei zōho kokushi taikei,* vol. 4.

Nihon shoki. Toneri Shinnō et al. 720 C.E. In *Shintei zōho kokushi taikei,* vol. 1.

Nihonkoku genzaisho mokuroku. Fujiwara no Sukeyo. Circa 891 C.E. In *Nihonkoku genzaisho mokuroku kaisetsu kō.* Tōkyō: Komiyama shoten, 1976.

Nosongdong Ilbon haengnok. Song Hu-gyông. 1420 C.E. In Murai Shōsuke, trans. *Rōshōdō nihon kōroku: Chōsen shisetsu no mita chūsei no nihon.* Tōkyō: Iwanami shoten, 1987.

Ouyang wenzhonggong ji. Ouyang Xiu. 11th century C.E. Qing-dynasty Kangxi imperial edition preserved in the Tōyō Bunko, Tōkyō.

Qixiu leigao. Lang Ying et al. 16th century and 1880 C.E. Qing-dynasty edition preserved in the Tōyō Bunko, Tōkyō.

Ruiju kokushi. Comp. Sugawara no Michizane. 892 C.E. In *Shintei zōho kokushi taikei,* vols. 5–6.

Ruiju sandai kyaku. 11th century C.E. In *Shintei zōho kokushi taikei,* vol. 25.

Sakeiki. Minamoto no Tsuneyori. 1016–1036 C.E. In *Zōho shiryō taisei,* vol. 6.

Samguk sagi. Comp. Kim Pu-sik. Mid-12th century C.E. In Nihon shiryō shūsei hensankai, *Chūgoku-chōsen no shiseki ni okeru nihon shiryō shūsei, sangoku kōrai no bu.* Tōkyō: Kokusho kankōkai, 1978.

Samuraidokoro satahen. In *Gunsho ruijū,* vol. 22, Bukebu.

San tendai godaisan ki. Jōjin. 1072–1073 C.E. In *Dai nihon bukkyō zensho,* vol. 115. Tōkyō: Bussho kankōkai, 1979.

Sankaiki. Nakayama Tadachika. 1151–1195 C.E. In *Zōho shiryō taisei,* vols. 26–28.

Sennyūji fukaki hōshi den. Shinzui. 1244 C.E. In *Dai nihon bukkyō zensho,* vol. 115. Tōkyō: Bussho kankōkai, 1979.

Shimai monjo. In *Fukuoka-ken shi shiryō,* vol. 6. Fukuoka: Fukuoka-ken, 1932–1943.

Shimazu-ke monjo. 3 vols. In *Dai nihon komonjo.* Tōkyō: Tōkyō daigaku shiryō hensanjo, 1942–1943.

Shinsarugakuki. Attributed to Fujiwara no Akihira. 11th century C.E. Tōkyō: Heibonsha, 1983.

Shinsen shōjiroku. Manta Shinnō et al. 815 C.E. In Saeki Arikiyo. *Shinsen shōjiroku no kenkyū,* 10 vols. Tōkyō: Yoshikawa kobunkan, 1962–2001.

Shōichi kokushi nenpu. Comp. Tetsugyū Enshin. 1281 C.E. In *Dai nihon bukkyō zensho,* vol. 95. Tōkyō: Bussho kankōkai, 1912–1922.

Shoku nihon kōki. Fujiwara no Yoshifusa et al. 869 C.E. In *Shintei zōho kokushi taikei,* vol. 3.

Shoku nihongi. Ishikawa no Natari et al. 797 C.E. In *Shintei zōho kokushi taikei,* vol. 2.

Shōyūki. Fujiwara no Sanesuke. 978–1032 C.E. 3 vols. In *Zōho shiryō taisei,* bekkan. Tōkyō: Iwanami shoten, 1959–1986.

Sochiki. Minamoto no Tsunenobu. 1065–1088 C.E. In *Zōho shiryō taisei,* vol. 5.

Song shi. Comp. Tuo Tuo. 1345 C.E. 20 vols. Beijing: Zhonghua shuju, 1977.

Sui shu. Comp. Wei Zheng. 656 C.E. 6 vols. Beijing: Zhonghua shuju, 1973.

Suisaki. Minamoto no Toshifusa. 1062–1086 C.E. In *Zōho shiryō taisei,* vol. 8.

Taiheiki. 14th–15th century C.E. In *Nihon koten bungaku taikei,* vols. 34-36.

Taihō ritsuryō. Fujiwara no Fuhito et al. 701 C.E. In *Nihon shisō taikei,* vol. 3.

Taiki. Fujiwara no Yorinaga. 1136–1155 C.E. In *Zōho shiryō taisei,* vols. 23-25.

Teikin ōrai. Attributed to Gen'ei. 14th century C.E. In Ishikawa Matsutarō, ed. *Tōyō bunko* 242. Tōkyō: Heibonsha, 1973.

Teishinkō ki. Fujiwara no Tadahira. 907–948 C.E. In *Dai nihon kokiroku,* vol. 8. Tōkyō: Iwanami shoten, 1956.

Tōfukuji monjo. 5 vols. In *Dai nihon komonjo,* Iewake. Tōkyō: Tōkyō daigaku shiryō hensanjo, 1956–1972.

Tsurezuregusa. Yoshida Kenkō. Ca. 1330–1335 C.E. In *Nihon koten bungaku taikei,* vol. 30.

Uji shūi monogatari. Ca. 13th century C.E. In *Nihon koten bungaku taikei,* vol. 27.

Ukaikishō. Sanjōnishi Kin'eda. 1517 C.E. In *Zōho shiryō taisei,* vol. 25.

Unshū shōsoku. Fujiwara no Akihira. 11th century C.E. In *Gunsho ruijū,* vol. 9, Shōsokubu.

Utsubo monogatari. Anonymous. 10th–11th century C.E. In *Nihon koten bungaku taikei,* vols. 10-12.

Wei shu. Comp. Wei Shou. 554 C.E. 8 vols. Beijing: Zhonghua shuju, 1974.

Wenguo wenzheng Sima Guang ji. 12th century C.E. Qing-dynasty Kangxi imperial edition preserved in the Tōyō Bunko, Tōkyō.

Xin tang shu. Comp. Ouyang Xiu et al. 1060 C.E. 20 vols. Beijing: Zhonghua shuju, 1975.

Xu zizhi tongjian changbian. Li Tao. 12th century C.E. Beijing: Zhonghua shuju, 1979.

Yōkōki. By Hamuro Tadatsugu. 1230–1249 C.E. In *Shiryō sanshū.* Tōkyō: Zoku gunsho ruijū kanseikai, 1971–

Yuan dianzhang. 1322 C.E. Beijing: Zhongguo shudian, 1990.

Yuan shi. Comp. Song Lian et al. 1369–1370 C.E. 15 vols. Beijing: Zhonghua shuju, 1976.

Yuehaiguan zhi. Liang Tingnan. 19th century C.E. Qing-dynasty edition preserved in the Tōyō Bunko, Tōkyō.

Zenrin kokuhōki. Zuikei Shūhō. 1470 C.E. In Hanawa Hokiichi, comp. *Zoku gunsho ruijū,* vol. 30, part 1. Tōkyō: Zoku gunsho ruijū kanseikai, 1974.

Zhizheng Siming xuzhi. Wang Yuan'gong. 1341–1367 C.E. In *Song Yuan fangzhi congkan,* vol. 7. Beijing: Zhonghua shuju, 1990.

Zhufan zhi. Zhao Rugua. 1225 C.E. Taibei: Taiwan shangwu yinshuguan, 1940, 1967.

SECONDARY SOURCES (AS IN THE ORIGINAL EDITION)

Akiyama Ken, et al., eds. *Heian*. In *Zusetsu nihon bunka no rekishi*, vol. 4. Tōkyō: Shōgakkan, 1979.

Arakawa Hirokazu. "Makie." *Nihon no bijutsu* 35 (March 1969). Special issue.

Balazs, Étienne. "Beiträge zur Wirtschaftsgeschichte der T'ang-Zeit (618–906)." *Mitteilungen des Seminars für Orientalische Sprachen* 34 (1931): 1-92; 35 (1932): 1-73; 36 (1933): 1-62.

Bauer, Wolfgang, ed. *China und die Fremden: 3000 Jahre Auseinandersetzung in Krieg und Frieden*. Munich: Beck, 1980.

Beaujard, André, trans. *Notes de chevet*, Paris: Gallimard, 1966.

Cheng Liang-sheng. *Min-nichi kankeishi no kenkyū*. Tōkyō: Yūzankaku, 1985.

Ch'oe Sangsu. "Les éventails." *Revue de Corée* 13:2 (1981): 63-70.

Cordier, Henri, and Sir Henry Yule, trans. *The Travels of Marco Polo: The Complete Yule-Cordier Edition*. New York: Dover Publications, 1993.

Earle, Joe, trans. *The Japanese Sword*. Tōkyō and New York: Kōdansha International, 1983.

Gernet, Jacques. *Le monde chinois*. Paris: A. Colin, 1972.

Geyger-Klein, Bettina. "Japanese Kinbyōbu: The Gold-Leafed Folding Screens of the Muromachi Period (1333–1573)." *Artibus Asiae* (1984). Special issue.

Haguenauer, Charles. "Relations du royaume des Ryūkyū avec les pays des mers du Sud et la Corée." *Bulletin de la Maison Franco-Japonaise* III: 1-2 (1931): 4-16.

Hayashi Ryōichi. *The Silkroad and the Shōsōin*. In *The Heibonsha Survey of Japanese Art*, vol. 6 . New York: Weatherhill, 1975.

Hayashiya Shōzō. "Chawan." *Nihon no bijutsu* 14 (June 1967). Special issue.

Hérail, Francine. "La circulation des biens au Japon aux Xᵉ et XIᵉ siècles." Unpublished seminar paper. Paris: École Pratique des Hautes Études, 1983.

_____, trans. *Notes journalières de Fujiwara no Michinaga, ministre à la cour de Heian (995–1018): Traduction du Midō kanpaku ki*. 3 vols. Geneva: Droz, 1987–1991.

Hirth, Friedrich, and W. W. Rockhill, trans. *Chau Ju-kua: His Work on the Chinese and Arab Trade in the Twelfth and Thirteenth Centuries, Entitled Chu-fan-chi*. 1911. Reprint. Taibei: Ch'eng-wen Publishing, 1967.

Hunter, Dard. *Papermaking: The History and Technique of an Ancient Craft*. 1943. Reprint. New York: Dover Publications, 1978.

Ikeda On. "Gudai Riben shequ Zhongguo dianji wenti." In *International Conference on Sinology*, ed. *Zhongyang yanjiuyuan guoji Hanxue huiyi lunwenji*, part 1 (lishi kaogu). Taibei: Academia Sinica, 1981.

_____. "Zenkindai tōa ni okeru kami no kokusai kōryū." In Tōhō gakkai, ed. *Tōhō gakkai sōritsu yonjisshūnen kinen Tōhōgaku ronshū.* Tōkyō: Tōhō gakkai, 1987.

Ishihara Michihiro. "Nihontō ka nanashu." *Ibaragi daigaku bunrigakubu kiyō* 11 (December 1960): 17-26.

Ishii Masatoshi. "Chronicle of Sino-Japanese Relations in the Heian Period." Japanese unpublished file, 1981.

Ishii Masatoshi, and Kawagoe Yasuhiro, eds. *Zōho kaitei nitchū kankei kenkyū bunken mokuroku.* 1976. 2nd ed. Tōkyō: Kokusho kankōkai, 1996.

Ishino Tōru, ed. *Nara.* In *Zusetsu nihon bunka no rekishi,* vol. 3. Tōkyō: Shōgakkan, 1979.

Jugaku Bunshō. *Nihon no kami.* Tōkyō: Yoshikawa kōbunkan, 1967.

Kawada Sadamu. "Raden." *Nihon no bijutsu* 211 (December 1983). Special issue.

Kawahara Sumiyuki. "Ichijōdani iseki." *Nihon no bijutsu* 214 (1984). Special issue.

Kawahara Yoshirō. *Sōdai shakai keizaishi kenkyū.* Tōkyō: Keisō shobō, 1980.

Kimiya Yasuhiko. *Nikka bunka kōryūshi.* 1955. Reprint. Tōkyō: Fuzanbō, 1977.

Kimiya Yukihiko. *Nissō sō chōnen no kenkyū: shu to shite sono zuishinhin to shōraihin.* Tōkyō: Kashima shuppankai, 1983.

Kobata Atsushi. *Chūsei nisshi tsūkō bōekishi no kenkyū.* 1941. Reprint. Tōkyō: Tōkō shoin, 1969.

_____. *Nihon no kahei.* Tōkyō: Shibundō, 1958.

Kobayashi Yukio. *Kodai no gijutsu.* 1962. Reprint. Tōkyō: Hanawa shobō, 1994.

Kokushi daijiten henshū iinkai, ed. *Kokushi daijiten.* 15 vols. Tōkyō: Yoshikawa kōbunkan, 1979-1997.

Kuwabara Jitsuzō. "On P'u Shou-keng." *Memoirs of the Research Department of the Tōyō Bunko* 2 (1928): 1-79.

Matsushita Masashi. "Kusado-Sengen machi iseki." *Nihon no bijutsu* 215 (April 1984). Special issue.

Mélanges offerts à Charles Haguenauer, en l'honneur de son quatre-vingtième anniversaire: Études japonaises. Paris: Asiathèque, 1980.

Mende, Erling von. *China und die Staaten auf der koreanischen Halbinsel bis zum 12 Jahrhundert: Eine Untersuchung zur Entwicklung der Formen zwischenstaatlicher Beziehungen in Ostasien.* Wiesbaden: Steiner, 1982.

Minkoku to nihon. Exhibition catalog. Ōsaka: Ōsaka shiritsu hakubutsukan, 1986.

Mori Katsumi. *Nissō bōeki no kenkyū.* Tōkyō: Kokuritsu shoin, 1948.

_____. *Nissō bunka kōryū no shomondai.* Tōkyō: Tōkō shoin, 1950.

_____. *Kentōshi.* 1955. Reprint. Tōkyō: Shibundō, 1966.

_____. "Nitchū bunka no kōryū." *Gekkan bunkazai* 62 (November 1968): 10-16.

_____. *Zoku nissō bōeki no kenkyū.* In *Mori Katsumi chosaku senshū,* vol. 2. 1975. Reprint. Tōkyō: Kokusho kankōkai, 1986.

_____. *Zokuzoku nissō bōeki no kenkyū.* In *Mori Katsumi chosaku senshū,* vol. 3. 1975. Reprint. Tōkyō: Kokusho kankōkai, 1986.

Mori Katsumi, and Tanaka Takeo, eds. *Kaigai kōshōshi no shiten,* vol. 1. Tōkyō: Nihon shoseki, 1975.

Mori Katsumi, and Numata Jirō, eds. *Taigai kankeishi.* Tōkyō: Yamakawa shuppansha, 1978.

Morris, Ivan I. *The World of the Shining Prince: Court Life in Ancient Japan.* 1964. Reprint. Rutland, Vt.: Charles E. Tuttle, 1978.

Morris, V. Dixon. "Sakai: From Shōen to Port City." In John Whitney Hall and Toyoda Takeshi, eds. *Japan in the Muromachi Age.* Berkeley: University of California Press, 1977.

Nagata Seiji. "Ōgi no hensen to kinsei kami ōgi ni tsuite." *Kobijutsu* 75 (July 1985): 4-52.

Nakamura Hidetaka. *Nissen kankeishi no kenkyū.* 3 vols. Tōkyō: Yoshikawa kōbunkan, 1965-1969.

_____. *Nihon to chōsen.* Tōkyō: Shibundō, 1966.

Nakamura Kiyoe. *Nihon no ōgi.* Kyōto: Kawahara shoten, 1942.

Nakazawa Fujio et al. "Sō gen no tōji kōeki." *Kobijutsu* 68 (October 1983): 52-71.

Netolitsky, Almut, trans. *Das Ling-wai tai-ta von Chou Ch'ü-fei: Eine Landeskunde Südchinas aus den 12. Jahrheindert.* Wiesbaden: Steiner, 1977.

Nihon shiryō shūsei hensankai. *Chūgoku-chōsen no shiseki ni okeru nihon shiryō shūsei, seishi no bu.* 2 vols. Tōkyō: Kokusho kankōkai, 1975-1976.

_____. *Chūgoku-chōsen no shiseki ni okeru nihon shiryō shūsei, sangoku kōrai no bu.* Tōkyō: Kokusho kankōkai, 1978.

Nishimura Heibe. "Orimono." *Nihon no bijutsu* 12 (April 1967). Special issue.

Ogasawara Sae, ed. *Hakusai no senshoku.* Tōkyō: Chūō kōronsha, 1983.

Omori, Annie Shepley, and Kochi Doi, trans. *Diaries of Court Ladies of Old Japan.* Boston: Houghton Mifflin, 1920.

Osa Setsuko. *Chūsei nitchō kankei to Tsushima.* Tōkyō: Yoshikawa kōbunkan, 1987.

Paul-David, Madeleine. "L'évolution de la céramique japonaise de l'époque des grandes sépultures à celle de Heian," in *Mélanges offerts à M. Charles Haguenauer, en l'honneur de son quatre-vingtième anniversaire: Études japonaises.* Paris: Asiathèque, 1980.

Ragué, Beatrix von. *Geschichte der japanischen Lackkunst.* Berlin: W. de Gruyter, 1967.

Reischauer, Edwin O. *Ennin's Travels in T'ang China.* New York: Ronald Press, 1955.

Rossabi, Morris, ed. *China among Equals: The Middle Kingdom and Its Neighbors, 10th-14th Centuries.* Berkeley: University of California Press, 1983.

Samurai. Exhibition catalog. Brussels: Credit Communal de Belgique, 1984.

Satō Kanzan. "Tōken." *Nihon no bijutsu* 6 (October 1966). Special issue.

Satō Shinichi and Ikeuchi Yoshisuke, eds. *Chūsei hōsei shiryōshū,* vol. 1. Tōkyō: Iwanami shoten, 1955.

Schafer, Edward. *The Golden Peaches of Samarkand: A Study of T'ang Exotics.* 1963. Reprint. Berkeley: University of California Press, 1985.

Schurmann, Herbert Franz. *Economic Structure of the Yüan Dynasty: Translation of Chapters 93 and 94 of the Yüan shih.* Cambridge, Mass.: Harvard University Press, 1967.

Seidensticker, Edward G., trans. *The Tale of Genji.* New York: Alfred A. Knopf, 1987.

Serruys, Henry. *Sino-Mongol Relations during the Ming: The Tribute System and Diplomatic Missions (1400–1600).* Brussels: Institut Belge des Hautes Études Chinoises, 1967.

Shiba Yoshinobu. *Sōdai shōgyōshi kenkyū.* Tōkyō: Kazama shobō, 1968.

Shōsōinten mokuroku. Exhibition catalog. Nara: Nara kokuritsu hakubutsukan, 1981.

Sō gen bunka to Kanazawa bunkoten. Exhibition catalog. Yokohama: Kanagawa kenritsu Kanazawa bunko, 1977.

Tamura Hiroyuki. *Chūsei nitchō bōeki no kenkyū.* Kyōto: Sanwa shobō, 1967.

Tanaka Takeo. *Chūsei kaigai kōshōshi no kenkyū.* Tōkyō: Tōkyō daigaku shuppankai, 1959.

_____. *Chūsei taigai kankeishi.* Tōkyō: Tōkyō daigaku shuppankai, 1975.

_____. *Taigai kankei to bunka kōryū.* Kyōto: Shibunkaku shuppan, 1982.

_____, ed. *Kamakura bakufu to mōko shūrai.* In *Kaigai shiten nihon no rekishi,* vol. 6. Tōkyō: Gyōsei, 1986.

_____, ed. *Dai minkoku to wakō.* In *Kaigai shiten nihon no rekishi,* vol. 7. Tōkyō: Gyōsei, 1986.

_____, ed. *Nihon zenkindai no kokka to taigai kankei.* Tōkyō: Yoshikawa kōbunkan, 1987.

_____, and Ishii Masatoshi et al. *Kentōshi kenkyū to shiryō.* Tōkyō: Tōkai daigaku shuppankai, 1987.

Tanaka Takeo, and Robert Sakai. "Japan's Relations with Overseas Countries." In John Whitney Hall and Toyoda Takeshi, eds. *Japan in the Muromachi Age.* Berkeley: University of California Press, 1977.

Tōkyō kokuritsu hakubutsukan. *Shin'an kaitei hikiage bunbutsu: The Sunken Treasures off the Sinan Coast.* Exhibition Catalog. Nagoya: Chūnichi shinbunsha, 1983.

Toyoda Takeshi, et al., eds. *Ryūtsūshi.* 2 vols. Tōkyō: Yamakawa shuppansha, 1969–1975.

Tsuchida Naoshige, et al., eds. *Kaigai shiten nihon no rekishi.* 15 vols. Tōkyō: Gyōsei, 1986–1987.

Tsuchida Naoshige, and Ishii Masatoshi, eds. *Kentōshi to Shōsōin.* In *Kaigai shiten Nihon no rekishi,* vol. 4. Tōkyō: Gyōsei, 1986.

_____, eds. *Heian bunka no kaika.* In *Kaigai shiten nihon no rekishi,* vol. 5. Tōkyō: Gyōsei, 1987.

Umehara Kaoru. *Sō ōchō to shinbunka.* In *Zusetsu chūgoku no rekishi,* vol. 5. 1977. Reprint. Tōkyō: Kōdansha, 1981.

Uwayokote Masataka, ed. *Kamakura.* In *Zusetsu nihon bunka no rekishi,* vol. 5. Tōkyō: Shōgakkan, 1979.

Verschuer, Charlotte von. *Les relations officielles du Japon avec la Chine aux VIIIe et IXe siècles.* Geneva, Paris: Droz, 1985.

_____. *Le commerce extérieur du Japon des origines au XVIe siècle.* Paris : Maisonneuve & Larose, 1988.

Wada Hisatoko. "Nanbansen no nihon kaigan raichaku." In Tanaka Takeo, ed. *Dai minkoku to wakō.* In *Kaigai shiten nihon no rekishi,* vol. 7. Tōkyō: Gyōsei, 1986.

Wada Sei, and Ishihara Michihiro, trans. *Gishi wajin den, Gokanjo wa den, Sōsho wakoku den, Zuisho wakoku den.* Tōkyō: Iwanami shoten, 1951.

Wada Sei, and Ishihara Michihiro, eds. *Kyū Tōjo wakoku nihon den, Sōshi nihon den, Genshi nihon den.* 1956. Reprint. Tōkyō: Iwanami shoten, 1986.

Wang Yi-t'ung. *Official Relations between China and Japan, 1368–1549.* Cambridge, Mass.: Harvard University Press, 1953.

Washi no bi. Exhibition catalog. Tōkyō: Suntory bijutsukan, 1983.

Weapons and Armor of Ancient Japan. Exhibition catalog. Paris: Cernuschi Museum, 1979–1980.

Wei Jung-chi [Gi Eikichi]. *Gen nichi kankeishi no kenkyū.* Tōkyō: Kyōiku shuppan senta, 1985.

Yabe Yoshiaki. "Tōyō no sometsuke, Minchō zenki no sometsuke jiki no nishi ajia." *Kobijutsu* 68 (October 1983): 72-87.

_____. "Tōji chūsei hen." *Nihon no bijutsu* 236 (January 1986). Special issue.

Yutani Minoru. *Nichi min kangō bōeki shiryō.* Tōkyō: Kokusho kankōkai, 1983.

Newly Added Secondary Sources: A Selective Bibliography

Adami, Norbert R. *Bibliography on Parhae: A Medieval State in the Far East.* Wiesbaden: Harrassowitz Verlag, 1994.

Akiyama Kenzō. *Nisshi kōshō shiwa.* Tōkyō: Nagai shoseki kabushiki kaisha, 1935.

Amino Yoshihiko. *Chūsei saikō: Rettō no chiiki to shakai.* Tōkyō: Nihon edita sukūru, 1986.

_____. "Kitaguni no shakai to nihonkai." In Amino Yoshihiko, et al., eds. *Nihonkai to hokkoku bunka. Umi to rettō bunka,* vol. 1. Tōkyō: Shōgakkan, 1990.

Andō Kōsei. *Ganjin daiwajōden no kenkyū.* Tōkyō: Heibonsha, 1960.

Araki Kazunori. "16 seiki zenhan Tsushima no seihen to sanpo no ran." *Higashi Ajia to Nihon* 2 (February 2005).

Arano Yasunori. "Kokusai ninshiki to taminzokukan." In Rekishi kagaku kyōgikai, ed., *Gendai o ikiru rekishi kagaku*, vol. 2. Tōkyō: Ōtsuki shoten, 1987.

Arano Yasunori, Ishii Masatoshi, and Murai Shōsuke, eds. *Ajia no naka no nihonshi*. 6 vols. Tōkyō: Tōkyō daigaku shuppankai, 1992–1993.

Batten, Bruce. "Foreign Threat and Domestic Reform: The Emergence of the Ritsuryō State." *Monumenta Nipponica* 41:2 (Summer 1986): 199–219.

_____. "Provincial Administration in Early Japan: From *Risturyō kokka* to *Ōchō kokka*." *Harvard Journal of Asiatic Studies* 53: 1 (1993): 103–134.

_____. *To the Ends of Japan: Premodern Frontiers, Boundaries, and Interactions*. Honolulu: Hawaii University Press, 2003.

Best, Jonathan W. "Diplomatic and Cultural Contacts between Paekche and China." *Harvard Journal of Asiatic Studies* 42: 2 (1982): 443-501.

Borgen, Robert. "The Japanese Mission to China of 801-806." *Monumenta Nipponica* 37:1 (Spring 1982): 1-28.

_____. "The Case of the Plagiaristic Journal: A Curious Passage from Jōjin's Diary." In Aileen Gatten and Anthony Hood Chambers, eds. *New Leaves: Studies and Translations of Japanese Literature in Honor of Edward Seidensticker*. Ann Arbor: Center for Japanese Studies, University of Michigan, 1993.

_____. *Sugawara no Michizane and the Early Heian Court*. 1986. Reprint. Honolulu: University of Hawaii Press, 1994.

_____. "Japanese Nationalism: Ancient and Modern." *Annual Report of the Institute for International Studies* [Meiji Gakuin University] 1 (December 1998): 49-59.

Bussho kankōkai, ed. *Yūhōhōden sōsho*. In *Dai nihon bukkyō zensho*, vols. 113-116. 1915–1922 Reprint. Tōkyō: Daiichi shobō, 1979.

Dazaifu-shi hensan iinkai, ed. *Dazaifushi-shi, Kodai shiryōhen*. Dazaifu: Dazaifu-shi, 2005.

Dykstra, Yoshiko, trans. *The Konjaku Tales*. 6 vols. Honolulu: Kanji Press, 2004 (Distributed by University of Hawai'i Press).

Emori Susumu. "Jūsan-jūroku seiki no tōhoku ajia to ainu minzoku." In Haga Norihiko, ed. *Kita nihon chūseishi no kenkyū*. Tōkyō: Yoshikawa kōbunkan, 1990.

Enomoto Wataru. "Nihon ensei igo ni okeru gen-chō no wa-sen taisaku." *Nihonshi kenkyū* 470 (October 2001): 58-82.

_____. "Minshū shihakushi to higashi shinakai kōtsūken." *Rekishigaku kenkyū* 756 (November 2001): 12-22.

_____. "Gen matsu nairanki no nichi-gen kōtsū." *Tōyō gakuhō* 84: 1 (June 2002): 1-31.

Fairbank, John King, ed. *The Chinese World Order: Traditional China's Foreign Relations*. Cambridge, Mass.: Harvard University Press, 1968.

Fujita Akiyoshi. "Jūgoseiki no utsuryōtō to nihonkai seiiki no kōryū." *Kōbe daigaku shigaku nenpō* 8 (1993): 23-48.

Fujiyoshi Masumi. "Jōjin to Yō Bunkō dan'en." In Kansai daigaku tōzai gakujutsu kenkyūjo, ed. *Kansai daigaku tōzai gakujutsu kenkyūjo sōritsu sanjisshūnen kinen ronbunshū*. Suita: Kansai daigaku shuppanbu, 1981.

_____. "Nissō kōtsūro no saikentō (zoku): San tendai godaisan ki sakki 2." *Shisen* 67 (March 1988): 1-18.

_____. "Fuki no kyaku." In Nakanishi Susumu and Ō Yū, eds. *Jinbutsu. Nitchū bunka kōryūshi sōsho*, vol. 10. Tōkyō: Taishūkan, 1996.

_____, trans. *Shobanshi (Zhufan zhi)*. Ōsaka: Kansai daigaku shuppanbu, 1991.

Goble, Andrew Edmund. "War and Injury: The Emergence of Wound Medicine in Medieval Japan." *Monumenta Nipponica* 60: 3 (Autumn 2005).

Hamada Kōsaku. *Shiragikoku shi no kenkyū, higashi ajia no shiten kara*. Tōkyō: Yoshikawa kōbunkan, 2002.

Han-Il kwan'gyesa yôn'guhoe. *Han-Il kwan'gyesa nonjô mongnok*. Seoul: Hyônômsa, 1993.

Hashimoto Yū. "Muromachi-sengokuki no shōgun kenryoku to gaikōken." *Rekishigaku kenkyū* 708 (March 1998): 1-18.

_____. *Chūsei nihon no kokusai kankei*. Tōkyō: Yoshikawa kōbunkan, 2005.

Hattori Hideo. "Sō bōeki no jittai—shokoku raichaku no ikyakutachi to 'chinatown' tōbō." *Higashi ajia to nihon* 2 (February 2005).

Herbert, Penelope A. "Japanese Embassies and Students in T'ang China." Nedlands: University of Western Australia Centre for East Asian Studies, Occasional Paper no. 4, n.d.

Hirano Kunio. *Taika zendai shakai soshiki no kenkyū*. Tōkyō: Yoshikawa kōbunkan, 1969.

Hokkaidō Tōhokushi Kenkyūkai, ed. *Kita kara no nihonshi*. 2 vols. Tōkyō: Sanseidō, 1988–1990.

Hotate Michihisa. "Tora, Onigashima to Nihonkai kaiikishi." In Toda Yoshimi, ed. *Chūsei no seikatsu kūkan*. Tōkyō: Yūhikaku, 1993.

I Yon. *Wakō to nichi-rei kankeishi*. Tōkyō: Tōkyō daigaku shuppankai, 1999.

Ishihara Michihiro. "Chūgoku ni okeru nihonkan no tenkai." *Shigaku zasshi* 59: 12 (December 1950).

Ishii Masatoshi. *Nihon-bokkai kankeishi no kenkyū*. Tōkyō: Yoshikawa kōbunkan, 2001.

_____, et al. "Kodai nitchū kankei hennen shiryōkō." In Mozai Torao et al., eds. *Kentōshi kenkyū to shiryō*. Tōkyō: Tōkai daigaku shuppankai, 1987.

_____. "Iwayuru kentōshi no teishi ni tsuite." *Chūo daigaku bungakubu kiyō* 136 (February 1990).

_____. "Gaikō kankei: Kentōshi o chūshin ni." In Ikeda On, ed. *Kodai o kangaeru: Tō to nihon*. Tōkyō: Yoshikawa kōbunkan, 1992.

_____. "Jūsseiki no kokusai hendō to nissō bōeki." In Tamura Kōichi and Suzuki Yasutami, eds. *Ajia kara mita kodai, Shinpan kodai no nihon*, vol. 2. Tōkyō: Kadokawa shoten, 1992.

_____. "Nissō junreisō." In Arano Yasunori, Ishii Masatoshi, and Murai Shōsuke, eds. *Ajia no naka no nihonshi*, vol. 5. Tōkyō: Tōkyō daigaku shuppankai, 1992–1993.

_____. "Zenrin kokuhōki." In Tanaka Takeo, ed. *Zenrin kokuhōki, Shintei zoku zenrin kokuhōki*. Tōkyō: Shūeisha, 1995.

Ishimoda Shō. *Nihon no kodai kokka*. Tōkyō: Iwanami shoten, 1971.

Itō Kōji. *Chusei nihon no gaikō to zen shū*. Tōkyō: Yoshikawa kōbunkan, 2002.

Iwami Kiyohiro. *Tō no hoppō mondai to kokusai chitsujo*. Tōkyō: Kyūko shoin, 1998.

_____. "Tō no kinu bōeki to kōken sei." *Tōyōshi ronshū* 33 (May 2005).

Kamei Meitoku. *Nihon bōeki tōjishi no kenkyū*. Kyōto: Dōhōsha, 1986.

Kawazoe Fusae. "Karamono to bunkateki jenda—: Wa to kan no hazama de." *Kokubungaku* 44:4 (April 1999): 61-68.

Kitajima Manji. *Toyotomi Hideyoshi no chōsen shinryaku*. Tōkyō: Yoshikawa kōbunkan, 1995.

Kornicki, Peter F. *The Book in Japan: A Cultural History from the Beginning to the Nineteenth Century*. Leiden and Boston: Brill, 1998.

Makita Tairyō. *Sakugen nyūminki no kenkyū*. 2 vols. Kyōto: Hōzōkan, 1955–1959.

Minoshima Hideki. *Kodai kokka to hoppō shakai*. Tōkyō: Yoshikawa kōbunkan, 2001.

Mori Kimiyuki. *Kodai nihon no taigai ninshiki to kōtsu*. Tōkyō: Yoshikawa kōbunkan, 1998.

Morris, Ivan, trans. *Pillow Book of Sei Shonagon*. 2 vols. New York: Columbia University Press, 1967.

Murai Shōsuke. *Ajia no naka no chūsei nihon*. Tōkyō: Azekura Shobō, 1988.

_____. *Chūsei wajinden*. Tōkyō: Iwanami shoten, 1993.

_____. "Ekisei kakumei no shisō to tennōsei." In Ishigami Eiichi, Murai Shōsuke, et al., eds. *Sekaishi no naka no tennō*. In *Kōza zenkindai no tennō*, vol. 5. Tōkyō: Aoki shoten, 1995.

_____. *Kokkyō o koete: Higashi ajia kaiiki sekai no chūsei*. Tōkyō: Azekura shobō, 1997.

Murai Shōsuke, Satō Makoto, and Yoshida Nobuyuki, eds. *Kyōkai no nihonshi*. Tōkyō: Yamakawa shuppansha, 1997.

Nakanishi Susumu, and Zhou Yiliang, eds. *Nitchū bunka kōryūshi sōsho*. 10 vols. Tōkyō: Taishūkan shoten, 1995–1998.

Nishijima Sadao. "Roku-hasseiki no higashi ajia." In Ienaga Saburō et al., eds. *Iwanami kōza nihon rekishi*, vol. 2. Tōkyō: Iwanami shoten, 1962.

Nishio Kenryū. *Chūsei no nitchū kōryū to zenshū*. Tōkyō: Yoshikawa kōbunkan, 1999.

Ō Reihei [Wang Liping]. *Sōdai no chū-nichi kōryūshi kenkyū*. Tōkyō: Bensei shuppan, 2002.

Ō Yū [Wang Yong] et al. "Gen sō no ōkan." In Nakanishi Susumu and Ō Yū, eds. *Jinbutsu*. In *Nitchū bunka kōryūshi sōsho*, vol. 10. Tōkyō: Taishūkan, 1996.

_____. *Tō kara mita kentōshi: konketsujitachi no dai tō teikoku.* Tōkyō: Kōdansha, 1998.

_____, and Tanaka Takaaki. *Zui-tō jidai ni okeru chūnichi kankeishi kenkyū bunken mokuroku.* Hangzhou daxue Riben wenhua yanjiusuo, 1998.

_____, eds. *Higashi ajia no kentōshi. Ajia yūgaku 3.* Tōkyō: Bensei shuppan, 1999.

_____, Kuboki Hideo, eds. *Nara heian ki no nitchū bunka kōryū: Book road no shiten kara.* Tokyo: Nōsan gyoson bunka kyōkai, 2001.

Ōba Osamu. *Kanseki yunyū no bunkashi: Shōtoku taishi kara Yoshimune e.* Tōkyō: Kenbun shuppan, 1997.

Ogawa Hiroshi. "Nantō kankei bunken mokuroku." *Nantō shigaku* 50 (October 1997).

Okladnikov Aleksei Pavlovich. "The Mo-ho Tribes and the P'o-hai State." In Aleksei Pavlovich Okladnikov, and Henry N. Michael, eds. *The Soviet Far East in Antiquity: An Archaeological and Historical Study of the Maritime Region of the U.S.S.R.* Toronto: University of Toronto Press, published for the Arctic Institute of North America, 1965.

Ono Katsutoshi. *Nittō guhō junrei gyōki no kenkyū.* 4 vols. Tōkyō: Suzuki gakujutsu zaidan, 1964–1969.

_____. *Nittō guhō gyōreki no kenkyū: Chishō Daishi Enchin hen.* 2 vols. Kyōto: Hōzōkan, 1982–1983.

Pack, Tchi-ho, trans. *Bericht des Nosongdong über seine Reise nach Japan aus dem Jahre 1420 (Nosongdong Ilbon haengnok).* Wiesbaden: Harrassowitz, 1973.

Pan Yihong. *Son of Heaven and Heavenly Qaghon: Sui-Tang China and Its Neighbors.* Bellingham: Western Washington University Press, 1997.

Pearson, Richard. "Port, City and Hinterlands: Archaeological Perspectives on Quanzhou and Its Overseas Trade," in Angela Schottenhammer, ed., *Emporium of the World: Maritime Quanzhou, 1000–1400*, pp. 177-235.

Pollack, David. *The Fracture of Meaning: Japan's Synthesis of China from the Eighth through the Eighteenth Centuries.* Princeton: Princeton University Press, 1986.

Read, Bernard E. *Chinese Medical Plants from the Pen Ts'ao Kang Mu A.D. 1596.* Taipei: Southern Materials Center Inc., 1982 (Reprint).

Reischauer, Edwin O, trans. *Ennin's Diary: The Record of a Pilgrimage to China in Search of the Law.* New York: Ronald Press, 1955.

Ri Sonshi [Yi Song-si]. *Higashi ajia no ōken to bōeki: Shōsōin no hōmotsu ga kita mō hitotsu no michi.* Tōkyō: Aoki shoten, 1997.

Robinson, Kenneth R. "From Raiders to Traders: Border Security and Border Control in Early Chosôn, 1392–1450." *Korean Studies* 16 (1992): 94-115.

_____. "The Tsushima Governor and Regulation of Japanese Access to Chosôn in the Fifteenth and Sixteenth Centuries." *Korean Studies* 20 (1996): 23-50.

_____. "The Jiubian and Ezogachishima Embassies to Chosôn, 1478–1482." *Chōsenshi kenkyūkai ronbunshū* 35 (October 1997): 55–86 (234–203).

_____. "Centering the King of Chosôn: Aspects of Korean Maritime Diplomacy, 1392–1593." *Journal of Asian Studies* 59:1 (February 2000): 109–125.

Saeki Arikiyo. *Hiun no kentōsō: Ensai no sūki na shōgai.* Tōkyō: Yoshikawa kōbunkan, 1999.

Saitō Enshin, trans. *San tendai godaisan ki,* vol. 1. Tōkyō: Sankibō busshorin, 1997.

Sakayori Masashi. *Bokkai to kodai no nihon.* Tōkyō: Azekura shobō, 2000.

_____. "Gagaku Shinmakkatsu ni miru kodai nihon to tōhoku ajia." In Takeda Yukio, ed. *Chōsen shakai no shiteki tenkai to higashi ajia.* Tōkyō: Yamakawa shuppansha, 1997.

Schottenhammer, Angela, ed. *The Emporium of the World: Maritime Quanzhou, 1000–1400.* Leiden: Brill, 2001.

_____, ed. *Trade and Transfer across the East Asian Mediterranean.* Wiesbaden: Harrassowitz, 2005.

Seki Shūichi. "Chūsei kōki ni okeru tōjin o meguru ishiki." In Tanaka Takeo, ed. *Zenkindai no nihon to higashi ajia.* Tōkyō: Yoshikawa kōbunkan, 1995.

_____. *Chūsei nitchō kaiikishi no kenkyū.* Tōkyō: Yoshikawa kōbunkan, 2002.

Seno Seiichirō, ed. *Matsura-tō kankei shiryōshū,* 5 vols. Tōkyō: Zokugunshoruijū kanseikai, 2005–2006 (3 vols. published to date).

Senshū daigaku/Seihoku daigaku kyōdō purojekuto, eds. *Kentōshi no mita chūgoku to nihon.* Tōkyō: Asahi shinbunsha, 2005.

Shimazu Sōko. *Jōjin Ajari haha no shū, San tendai godaisan ki no kenkyū.* Tōkyō: Daizō shuppan, 1959.

Shimizu, Isamu, trans. "Priest Takaoka Shinnyo." *Transactions of the Asiatic Society of Japan,* 3rd series, vol. 5 (1957): 1–35.

Sō Fuku [Cao Fu]. *Kentōshi ga aruita michi.* Tōkyō: Nigensha, 1999.

Sugimoto Naojirō. *Shinnyo Shinnō den kenkyū: Takaoka shinnō den kō.* Tōkyō: Yoshikawa kōbunkan, 1965.

Suzuki Yasutami. *Kodai taigai kankeishi no kenkyū.* Tōkyō: Yoshikawa kōbunkan, 1985.

_____. "Nantōjin no raichō o meguru kisoteki kōsatsu." In Tamura Enchō Sensei koki kinenkai, ed. *Higashi ajia to nihon: Rekishi hen.* Tōkyō: Yoshikawa kōbunkan, 1987.

_____, ed. *Kodai ezo no sekai to kōryū. Kodai ōken to kōryū,* vol. 1. Tōkyō: Meicho shuppan, 1996.

_____. "Bokkai kokka no kōzō to tokushitsu." *Chōsen gakuhō* 170 (January 1999): 1–28.

_____, ed. *Bokkai to kodai higashi ajia. Ajia yūgaku* 6. Tōkyō: Bensei shuppan, 1999.

Suzuki Yasutami et al. eds. *Kentōshi boshi o meguru nitchū kōryūshi.* A special issue of *Higashi ajia no kodai bunka,* Spring 2005.

Taigai kankeishi sōgō nenpyō henshūkai, comp. *Taigai kankeishi sōgō nenpyō.* Tōkyō: Yoshikawa kōbunkan, 1999.

Tajima Isao. "Nihon, chūgoku, chōsen taigai kōryūshi nenpyō." In Nara kenritsu Kashihara kōkogaku kenkyūjo fuzoku hakubutsukan, ed. *Bōeki tōji: Nara Heian no chūgoku tōji.* Kyōto: Rinsen shoten, 1993.

Takahashi Tomio, ed. *Tōhoku kodaishi no kenkyū.* Tōkyō: Yoshikawa kōbunkan, 1986.

Takahashi Kimiaki. "Chūsei higashi ajia kaiiki ni okeru kaimin to kōryū." *Nagoya daigaku bungakubu kenkyū ronshū, shigaku* 33 (1987): 1-20.

Takakusu, J., trans. "Le voyage de Kanshin au Japon." *Bulletin de l'École Française d'Extrême Orient* 28, 29 (1928, 1929).

Takara Kurayoshi. *Ajia no naka no ryūkyū ōkoku.* Tōkyō: Yoshikawa kōbunkan, 1998.

Tamura Kōichi and Suzuki Yasutami, eds. *Ajia kara mita kodai nihon.* In *Shinpan kodai no nihon,* vol. 9. Tōkyō: Kadokawa shoten, 1992.

Tanaka Takaaki, and Ō Yu, eds. *Nihon no kentōshi. Ajia yūgaku* 4. Tōkyō: Bensei shuppan, 1999.

Tanaka Takeo, trans. *Kaitō shokokuki: Chōsenjin no mita chūsei no nihon to ryūkyū (Haedong chegukki).* Tōkyō: Iwanami shoten, 1991.

_____, ed. *Zenkindai no nihon to higashi ajia.* Tōkyō: Yoshikawa kōbunkan, 1995.

_____, ed. *Zenrin kokuhōki, Shintei zoku zenrin kokuhōki.* Tōkyō: Shūeisha, 1995.

_____. *Higashi ajia tsūkōken to kokusai ninshiki.* Tōkyō: Yoshikawa kōbunkan, 1997.

Toby, Ronald P. *State and Diplomacy in Early Modern Japan: Asia in the Development of the Tokugawa Bakufu.* Princeton: Princeton University Press, 1984.

Tōno Haruyuki. *Kentōshi to Shōsōin.* Tōkyō: Iwanami shoten, 1992.

_____. "Japanese Embassies to T'ang China and their Ships." *Acta Asiatica* 69 (1995): 39-62.

_____. *Kentōshisen: Higashi ajia no naka de.* Tōkyō: Asahi shinbunsha, 1999.

Tsuji Zennosuke. *Zōtei kaigai kōtsū shiwa.* Tōkyō: Naigai shoseki kabushiki kaisha, 1930.

Tsunoda, Ryūsaku, trans., and L. Carrington Goodrich, ed. *Japan in the Chinese Dynastic Histories: Later Han through Ming Dynasties.* South Pasadena, Calif.: Perkins, 1951.

Uraki, Ziro, trans. *Tale of the Cavern (Utsuho Monogatari).* Tōkyō: Shonozaki shorin, 1984.

Ury, Marian, trans. *Tales of Times Now Past.* Berkeley: University of California Press, 1979.

Verschuer, Charlotte von. "Le voyage de Jōjin au mont Tiantai." *T'oung pao* 77: 1-3 (1991): 1-48.

_____. "Le Japon, contrée du Penglai? Note sur le mercure." *Cahiers d'Extrême-Asie* 8 (1995): 439-452.

_____. "Jōjin découvre la ville de Hangzhou en 1072." In Jacqueline Piegot, and Hartmut O. Rotermund, eds. *Le vase de béryl: Études sur le Japon et la Chine en hommage à Bernard Frank*. Arles: Philippe Piquier, 1997.

_____. "Tō sō ni okeru nihon Hōrai kan to suigin yu'nyū ni tsuite." In Ō Yu, and Tanaka Takaaki, eds. *Higashi ajia no kentōshi. Ajia yūgaku* 3 (1999): 151-170.

_____. "Japan's Foreign Relations 600 to 1200: A Translation of *Zenrin kokuhōki.*" *Monumenta Nipponica* 54:1 (Spring 1999): 1-39.

_____. "Kōshū Ninbo Fudasan o tazunete." *Nihon rekishi* 613 (June 1999): 44-47.

_____. "Looking from Within and Without: Ancient and Medieval External Relations." *Monumenta Nipponica* 55:4 (Winter 2000): 537-566.

_____. "Le moine Shunjō (1166–1227): Sa jeunesse et son voyage en Chine." *Bulletin de l'École Française d'Extrême Orient* 88 (2001): 161-190.

_____. "Japan's Foreign Relations 1200–1392 A.D. A Translation from *Zenrin kokuhōki.*" *Monumenta Nipponica* 57:4 (Winter 2002): 413-445.

_____. "Journal de voyage de Jōjin en 1072: la vie sur le Grand Canal dans la Chine des Song," *Revue d'Etudes Japonaises du CEEJA* (2005): 79-124.

Wang, Zhen-ping. "Sino-Japanese Relations before the Eleventh Century: Modes of Diplomatic Communication Reexamined in Terms of the Concept of Reciprocity." Ph.D. diss., Princeton University, 1989.

_____. "Act on Appropriateness and Mutual Self-Interest: Early T'ang Diplomatic thinking A.D. 618-49." *Medieval History Journal* 1:2 (1998): 165-94.

_____. *Ambassadors from the Islands of Immortals: China-Japan Relations in the Han-Tang Period*. Honolulu: Association for Asian Studies and University of Hawaii Press, 2005.

Yamanaka Yutaka. "Genji monogatari no Kōraijin ni tsuite." In Mori hakase kanreki kinenkai, ed. *Taigai kankei to shakai keizai: Mori Katsumi hakushi kanreki kinen ronbunshū*. Tōkyō: Hanawa shobō, 1968.

Yamauchi Shinji. "Jū-jūisseiki no taigai kankei to kokka: Chūgoku shōnin no raikō o megutte." *Hisutoria* 141 (1993): 1-22.

_____. *Nara heianki no nihon to higashi ajia*. Tōkyō: Yoshikawa kōbunkan, 2003.

Yamazato Jun'ichi. *Kodai nihon to nantō no kōryū*. Tōkyō: Yoshikawa kōbunkan, 1999.

Yonetani Hitoshi. "Tōdai shiryō hensanjo kazō 'Nihon kankei chōsen shiryō.'" *Komonjo kenkyū* 48 (October 1998): 74-110.

INDEX

Page numbers in italics refer to tables

CORNELL EAST ASIA SERIES

CPSIA information can be obtained
at www.ICGtesting.com
Printed in the USA
LVHW091936151119
637499LV00007B/50/P